Behind Colorful Doors

A Collection of 14
Remarkable Short Stories

Deleen Wills

This book is a collection of works from storytellers based on their lives and experiences.

Copyri ght © 2016 DFWills Publishing
Printed by Createspace

ISBN: 1530557879

ISBN-13: 9781530557875

First Edition

If you have any comments or questions, please contact Deleen Wills through Facebook at Behind Colorful Doors.

DEDICATION & THANKS

This book is dedicated to my parents, Del and Patty Riley, who instilled in me the love for storytelling and wanderlust at a very young age. My parents, two younger brothers, Mark and Bruce, and I camped in a 15-foot travel trailer while we roamed Oregon and the Pacific Northwest, rambled through the western United States as far east as Nebraska, and wandered in western Canada. They have loved me unconditionally, encouraged me to always do my best, and supported me through everything.

Special Thanks to my husband Mark, for traveling life with me the past 42 years, exploring the world as I discover new colorful doors and for supporting my unending adventures.

Sincere Thanks To:

Beth E. Pitcher	Copy Editor
J. Steven Hunt	Cover Illustration
Jessica Marple	Cover Design and Deleen Wills Portrait
NiCole Anderson	Interior Design
Alex Christie	Photo of the Blue Cardinal
Writers	Photos for Their Stories

Behind Colorful Doors

ACKNOWLEDGMENTS

Behind Colorful Doors is very much a collaborative effort, as
there would be no stories were it not for the storytellers who
have their own colorful doors they were willing to share from
their life experiences. They are: NiCole Anderson, Dr. Leroy
Goertzen, Carol Crespi Green, Rebecca L. Hillyer, Bonnie Hull,
Dr. Katie Hunsucker-Brown, J. Steven Hunt, MAD MacNeill,
Laura Alyson Manger, Jovanka Mrdja, Robin Richardson, Del
Riley, Patty Riley, R. D. Roberts and Deleen Wills.

My deepest appreciation to my very patient and loving family
and friends who went on this new journey with me. They are
included but are not limited to:

• *Beth E. Pitcher*, for expertly and patiently editing each story and
allowing me to bounce all kinds of thoughts by her. A dear
friend who I would never know if we hadn't met in an elevator
in Quito, Ecuador before our Galapagos expedition—
serendipity at its finest.
• *Jon D. Pitcher*, for his extreme patience and tech support.
• *NiCole Anderson*, for her talent with technology, crafting the
interior design, and for being such a loyal friend.
• *Jessica Marple*, cover designer, photographer, graphic designer,
artist and friend. See her work at greengatephoto.com.
• *J. Steven Hunt*, illustrator, artist and longtime friend. I am
indebted to Steve, a man of many talents and gifts, as a mentor
and champion, both personally and professionally.
• To my cheerleaders for their continued encouragement: *Alyssa,
Bonnie, Darrel, Heather, Jeannie, Joyce, Michelle, Nancy, NiCole and
Sandy*. My "Sisterchicks" *Nita, Sherrie, Sue* and *Suzanne* and thirty-
year dear friend, travel-mate and mentor, *Carol Crespi Green*, with
whom I first shared the dream of writing a book and they
encouraged me to Just Do It.

CONTENTS

	Acknowledgments		v
1	The Sapphire Door	Deleen Wills	2
2	The Orange Door	J. Steven Hunt	44
3	The Blue Cardinal Door	R. D. Roberts	66
4	The Gray Door	Del Riley	92
5	The Emerald Door	NiCole Anderson	126
6	The Faded Red Door	Rebecca L. Hillyer	148
7	The Acorn Door	Robin Richardson and MAD MacNeill	166
8	The Pale Green Door	Dr. Leroy Goertzen	190
9	The Black Door	Bonne Hull	216
10	The Slate Door	Dr. Katie Hunsucker-Brown	224
11	The Lime Green Door	Jovanka Mrdja	254
12	The Green and Gray Door	Laura Alyson Manger	280
13	The Boise Green Door	Patty Walker Riley	300
14	The Weathered Gray Door	Carol Crespi Green	338

1

The Sapphire Door
Deleen Wills

Wanderlust (n): A strong desire for or impulse to wander or travel and explore the world.

My parents had instilled wanderlust in me from an early age when our family of five went gallivanting in our 15-foot travel trailer around the western United States and Canada. We once ventured as far as Nebraska where my mother spent her childhood. These vacations bonded our happy-go-lucky, yet sometimes naïve family, as it was us against the elements. Yet it instilled in me the quest for exploration that only travel can quench. I was bitten by the travel bug as a youngster.

In 40 years of employment, 30 of those working at nonprofit educational institutions, I organized and implemented events, established friendships, raised funds and coordinated travel programs. The most enjoyable was organizing voyages on many cruises and land tours for groups of alumni and friends so that they, too, could experience the world. Retirement was upon me and the new chapter in life happily included volunteering at worthwhile nonprofit organizations and spending more time with family and friends. Also I work on a part-time basis coordinating journeys for groups,

3

families and friends, including this one for my husband and me and another special couple. It was a momentous fortieth wedding anniversary for us and a monumental birthday for me. We were on this vacation with our favorite traveling companions, Scott and Heather. Heather was also celebrating a milestone birthday, but one decade younger than me.

After transiting from Salem, Oregon to Portland International Airport, arriving three hours early for international check-in and surviving the security gauntlet, I was nestled in a window seat on a crystal clear night and I could see 40,000 feet down. The smooth nine-hour flight over Canada, the Northwest Territories, looping down over Greenland and at midnight viewing Iceland awash in light due to the brilliance of a full moon, I said to my dozing husband, "We've got to go to Iceland." Each time we flew to Europe I said that. There is nothing like that feeling you get when you arrive at a place you've never been before. I could spend my life traveling toward that feeling. We caught up with the sunrise as our flight continued over the tip of Northern Ireland, cutting across Scotland as we dropped uneventfully, fortunately, into Amsterdam, where we would waste a couple of hours until our next short flight to Venice. Customs was relatively painless, and even though we were a weary group of four, we became reenergized anticipating what was to come.

As we flew over the German, Austrian and Italian Alps, quickly the terrain flattened out, and in the distance I spotted the clock tower at Saint Mark's Square. Even though we were fatigued vacationers due to sleeplessness and eagerness about our upcoming adventure to Italy, Croatia and Slovenia, after 20 hours of international travel we now seemed wide awake with great expectations. The Dalai Lama said, "Once a year go someplace you've never been before." We were.

We were savvy travelers and knew that after the length of the flights this would be the time to spend some Euros hiring someone who knew where he was going to transport us to our hotel. Carrying our luggage, even though we'd adhered to our motto and vow of packing fairly light, the tasks of figuring out transportation to the dock, a water taxi or water bus, deciphering a map and finding the correct alley in the Venetian maze to our hotel, seemed unfathomable after traveling almost an entire day.

After touching down at Aeroporto Marco Polo, retrieving our luggage and going through immigration, we were in a steady stream of soon-to-be-explorers shuffling our way down the corridor. Standing in a continuous line, we saw many good-looking Italian men wearing fashionable Italian sunglasses and holding signs indicating the last names of their would-be arrivals. We spotted our very own Italian holding a sign that read KING WILLS in big, bold letters. Yes, we certainly felt like royalty with our very own personal chauffeur. The fact that it was merely a combination of our two last names was not lost on us. Still, this splurge turned out to be an excellent investment and part of our trip of a lifetime.

In the back of a spacious black car driven by our handsome Italian protector, we went a short distance to our awaiting water taxi. We climbed in for what should have been about a 30-minute ride through the Venetian Lagoon into the city. We sat on comfortable, cushioned seats in the rear of the boat which was open to fresh air and sunshine plus easy access for me to pop up and down for photos. The boat was beautifully crafted with multicolored inlaid woods with polished shiny railings and handles. Pinch me. Was I really riding in a water taxi in the largest wetlands in the Mediterranean basin driven by yet another attractive young Italian man, and spotting the islands of Burano, Mazzorbo and Torcello in the distance?

We saw several types of birds sunning themselves on top of the short trees and bushes in the marshes of tall grasses. We recognized a great grey heron, white egrets standing in mud flats, kingfishers diving for lunch, along with what would be a frequent sighting, a Eurasian magpie. We passed other water taxis, sailboats, yachts and, wait! A gondola. Then we spotted the small Isola (island) di Tessera and Isola Carbonera. We were almost there; we could see the top of the clock tower in Saint Mark's Square in the distance.

Loud clunk--then nothing. Complete silence from the motor of our watercraft. While the four of us were glancing at each other with raised eyebrows wondering what in the world that noise was, our driver guided the dead-in-the-water boat over to a tall wood piling about the size of an oak tree and tossed a rope around it. My camera was ready as I was taking lots of photos to help remind me of everything we experienced. Copious photos are part of my souvenirs from any trip. If I were to forget anything about the trips in years to come, I'd have my thousands of photos to back up my fading memories. One can only retain so many snapshots or postcards in one's mind.

I was clicking photos of our driver from all angles as he scooted forward inch by inch, not wanting to scuff the front of his beautifully crafted water taxi. Precariously perched over the front of the boat, he was so far forward that I was afraid he'd fall in. Then we'd really be up a creek or a lagoon, in this case, without a paddle. He fiddled with something and then pushed himself backward, stood up as he raised his hands upward gesturing somewhere towards the heavens. It seemed a good thing we weren't fluent in the Italian language at this point. However, we could certainly translate "quattro Americani" as he was speaking quickly on his cell phone.

All of the working water taxis transporting visitors either coming or going kindly slowed down to inquire whether we were okay. While our driver seemed perturbed--obviously time was money--we were laughing and having a remarkable escapade. I mean, who gets to break down in the Venetian Lagoon in a water taxi? Turns out we quickly learned why he was a bit troubled. He explained that some taxis were owned by companies and many were owned independently, which was his situation.

He and his father were co-owners and even though he did most of the taxi driving his father was due to take over the slower evening shift. Between the two of them they drove their boat almost 20 hours per day to provide a living for both families. He, being younger, worked longer hours especially in the summertime. He told us his grandfather and two uncles had built the boat as they had been in the boat construction business since the mid-1960s. This was his father's third boat over the decades and this particular boat was built in 2001 with the hull comprised of olive, poplar, cypress and pine woods.

Since we were sitting there in our broken down water taxi with nowhere to go, he pointed out the six different types of wood used in their vessel. First was olive wood, which was golden brown with streaks of brown and black. Then cypress, a pale or blond color with straight grain, was the ideal wood for coastal locations with constant heat and humidity. The poplar was a hard wood of light cream to yellowish brown with ribbons of gray or green and the most common in boat building.

He explained that along with these woods there were three types of pine used in this more distinctive boat, more than we could ever imagine. The aleppo pine, with its honey-colored wood, is native to the Mediterranean region and found throughout Italy. It grows to over 90 feet tall and is marked with orange-red bark that is thick and cracked in appearance and has been manufactured for an estimated 2,000 years. The maritime pine, with light reddish-to-brown coloring, another native of the Mediterranean, could reach 100 feet and is similar to the aleppo in appearance and use. The third pine was from the Italian stone pine, with white to soft yellow coloring, sometimes called the umbrella pine, also native to the region. The needles are different than other pines and some stone pine are grown for their edible nuts, called pine nuts, which are actually the seeds of the trees and found in the broad, oval-shaped cones of the trees. We were so surprised and elated by our impromptu arborist sharing all this history and the bonus tree education. The boat certainly took on an exceptional individuality to us after this enlightenment that reminded me there is a story behind everything, but you have to get out there to find it.

Too soon to us, it seemed, another taxi pulled alongside and the two drivers hoisted our luggage across and then assisted us as we carefully stepped across from our bobbing, conked out taxi to the operational one. Our driver was repeatedly apologetic but we assured him it was a grand incident and said our grazies and waved farewell. As we pulled away I felt a bit sad because he looked so forlorn in his boat dipping up and down in the lagoon waiting for help to arrive.

That sad feeling didn't last long, however, as another fine-looking Italian was transporting us to our final destination as we viewed the island of Murano that we would visit later. We zipped by Isola Campalto as we entered one of several busy canals, the Canale di Cannaregio, which would take us to the Grand Canal. Now this was eventful.

Venice, Venezia. Cruising down the Grand Canal in our second private water taxi of the afternoon, we were gawking at the buildings, one-of-a-kind bridges and all types of bustling watercraft. It had been more than 19 years since our first, brief visit when we realized it wasn't nearly enough time to properly visit this historic, beautiful city on the Adriatic Sea. We determined that we must come back one day. That day had arrived.

We were looking forward to a leisurely pace exploring this unique city on our own and purposely had a goal of getting lost in Venice. We were immersing ourselves spending a week living amongst Venetians, observing how they lived, worked, ate and shopped. We knew we were tourists but somehow thought ourselves above the typical ones, especially those getting off for six to seven hours from the cruise ships and seeing only Saint Mark's Square.

We were staying at the hotel A La Commedia, located in a quiet square between the Rialto Bridge and Saint Mark's in the San Marco district. The hotel had a marvelous rooftop terrace where we spent each evening watching the sun go down and the ever-changing, puffy multicolored cumulus clouds against the cobalt sky. The clouds seemed to form a lacy pattern of marigold to rosy plum to crimson, creating breathtaking Venetian sunsets. "Our" terrace, where we lounged on comfy overstuffed chairs, was appointed with flower boxes of black-bearded yellow pansies, lush palms and red geraniums. There were three wooden planters with fragrant mint that our waiter, Efram, used in assorted beverage concoctions. He automatically delivered munchies of roasted corn nuts, pistachios and squares of dark chocolates every time we appeared. Our view overlooked tiled rooftops and church steeples, and seemed about level with the clock tower in the square.

Our hotel was conveniently located at the Del Carbon Grand Canal stop and made for an easy walk to just about anywhere, including the opposite direction from the busy Saint Mark's where the tourists generally would venture only several canals from the pier or their hotels. Our cut-through was under the clock tower erected at the end of the 15th century and had the phases of the moon, sun and Zodiac displayed on its colorful face.

During the week our explorations took us to each neighborhood but we started with the diverse districts of San Polo and Santa Croce. It was hard to tell where one began and the other ended. They are located inside the first bend of the Grand Canal, enclosed between Cannaregio and San Marco. Exploring the outdoor markets, filled with fresh fruits and vegetables plus a variety of unidentifiable smelly fish, was an experience in itself. This was our first opportunity for homemade gelato and our first scoop or two, would be at Gelateria il Doge. I had done my research. I had a special map all marked up and knew exactly where several gelaterias that made their own gelato were located. I was a gelato snob as an outcome from past visits to Italy but I didn't care, I wanted only homemade. Even with their dozens of choices my favorite was lemon, "limone" in Italian, and I was looking forward to consuming a lot and frequently. The easy decision was limone; the hard choice was what the second scoop would be. It would be my only angst on the entire trip. I did vow the second (or third) scoops would always be something extraordinary and the pomegranate popped with flavor.

Historical San Polo is the commercial heart of the city where banking and trading happens. It is connected to Cannaregio by the Scalzi and Rialto bridges. Whenever we felt disoriented and couldn't decipher our maps, we'd look up and see the words

"Per Rialto" with an arrow painted on the side of a building. With the arrows' guidance we could always find our way out of the maze of canals, ornate bridges and dead ends. The San Polo district of today has many food shops, markets and old style bars called bacari, where you can stand to eat and drink and where you meet the real Venetians.

Another day we explored the district of Dorsoduro, one of the oldest in Venice. Its name refers to the firmness of the ground on which it was built. Its massive buildings, with one-of-a kind architecture and history galore, grace the Grand Canal. Several times we cut through the Palazzo Venier dei Leoni which houses the Peggy Guggenheim collection. In the middle of the district is Campo Santa Margherita and is the heart of the district with numerous cafes, stalls and shops. Venice's top art museum, the Accademia, always packed with highlights of the Venetian Renaissance, paintings by the Bellini family, Titian, Tintoretto, Veronese, Tiepolo, Giorgione, Calalette and Testosterone, seemed a step back in time. It was just across the wooden Accademia Bridge from all the San Marco craziness.

While in Venice we knew we must take the touristy gondola ride and, even though the canals seemed almost overflowing because of tourists in these unique handcrafted boats, who cared? We climbed in and navigated a portion of the Grand Canal viewing buildings that once were private, wealthy family palaces. Our gondola was propelled by a very dashing man with a straw hat that had a ribbon around the brim and down his back that matched the black striped color of his shirt. This was accented with a bright red scarf that most gondoliers wore. He stood facing the bow and rowed with a forward motion then a backward stroke. We noticed that the attire the gondoliers wore was red and white, blue and white, or black and white striped shirts and always black pants.

We shared the water with tragettos, gondolas that operated as ferries where you stand up while crossing the canal (usually backward with nothing to hold on to except other unsteady passengers), vaporettos, a public water bus carrying hundreds of passengers, delivery boats, barges, police boats and locals with their own motorized boats. We soon ducked into Rio Marin. The interior canals were much quieter but tighter. Each time we'd go around a sharp corner the gondolier would shout some word that we couldn't quite understand but guessed it was a warning to others with equally limited sight distance. Our gondola was shiny ebony with gold railings and carvings. Our gondolier told us that gondolas' earliest recorded use dates back to 1094 and that today all gondolas are black after a decree in the 16th century to stop the rich and famous from trying to outdo each other with ostentatious colors and ornamentation. The small boats were handmade, not far from where we were cruising, with eight different types of wood and composed of 280 separate pieces of wood. The left side of the gondola was made longer than the right side which helped the gondola resist the tendency to turn toward the left at the forward stroke or going in a circle.

He said he went through a lot of training and apprenticeship, followed by a major comprehensive examination which tested his knowledge of Venetian history, landmarks, foreign languages, plus skills in handling the craft necessary in the tight spaces of canals. The profession of gondolier is licensed by a guild, which issues a limited number of licenses (425) granted after passing the exam. He felt fortunate to have his license which he had gotten nine years earlier. He explained that every detail of the gondola has its own symbolism. The iron head of the gondola is needed to balance the weight of him at the stern and has an "S" shape, symbolic of the twists in the Grand Canal. Under the main blade there is a type of comb with six teeth or prongs representing the six districts of Venice. The curved top signifies the Doge's cap. The semicircular break between the curved top and the six teeth is supposed to represent the Rialto Bridge. That seemed like a lot of detailed work on each boat but he noted that each one is a piece of art and unique unto its own. On each side of our gondola was a 10-inch high gold half-horse and half-bottom of a mermaid.

As we rode quietly through the water we looked straight up to see windows full of colorful, overflowing flower boxes, and clotheslines pulled between one window and the next with all sizes of laundry. Red and white poles were prominent, and rowing by well-worn, vintage closed doors caused me to wonder where they led. Several windows were open where we could see frescos painted on the ceilings and walls. Who knew how old they might be or who painted them? The flag of Venice was flown proudly everywhere and appeared reddish-orange with gold ornamentation and a lion. Our gondolier gave us some historical background which turned out to be much more significant than just a lion on a flag.

As we continued our ride, some bridges were so short that our gondolier had to squat to get under. We were passing a gondola going in the opposite direction with a typical looking young couple when we noticed the man getting down on one knee, pulling a box from his pocket and saying something to the young lady who threw her arms around him and, we guessed, said yes. As they floated underneath the next bridge there was draped a big pink and purple banner that read "Rosella, will you marry me?" A sweet story for us to remember from this excellent adventure.

Piazza San Marco, with the Basilica of Saint Mark and the Palazzo Ducales, is the judicial and political heart of the city. Behind Saint Mark's Basilica is the much photographed Bridge of Sighs, which connects the Doge's Palace with the horrible, dark stone prison. One could only imagine what happened in there. This is also not the place to go if you want to avoid tourists. Going early, we'd always beat the crowds and that morning we took the elevator to the top of the clock tower where we could see the landscape of colorful buildings, water, islands and miles out to sea. Then we got off the beaten path (canal), and headed for the outlying neighborhoods as fast as we could. Castello district is right next to San Marco and is the only one which does not face the Grand Canal. Here is the most famous walk in Venice, the ever-crowded Riva degli Schiavoni. The shops of Italian shoes, purses, jewelry and anything else you'd desire, are there. However, the interior of the district was peaceful, and great for discovering all sorts of charming characteristics along with its numerous restaurants, churches and buildings.

Libreria Acqua Alta, or Library of High Water, self-proclaimed and rightly so, is one of the most beautiful bookshops in the world and has got to be one of the most original. We found new and used books in all languages. The originality comes not just from the books but from the shelves which were boats, canoes, bathtubs, gondolas and anything else in which they can possibly insert books and magazines. We were told that when the Acqua Alta pushes high water into the canals causing anywhere from inches to feet of water, the boats and bathtubs rise with the water. Some books have been turned into furniture. The old encyclopedias, the kind no one buys anymore because everything can be found on the internet, are steps in an amazing staircase and cover the walls in the outer courtyards, transforming them into multicolored surfaces. There are also poles, oars and mannequins to complete the treat for the eyes and book lover's soul. My extraordinary find and souvenir was a small book, "The Grand Canal, Palaces and Families," complete with photos of every building along the Canal, plus its history.

This area has two of several homemade gelato shops. Not far from the Rialto Bridge and certainly touristy, is the La Boutique del Gelato, where limone and raspberry were vibrantly flavorful. After several days' exploring, I had determined my favorite gelateria was Artigionale La Mela Verde, with many surprising, unusual flavors like a combination of lemon, fresh basil and mint. Not only were the flavors unusual but Davide, the owner, was very generous with samples of his creations. He reminded me of Michelangelo's statue of David (carved in the early 1500s and one of the most famous Renaissance sculptures to this day housed in the Accademia Gallery in Florence) but with dark hair and not quite as tall. And he had very charming staff, with patience for the perplexed tourists who had a hard time deciding which delicious delight to experience that day. They were very friendly and one in particular always had a quick smile, remembered me and was eager to help. Her name was Juanita and she dished up plentiful scoops. She told me that any kind of gelato was her preferred dessert but limone was her favorite. This was becoming my favorite neighborhood.

It was also interesting to discover that after several days of consuming local cuisine we could differentiate the herbs and spices that each neighborhood used in their pizza, pasta and salads that made their delicacies distinctive. It was a guessing game trying to figure out what those flavors might be.

We were down to our final few days and totally in denial about having to leave. Lazily sipping espresso and munching delectable delights of chocolate-filled croissants on the Grand Canal was exactly what my husband and friends were doing on this fine, late May morning while I wandered the back canals of Venice. It was my ritual to get out early before all the other tourists.

Plus, I was on a mission. Two, in fact. Mission #1 - shopping. We are talking serious business here.

We'd been island-hopping earlier in the week for a day to Burano, a quiet, quaint and colorful town where authentic lace is made and sold. Strolling the streets, we'd never seen such vibrant colorful buildings, windows and doors. As we stood in the middle of the square with the statue of the Mr. Burauella, (the father of Burano) Bladassare Guluppi, we could see a complete circle of brightly painted houses and shops of interesting color schemes such as purple with an expansive teal awning, Grey Poupon mustard with jade shutters, fuchsia with orange and yellow window shades, and a cobalt blue building with red and green canopies. These were just a few feasts for the eyes for those who appreciate color. Filled up from a delicious lunch of risotto, tortellini and spaghetti, with Friuli Colli Orientali Pinot Grigio, we thought this would be a fabulous place to stay when one wanted to escape from the crowds of Venice.

Then we were off to Murano to watch glass-blowing and do some shopping. I made the mistake of not buying something in particular there. Our compatriots, however, had scored big time with an exquisite piece of glass that they affectionately named Sophia. She was hand-carried for the rest of the trip and all the way home. Sophia weighed about seven pounds. Since I neglected picking up one item in particular, I was searching for a local, Made-in-Venice store, for this incredibly beautiful, one-of-a-kind-made glass.

Mission #2 - return to La Mela Verde for gelato. Our motto from our first trip to Italy over two decades before was "It's never too early for gelato."

And I already knew ahead of time what I would have. Yet another scoop of limone plus chocolate noir, made with dark Venezuelan cocoa and Costa Rican chocolate. It created an intense flavor not too sweet or too bitter. But it was also rich in antioxidants, low fat, and dairy-free. How did I know ahead of time? I'd had a sample last time we were there.

I love gelato because it's a different texture and more flavorful than we have in our ice cream products at home. Part of my process in becoming a gelato snob was discovering that while our ice cream legally has a minimum of 10 percent fat, gelato is made with a greater proportion of whole milk to cream, so it contains more like 5 to 7 percent fat. This was good news. Also, gelato is churned at a slower speed than ice cream, and it's denser because less air is whipped into the mixture. Gelato contains about 25 to 30 percent air while ice cream can contain as much as 50 percent. More good news. While ice cream is typically served frozen, gelato is usually stored and served at a slightly warmer temperature, so it's not completely frozen. And I learned that many of the concoctions are first cooked so that the flavors are tangier, sweet and tasty. Well, the healthier the better I say, especially at 10 a.m.

When completing my shopping mission, I would rendezvous with my coffee drinkers at 9:45 and we'd have enough time to be there when it opened at 10:00. It would be our mid-morning snack before exploring yet another district. Cannaregio, the most northerly district, stretched in the large arc from the railway station in the west to one of the oldest quarters of Venice in the east. It was known for its quiet areas with small, simple artisan workshops and stores. In Cannaregio, near the Rialto, the famous merchant Marco Polo was born in 1254.

It was about 8:30 on a bright, sunny morning when shafts of sunlight created shadows bouncing around on the periwinkle, amber and azure-tinted water and buildings. The colors of this city were always different and stunning depending on the time of day, sunshine or clouds. Sauntering down a narrow walkway, it was abundantly clear that it was a neighborhood and not the business district. I came upon a weather-beaten, sapphire-colored door. What caught my attention was the deep, vibrant sapphire color, the exact same blue of the waters of the Mediterranean and Caribbean we'd seen on trips before. On the sides of the door were a myriad of planter boxes of overflowing red and white ivy geraniums with dark green foliage and bunches of yellow freesia. The red, white and green jumble reminded me of the Italian flag. Mixed in was one lone rose bush in a clay pot. A thin wire stretched to the top of the right side of the door with a nail anchoring it securely. A climbing vine wound its way round and round and dipped several red roses into the right corner and one over the top. I saw that the left side of the door was closed but the right door was slightly ajar.

Glancing from side to side, I was relieved that I saw no one who might cause me to be arrested for breaking and entering. I'd done this before. With a gentle touch, or maybe a breeze caught it, the right door gently opened just a few inches. If my husband had been there he would have said I pushed it open. I

20

call this regular travel occurrence my made up word, "graviosity" (curiosity and gravity). He'd seen me in action before on many adventures where I simply HAD to discover what was behind that colorful door. That's why I'd learned it was best that I discover these revelations on my own.

As I peeked in before me was a surprisingly large courtyard bursting with cornflower blue and deep purple hydrangeas appearing six feet high mixed with patches of pink heather and all varieties of lilies, which I discovered later is the national flower. Also, multicolored hibiscus, trailing lavender wisteria along with flourishing boxes of petunias, and more geraniums that matched the colors of those outside the door. In one corner were several long wooden boxes full of herbs, including what seemed to be foot-tall mint. Ground cover popped up between the brick-toned cobblestones and created a soft saffron glow from the morning sunbeams between the buildings. I spotted two tricycles and a few toys scattered around. The flowers were very similar to those at home in the Pacific Northwest but much more lush and carefree.

As I was peering at all the flowers, architecture, and staircases leading to several floors and multiple doorways, I spotted a cinnamon-colored dachshund on the heels of small girl with brunette hair. She was wearing a thin, lacy white overcoat covering a sunflower print yellow dress and maybe three years old. She was struggling while pulling a bigger boy, who I guessed was her brother, in a well-worn red wagon. They were laughing and I guessed she was probably wondering, "How did I end up pulling him around again when he is older and bigger than I am?" His eyes twinkled at the younger girl. He seemed to be about five years old and had darker brown hair. He called, "Susi, vieni qui," to a fawn colored pug that came running from the back of a lemon tree growing in a large wooden planter box.

The morning giddiness changed quickly as a woman, dressed in classic Italian black blouse and pencil skirt and wearing heels (that made me question how in the world she was going to get around those streets in those shoes), bent down for hugs and kisses and said her good-byes. The little girl dramatically sobbed, "Momma, no! No, Momma, no!!" as she threw her pudgy, tanned arms around her momma's left leg. The little boy shook his head and said something sweetly to his baby sister. Even though I didn't understand any Italian, I knew enough that the daughter wasn't one bit happy her momma was leaving. Poppa appeared and said his farewell without the drama; obviously, he didn't stand for such outbursts.

To calm down the apparently expected episode, a woman with salt and pepper-colored hair, and dressed in a brightly colored blue and white flowered, short-sleeved print dress, entered the courtyard to distract the seemingly heartbroken little girl. My guess was this was grandma to the rescue. In her arms was a basket with a long loaf of bread, fruit and a jug of milk. She efficiently spread out the display on the mosaic-tiled table in the middle of the square and the children were eager to dig in and therefore easily sidetracked. Momma and Poppa signaled each other and made a speedy exit. They appeared to be in their early thirties.

This entire scene was no more than a couple of minutes in time but seemed longer as I intruded on their early morning family drama and ritual. I was elated that "graviosity" had once again intervened for me in yet another far-off location and I got a glimpse of a Venetian family living behind a colorful door.

I happily snuck away from the familial scene and continued strolling along the canal in pursuit of conquering my tasks: shopping, then gelato. I was on my trek for a special type of Venetian glass that I mistakenly hadn't purchased earlier when we were in Murano. I had previously seen several off-the-beaten-canal, Made-in-Venice stores, that shouldn't be as expensive as those where tourists would shop which meant anything around the Ferrari Store, which we did visit because half of our quartet were Ferrari addicts.

I spotted exactly what I was looking for in a window—a perfectly round, four-inch paperweight made from the Millefiori technique which produces distinctive patterns on glassware. It involves the production of canes or rods, known as murrine, with beautiful multicolored patterns which are only visible from the cut ends of the rod. The murrine is heated in a furnace and pulled until thin, while still keeping the cross section designs. Then the rods are fused together and when cooled, it looks like a kaleidoscope of varying patterns and colors.

The store wasn't open yet so I loitered patiently but was spotted by a woman who came and unlocked the door early. She greeted me with a gracious smile that somehow I thought I recognized. She said, "Buon giorno" and I replied in one of just a few words I knew in Italian, "Ciao." I always liked this word because it efficiently served as hi and bye.

As I entered the store that soon would be taking my Euros, birthday money from my mom and dad that I had saved and had earmarked for something very special, I took a closer look at the lovely, slightly familiar-looking woman and wondered could it be "Momma" working in this very store? I wasn't exactly sure so I decided to fess up and explain where I thought I might have recognized her. I spilled out the truth of me spying through the colorful door slightly ajar just 30 minutes earlier and she laughed out loud. Yes, it turned out Momma worked several canals away in this local store that sold handcrafted glassware from Murano. She was at work early because a cruise ship was due at 10 a.m., unloading three thousand passengers who would be in search of traditional, handmade souvenirs to remember their trip. Plus, with the regular tourists, it would be a busy and hopefully profitable day.

When she mentioned cruise ships it reminded me that we'd seen some local people waving signs with a picture of a cruise ship and a black line drawn through it. I was interested because we had cruised many times all over the world but never in or out of Venice, which had been a dream of mine.

She said that the rise in cruise ship traffic in 2013 alone had been around seven percent, which had seen the anti-cruise ship protesters up in arms yet again. Although everyone appreciated and enjoyed the economic benefits of cruise passengers buying souvenirs, taking tours with local operators, eating meals and generally contributing to the economy, many believed it was not worth it for the level of erosion that ships caused passing through the lagoon.

She said Venetian residents organized a flotilla of protestors who wanted to rid the cruise ships from the city and managed to hold up the departure of one of the ships. They believed that the large ships cause irreparable damage to the delicate foundations of the city and its canals. The mayor of Venice proposed that cruise ships dock at the nearby port of Porto Marghera instead of traveling through the lagoon, in front of Saint Mark's Square, easily dwarfing the entire city.

I told her we'd just witnessed a ship coming in the day before and it was shocking how the entire ship was longer than the width of the water entrance to Saint Mark's Square. It totally blocked the view of the lagoon for many minutes while it traversed and anchored. Since I couldn't tell how she stood on the subject, I certainly did not reveal that secretly I thought how awesome it would be to cruise in through the small islands in the lagoon and to see Saint Mark's from a ninth floor stateroom on one's own veranda.

She further enlightened me that there had also been calls to create a floating offshore port which would then deliver cruise passengers via smaller tender boats. But that would not be a viable option given the latest cutbacks on traffic in the waterways of the city. Another option was to dredge a completely different route for cruise ships to pass into the city and allow them to use the same port as they currently do. This newly dredged route would not see ships pass so close to the center of the city and Saint Mark's Square. Previous opinions were to ban cruise ships and move to another nearby port instead.

The government did cut by about 20 percent the number of ships into Venice in 2014. The Italian prime minister announced plans to open up a new canal route into Venice which would allow cruise ships to continue to visit this wonderful city but to enter by a completely different route, thereby completely cutting the damage to the foundations of the city. From November 2014, cruise ships larger than 96,000 tons were banned from entering the city via the lagoon especially even bigger cruise ships of more than 200,000 tons that carry more than 6,000 passengers and 5,000 crew.

People from the protest groups had commented in the press that this was a good first step in their fight to ban cruise ships from Venice, but that it was simply a first step and the campaign to ban ships completely would go on.

Wow, she knew a lot about this situation for sure. And I could totally understand the historic value of preserving this one-of-a-kind place in the world, now one of my top five favorite cities. I was ready to enlist, sign a petition and carry a sign, and vowed never to cruise in or out of Venice until remedies guaranteed the preservation.

After the cruise predicament education, which only took about five minutes as she spoke fast with very good English, she introduced herself as Carola and it turned out that she was proprietor of the store. She asked why I was visiting her city and I explained we were combining Venice with a tour of Croatia and Slovenia with longtime friends celebrating milestones in our lives. Because she arrived early and was ready for the onslaught of shoppers, it seemed she had time to visit with the tourist from Oregon. I was delighted to say the least and here's more of what I learned in the next five minutes.

Her children were Leonzio and Maddalena and I had accurately guessed their ages, three and five, and they both had birthdays coming up the next month. They were both born in June almost two years apart, June 3 and 14.

Her husband was named Roberto, or Berto, and oversaw a team of 10 workers who unload supplies and products and make deliveries for medical offices in the Castello neighborhood. She added that it is very hard work pushing and pulling carts loaded with heavy equipment. Nothing is motorized except the boats, and since this neighborhood didn't face the Grand Canal, all items are moved from barges to smaller motorized boats that fit into the smaller canals. This creates more distance to cover, and more bridges to cross, and they have to haul their items on their shoulders or pull carts to doctors' offices, clinics and hospitals. No wonder, even with my brief view of him, he looked so fit. I was really enjoying her story.

As a few shoppers started to trickle in, she asked if I'd like to come over that evening for antipasti and vino and bring my husband and friends. I was jolted that someone I had just encountered would be so welcoming and told her absolutely yes and asked what time we should come so she wouldn't change her mind—not even taking into consideration or consulting my other compatriots. I knew they would totally be "in" for this experience as we all loved to visit local people wherever we traveled. I asked if we could bring anything and she replied, "grazie but no," and that "Nona" would take care of everything. Of course, I didn't know who Nona was but that was fine with me. I recognized the first name as I had a childhood friend named Nona. Serendipity, I thought as I left her shop.

When telling my partners about this incredible encounter and invitation, they weren't at all surprised as things like this seemed to happen to me on occasion.

My now favorite gelateria La Mela Verde opened at 10 a.m., and our first gelato stop of the day was complete. I savored every lick of limone and dark chocolate. I did know that these daily splurges, sometimes more than once a day, were too quickly coming to an end. We spent time leisurely exploring Cannaregio and there seemed to be many historic small churches and cathedrals in this neighborhood. There was a plaque on the wall at the Foundation Studium Generale Marcianum that read, "Culture is that through which a person as person, becomes a real person. 1980 Pope John Paul II." Since this Pope was Polish, I thought something might have been lost in translation but I liked it anyway.

The Palazzo Labia was the point where the canal of Cannaregio flowed into the Grand Canal. We decided that if we ever got totally lost, we'd just head to the Grand Canal and follow it around to the Rialto Bridge, then we'd know where we were. We did have many adventures getting lost in Venice, which was one of our goals. We ate our share of hand-tossed, thin crust pizza with tomato sauce, herbs and cheese, including for lunch that day. Normally we'd each order a different kind and share slices. Another favorite was artichoke, Kalamata olive, prosciutto with a little cheese and tomato sauce. I am convinced that the best pizza in the world is made in Italy.

That afternoon as we crossed the Scalzi Bridge cutting through the Santa Croce district, I again checked my pre-marked gelato map for any sightings that we just couldn't pass up. And luckily for us there was one not far from where we were, called Gelateria Alaska. The owner, Carlo Pistacchi, seemed a colorful character yet an artisan who was passionate about his craft. Alaska seemed an odd name in Italy but they were known for their house-roasted local pistachio, and who could pass up a house specialty? Hard to believe that I was skipping limone but I did and the second scoop was mojito, which combined lime juice with plenty of spearmint leaves and pure sugar cane. I was not disappointed. On our way back to our hotel we discovered a perfect little square and made exquisite art purchases at Testolini located at 1911 Bottega dell' Arte, a fabulous art supply store established in 1911 with reasonably priced originals and prints, along with calendars and handmade cards, located right off of Piazza San Marco.

We stopped at the small, yet well-stocked grocer not far from our hotel and purchased a bottle of Callalto Supericre Prosecco, extra dry, to take to our adventure that evening. We knew it was good because we'd had some given to us at the hotel as a welcome gift.

When we arrived at 19:30 (7:30 p.m. our time) I eagerly entered through the sapphire wooden door and got to meet those who I peered in and spied on that very morning. Momma had shared the story of the peeping signora Americana and divine intervention of our encounter at her store. The entire Rossi famiglia was up to speed. Maddalena, who they called Maddy, and Leonzio shortened to Leo, were friendly, very outgoing youngsters and knew English very well especially when compared to our pitiful Italian language endeavors.

We met Nona and discovered "nonna" means grandmother in Italian. Her given name was Patrizia Circo, and Nonno (grandpa), was Vito Rossi. I told her I thought her name was beautiful and said that my mother's name was Patricia. She asked about my mother and I told her she was born in 1926, raised in the middle of the United States during what was known as the Depression, and traveled with her family of nine all in one car to Oregon to escape the Dust Bowl in her father's quest for a better lifestyle for his family. I explained a bit about the Depression and Dust Bowl as they weren't familiar with these events. My mother and father raised three children, and were gifted with 10 grandchildren and 14 great-grandchildren. She is the much-loved and godly matriarch of a larger family unit with dozens of nieces and nephews from eight siblings of which only one remained. Plus, my father's oldest sister, a favorite aunt of mine, was named Patricia. The name was used once more in our extended family for a cousin, but shortened to Patti.

Patrizia and Vito appeared to be in their mid-60s yet they weren't the elders of the family. Berto's great grandparents, Marco and Francesca, lived there, too, and we had the honor of meeting them. As it happened, there were four generations behind this colorful door, sharing a common area but each living in their own apartment. This large multigenerational home had belonged to their family since the 1940s when Marco and Francesca moved there to start their lives together.

Nonna and Nonno (Patrizia and Vito) raised four children, all now in their thirties. She said they were all out on their own except for Berto and his dear family, whom I guessed might be her favorite. Vito worked for 37 years for the Ministry of Infrastructure and Transport, which is responsible for roads, motorways, railways, ports and airports as well as general transportation planning and logistics. We found out that he worked specifically on building roads, and since three of our foursome had worked for Oregon's highway department, they peppered Vito with questions and he told us about the roadway system he helped build on the mainland.

I wasn't quite as intrigued as the trio about the Venetian road construction and this side conversation went on for some time while I learned from Patrizia about their children. She shared with me that their oldest son is an engineer working for the Venice Water Authority under the Ministry of Infrastructure and Transport on the controversial but hopefully successful project nicknamed MOse (modulo sperimentale elettromeccanico, or in English, the experimental electromechanical module). In other words, building the 78 inflatable gates to control tidal flooding which included a new breakwater, ship locks and even a fake island. The gates are supposed to make a huge difference. In theory, they lie flat on the seafloor at inlets and inflate on command to stop too much water flowing into the lagoon. They are supposed to inflate when tides rise 3.6 feet above average which usually happens about five times per year.

She remembered well the great flood of 1966 and said November 4 was just like any other Acqua Alta with water gurgling up drain holes and between stones, but before the morning tide had receded into the lagoon the afternoon tide came in, pouring over the paved streets along the water and covering Piazza San Marco. The city's oil storage tanks ruptured and a minor seafloor earthquake triggered a mini-tsunami. Venice was under more than six feet of stinking muck and black sludge which ruined thousands of pieces of art, inflicted over $6 billion in damages and left 5,000 Venetians homeless. Their home was spared except for a lot of cleanup of the bricks in the courtyard and lower part of the foundation. With the completion of MOse in the next year or so, she and everyone else hope it will never happen again.

Their second son lives in Vernazza, on the coast of the Cinque Terre, and is the owner of a prosperous olive grove producing some of the finest olive oil in the country. We were dipping our bread in his homemade oil, plus the olives were baked into the bread nonna had made. Their third child, and only daughter, is an artist residing in Florence. She specializes in handcrafting silver jewelry using local stones and Roman glass found in that area. She is also a popular watercolor painter with her gallery on the tourist ridden Ponte Vecchio Bridge. Berto is the baby of the family and clearly he and Carola were taking very good care of, and bringing joy to, the two older generations.

While drinking vino, a pitcher of sangria made with lemon, oranges and apples, and feasting on Italian appetizers of bite-size calzone with olives and artichokes, prosciutto with melon, Caprese salad, all kinds of mysterious looking seafood, a fruit medley of figs, apricots and dark cherries (it looked like nonna owned the local market in the square), and homemade gelato made just that afternoon, we learned a lot about their family and some history of Venice. It was the third time in one day I'd had gelato and nonna had prepared a smorgasbord of flavors including limone from their lemon tree, mixed berry made of raspberries and elderberries, and spearmint, fresh from their garden. I was in gelato heaven.

The great grandparents, Marco and Francesca Rossi (Rossi means red in Italian) explained that historically Italian last names were based on where a person lived or was born. The Rossi family originally grew red grapes in the interior of the country before Marco moved to Venice in the early 1940s for a job.

Marco Rossi and Francesca De Luca first met while in service to a wealthy family who lived at Cavalli Fanchetti Palace on the Grand Canal in 1941. His job was to catalog all music, instruments and art pieces, of which there were thousands in the palace. Her job was in the kitchen as the main cook; she had two other helpers. Son Vito laughed and said that everything any of them knew about cooking was due to Francesca.

They were married in 1946 and had twin sons, Vito and Giorgino. Sadly, tragedy struck the family early as Giorgy died at age 17 while fishing in the lagoon in his small boat. Speculation was that a wave from a larger vessel might have tipped it over and, like most Venetians, he didn't know how to swim.

Marco's history included serving in World War II fighting against Nazi Germany. He still felt indebted to the "Americano Liberatores," to whom he attributed turning the war around when arriving in Italy and ending the war sooner rather than later. He was honored to have helped protect his historic city of Venice that was largely free from attack. The only aggressive effort was Operation Bowler, a successful Royal Air Force precision strike on the German naval operations in the city in March 1945. The targets were destroyed with virtually no architectural damage to the city. However, the industrial areas in Mestre, Marghera and the railway lines to Padua, Trieste and Trento were repeatedly bombed. He recalled how on April 29, 1945, New Zealand Army troops arrived in Venice and relieved the city, which was already in partisan hands.

Marco was the same age as my father and I told him my father had served in the Army in the 10th Mountain Division C Company 85th ski and climbing troops that retook Mount Belvedere near Vidiciatico, in northern Italy. I shared that my father-in-law served in the Navy in the South Pacific. Marco recalled rumors that had circulated at the time about these soldiers on skis dressed in white and carrying rifles.

I explained to Marco what I recalled about my dad's time in the military. Dad left on January 4, 1945 on the USS West Point that several years earlier had been christened the SS America by President Roosevelt's wife Eleanor, and was one of the first passenger ocean liners. The ship was turned over to the Navy in 1941 and went through a massive conversion including painting it camouflage gray. It was the fastest ship in the fleet and arrived in Naples on January 13. Then soldiers were loaded onto Navy boats that held 200. They sailed up the Mediterranean to Leghorn (Livorno) on the western coast of Tuscany. They walked about 12 miles to Pisa where they camped for a week and were given a one-day pass to visit the Leaning Tower.

The war started for my dad in the Alps of Northern Italy. It was another 70 miles walking to Vidiciatico, a town at the base of Mount Belvedere. They camped at a nearby deserted private airport. The word had gotten out where the Americanos were because the next morning, as the soldiers came out of their tents, hundreds of barefoot children greeted them holding empty food cans, in spite of snow on the ground. The soldiers gave them all the food they could until they were instructed to stop because they needed food, too. They also stayed in a small town for two weeks doing reconnaissance with the local Italian Army scouting paths, trails and access through the mountains.

The 10th Mountain Division faced German positions along the five-mile long Monte Belvedere-

Monte della Torraccia ridge. Other divisions had attempted to assault Mount Belvedere three times, even holding it temporarily, but none had succeeded. To get to Mount Belvedere, the division first had to take a ridge line to the west known as Riva Ridge. The Germans had Riva Ridge protected because it was a perfect vantage point to see the approaches to Mount Belvedere and to shell and bomb the area below. After much scouting, it was decided the assault would be at night, a 1,500-foot vertical assent. The Germans considered it impossible to scale and manned it with only one battalion of mountain troops. The attack by the 86th Mountain Infantry on February 18 was a complete success and an unwelcome surprise to the Germans. Dad said they never would have taken Mount Belvedere two days later if the 86th Mountain Infantry hadn't taken the Riva Ridge. The main objective was capturing Mount Belvedere but it was heavily manned and protected with German minefields. On the night of February 19, the 85th and 87th Regiments spent part of the night trying to sleep on snowy, rocky ground with one GI blanket each. They were to attack shortly after midnight and when they got on their feet the shivering slowed down. Attacking at night was a new idea. They were to use only bayonets and hand grenades, since firing would reveal their position and they would be going in without coverage of artillery fire. Their success again depended on the element of surprise so all weapons were unloaded and were not to be fired until after daylight when an order would be given. This was unusual.

On February 20, my dad's unit filed toward the line of departure. When daylight came, the firing began. During the attack they encountered land mines and a buddy was killed instantly and Dad was hit with shrapnel in the right leg. While lying on the frozen ground in the snow for 12 hours waiting for help to arrive, he could only listen to gunfire and airplanes overhead, and prayed that the rest of the battalion reached the top of Mount Belvedere.

Medics arrived and put him onto a stretcher, placed him on the hood of a jeep and drove down the mountain to a first aid station and, after being treated, loaded him in an ambulance and delivered him to an evacuation hospital on the front lines, where he had his first surgery. His next stop was an Army hospital for another surgery, and after almost four weeks was loaded on the USS Shamrock Bay hospital ship on St. Patrick's Day, March 17. A doctor on the ship was Dr. Kelly and he introduced himself saying it was a good day for the Irish as my dad's last name is Riley. After two days the Shamrock arrived in Naples where he was transferred onto the USS Larkspur, a huge hospital ship with hundreds of injured. He and one other white man were in a ward with 38 black men from the 92nd Infantry Division nicknamed the Buffalo Division, for a 19-day trip to Charleston, South Carolina. I told Marco that Dad really liked those fellows and they had many good laughs and stories. That was the last time he saw any of those men because from there he went on a hospital train five days across the United States to Madigan Hospital at Fort Lewis, Washington, for treatment until October 2, 1945.

I told Marco that my dad, his two sons and two grandsons went to Querciola, the memorial site at Mount Belvedere, several years ago and they revisited the area where Dad had been. It was an emotional visit for my father. To this day he is afflicted with this war injury that required treatment throughout his entire life. He had been in and out of Army hospitals for years during my childhood and had eight surgeries on his leg. He received the Purple Heart and a Bronze Star. But we were thankful to God that overall his health and my mother's have been very good. About 20 years ago he was reunited for the first time with some of his Army buddies for a 50-year reunion. They filled him in on the rest of what happened that awful night and later. Marco bowed his head and quietly repeated the words "Americano Liberatores."

Marco told us he worked for decades as a police officer and later the chief of police at Carabinieri Camonda, Provincial Compagnia Stazione. The main duties were to enforce local regulations and traffic laws and he also dealt with petty crimes. I found this especially interesting as my youngest brother is a sheriff in a county in the Willamette Valley of Oregon. Marco saw plenty of crime in his decades as an officer but chuckled and said it was nothing as exciting as American movies such as "Moonraker," "Italian Job," and "The Tourist."

He shared a memory of working security on a movie made in 1955 starring Katharine Hepburn called "Summertime." Even though the movie title says summer, it was filmed in early spring. The movie studio used locals as extras and their sons, Vito and Giorgy, were in the scene where she fell into the canal. They only filmed it once. The filming took a little longer than expected due to Acqua Alta, which was a regular occurrence. He smiled as he recalled her traipsing around Saint Mark's Square wearing boots to her knees for a few days while they waited until the tide receded. He explained that Acqua Alta is fairly common and means "high water" due to exceptional tide peaks that occur once in a while. The phenomenon occurs mainly between autumn and spring, when the astronomical tides are reinforced by the prevailing seasonal winds which hamper the usual ebbing. The main winds involved are the Bora, which has a specific local effect due to the shape and location of the lagoon, and the Sirocco which blows northbound along the Adriatic Sea.

Francesca laughed and said Marco had a serious infatuazione with Katharine, the beautiful, very kind movie star who loved hats. The store owners appreciated her shopping sprees as she shipped boxes and boxes of handmade hats plus traditional Venetians masks back for family, friends and herself.

The City of Venice received its own copy of the movie on large reels and showed it many times in a local theater, always to a packed house. The family was very excited to see it and spotted the boys along with dozens of others they recognized. The town nicknamed her Kate the Great. I mentioned that I had a great aunt Katie and my brother named his youngest daughter Kate, combining Katharine and my name to make the name Kathleen.

Marco retired after 37 years of service. He had a sharp memory and wit and we couldn't believe he was 90 on May 12, just two weeks earlier. They had celebrated their 68th wedding anniversary on March 16. Five-year-old Leo proclaimed that he wanted to be a policeman, too, but Carola said they all knew it was because he wanted to ride in fast boats with sirens and bright flashing lights.

Francesca shared the history of the palace where she and Marco met. She said it was regarded as one of the most magnificent examples of the gothic architecture of the second half of the 15th century. The prestigious façade, perfectly proportioned, showed off the center of the two posh floors, rich with hand-carved knotted arches and indented patterns inspired by the Ducal Palace.

It belonged to the ancient family of Gussoni and was purchased afterwards by the Condottiere of the Venetian troupes, Cavalli. The count Alessandro Pepoli, who owned it next in 1780, called it the Academia dei Rinnoviat to use for concerts. It was successively the seat of Archduke Frederick of Austria (1846), of Court De Chambors, and lastly of Baron Franchetti, who had the interior restored by Camilla Boiti, brother of the musician Arrigo in 1890, although he did not change the exterior.

The baron, Alberto Franchetti, who lived 1860-1942, was a famous musician whose operas were very popular in his time. He bequeathed to Venice his large and splendid art collection together with the Ca' d'Oro that he owned. His son Raumondo, born 1891 and killed in a flying accident in 1935, was a famous explorer in Africa and Asia. Marco and Francesca worked for the baron Alberto and remembered how fondly he spoke of his son. Francesca sighed and said how sad it was that the son had perished at such a young age. Now the palace belonged to the bank.

They were very interested to hear about our families and lives. I thought about some of the similarities we'd learned that evening such as names, professions, parallel ages and dates. Even though we lived in a country 5,600 miles from Venice, it occurred to me that from their lives, and the other people I had encountered on numerous adventures around the globe, that the following adage holds true for everyone: Every person loves their family, their God, their home and a desire to support their family. We are not so different. The thing I had learned about Europeans was that they tend to take work less seriously, where work is part of your life but not your entire life. I like that a lot.

After hugs and kisses on both cheeks, we said our grazies and arrivedercis and promised to keep in contact. Because of this extraordinary experience, both my husband and I wished we had one drop of Italian blood in us, but sadly we knew we didn't.

Saint Augustine wrote, "The world is a book, and those who do not travel read only a page." This page with the Rossi family, this snapshot in time, would never have happened if the slightly ajar, sapphire-colored door hadn't mysteriously opened to remind me that this heart of mine was made to travel the world.

About the Author:

Deleen Wills had a dream to share stories about experiences and people she has encountered in her travels. This is her first attempt as a writer except for annual Christmas letters and fund-raising appeals. She grew up and still lives in the beautiful Willamette Valley in Oregon with her husband Mark. She worked in the nonprofit educational sector for 30 years in alumni relations, development, event planning and orchestrating travel programs.

Beginning a new chapter in 2015 and now officially retired from full-time employment, she enjoys spending more time with family and friends, working part-time as a travel coordinator, organizing and escorting adventures for friends and family, volunteering for several nonprofit organizations and her new passion, writing.

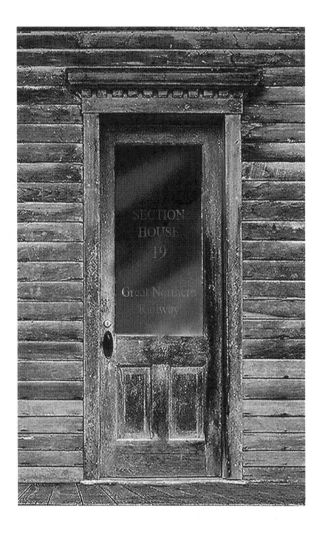

2

The Orange Door
J. Steven Hunt

There is a vintage cabinet in our living room that has long been a favorite conversation piece. Maybe that's because it has the markings of a long, hard-fought life. It has graced our home for 40 of my 68 years and still brings a smile as I think about the family gatherings it has seen. We've kept the silverware, cloth napkins and a salt and pepper shaker collection in it, along with a few other household essentials.

I remember the first time I saw it. From that day forward I began hearing many stories about it by my mother and relatives over the years. Most of the stories from the past few generations are true, but there is no way to verify the previous century's stories, so I assume they are lore rather than fact. But all in all, it has been an old friend for as long as I can remember.

The Door

My mother grew up in North-central Montana. To be exact, it was in a little whistle-stop town called Galata. As a child, I was there many times on family trips, visiting relatives during holiday weekends—usually the fourth of July. For a couple of weeks in the summers I made the trip by myself on the train. It was a great adventure, riding the Great Northern Railway from Whitefish past Glacier Park, through the Blackfeet Indian Reservation and across the plains to Shelby, where my aunt and cousins would meet me. I remember gawking at the wide open spaces north of Great Falls, especially the vast wheat farms, interspersed with large, untamed areas of prairie grass filled with all sorts of wildlife.

I learned a lot from my cousins during those stays, like the fact that running deer jump over a barbed wire fence but antelope squeeze under it. I had a lot of "firsts" back then, partly because I was away from my parents' watchful eyes and joined my daredevil cousins in doing crazy things usually considered too dangerous.

One of the old folks' favorite pastimes was to drive out to see abandoned homestead houses and recall stories about the people who had lived in them. One summer in the late '60s I visited my cousins, and, on one adventure trip, came within sight of an abandoned house standing alone, proudly defying wind and weather. After the usual admonitions by my aunt to watch out for rattlesnakes, we walked through the sand and prairie grass on a discovery mission.

It was then that I first saw the door. At the time, I had no way of knowing that tired-looking old door could introduce us to so much of what came later. It appeared to be nothing extraordinary—just a door on a building that should have been torn down long ago. Instead of the front door falling down, it had stubbornly held on to its doorjamb, trusting a lifelong partnership with rusting hinges. The door's orange paint was mostly chipped off, exposing the gray wood that had earlier been preserved by layers of paint. The bottom of the door was full of scratches, undoubtedly put there by a dog determined to wear down resistance to its requests to get in from the cold.

The doorknob and plate were gone, probably taken by souvenir hunters. I was surprised to see that we were actually looking at a railroad section house— a building usually located near a section of the rail route and used for housing railroad workers. I was told that this one had been retired and moved to this spot, which was nowhere near a rail line.

As is sometimes the case, the glass was still in the door. I was surprised to see that in spite of the porch missing, windows gone, sections of siding ripped away, and most of the roof shingles gone, the door glass remained. Faintly painted across the glass were the words "Section House 19, Great Northern Railway." Then I understood why the door was orange—the official color of the GNR.

As Auntie related memories we stepped up on a rock placed there as a substitute for the missing porch. Once inside, even without windows, there was a hush in the single-room layout. We all stood for a moment, in reverent silence as we pondered the history that was around us. Except for a built-in closet, there were no dividing walls, just a room about 18 by 30 feet in size. The floor showed varying degrees of disintegration—the main portion had worn boards, but the corners were covered with bits of surviving linoleum.

A Treasure Found

We began to look around, noticing old boards, strange knotholes and finding small items of interest.

"Look, here's an old fork," I said as I stooped to pick it up. I imagined it had been left there from days gone by when a family gathered for its daily meals. On some of our other house-hunting excursions we'd seen houses that had furnishings in them—pieces that had remained there for decades. This particular house contained only a low cabinet that begged my attention. It was worn and the finish was faded, dented and scratched. The cabinet was only about 14 inches high and 48 inches wide, with nine shallow drawers. Each of the drawers was marked with a labeled, brass pull.

I bent down to read the labels and discovered that there were a variety of subjects written on them, specifying things the drawers had held. All of them were empty except for a layer of prairie dust. I tipped the cabinet to see if it had any information on the back. Sure enough, faintly visible near the center was a stamp: "Western Maryland RY Company, 1858." There were other unique marks on it, including an almond-shaped gash that appeared to be caused by a knife or arrowhead.

"Wow, this is *old*!" I exclaimed. "…Like you!"

Auntie smiled at my one-upmanship. We had a habit of making playful jabs at each other.

"It's been here as long as I can remember," she said.

As I thought about the years it survived and the miles this cabinet had traveled, I wondered what stories it could tell. We dubbed it "The Cabinet" and listened as Auntie told stories that had been passed down to her. By the time we were ready to leave, she said if I had a desire to preserve it, I'd better take it before someone else did. I jumped at the chance, and since that time, it's been in our home.

Where it Began

The cabinet was originally part of the Western Maryland Railway Company office in Baltimore. The WMR operated in Maryland, West Virginia and Pennsylvania as a freight railroad, with only a small passenger operation around 1860. The Baltimore station was one of many along the route and served as a central routing office for lines running north and west. When each office was built it was furnished with a desk, a tall stool, a table and chairs set, and a cabinet that held documentation for tracking the commodities shipped in its rail cars.

When the railroad was later sold, the furnishings were put up for auction and the building dismantled. The furnishings were stockpiled for sale in a warehouse near Baltimore. On auction day, scores of people turned into scavengers as they toured the grounds and secretly noted their favorite items, preparing to bid on them.

During the early moments, the cabinet caught the interest of several people. Soon, a general store owner from Charles Town, West Virginia named

Francis Moorhead knew he just *had* to have it. After a flurry of bids the price climbed steadily until his offer of $2.50 eventually won out.

Francis loaded the cabinet into a buckboard and set out for home. He traveled three days to arrive at his store late one evening. After greeting Mrs. Moorhead and telling her about his trip, he proudly carried the cabinet into the store and then took care of the horses. He was just coming back into the store when he saw Mrs. Moorhead come over from the fabrics section to inspect the new acquisition. She immediately loved it and knew exactly what she wanted to do with it.

"Now, wait just a minute!" Francis protested. "I've hauled this all the way from Baltimore so I could store the cigar boxes in it."

"Oh, that's a horrible fate for such a lovely piece!" she intoned. A growing uneasiness gripped him as he saw the covetous look on Mrs. Moorhead's face. True, he'd had other ideas for his prize, but after a brief negotiation, Mrs. Moorhead won out and carefully loaded it with sewing notions.

Too proud to acknowledge defeat, Francis dealt with his epic arbitration failure by walking outside. As Mrs. Moorhead organized her sewing supplies, she saw Francis moping on the porch, smoking a cigar.

The Journey West

The cabinet proved to be the perfect centerpiece for the store and sales reflected that. Month after month, shoppers crowded around the cabinet to buy their thread, needles and other sewing supplies.

Francis had a stroke about a year later, so it was necessary to put the store up for sale. Friends and family posted flyers around Charles Town to spread the word about the sale. With Francis disabled, much of the task of selling the store fell on Mrs. Moorhead. Weeks passed. Then, on one rainy Saturday morning, an overly-large man named Herman Johnson stopped by and asked a lot of questions.

Mrs. Moorhead was puzzled. He didn't seem the sort to be taking on the purchase of a retail business. Furthermore, Herman lacked the social skills that would attract and keep customers. After their first meeting, as Mrs. Moorhead noted a distractive chewing tobacco stain on his beard, she found herself wishing someone else would magically appear to buy the store.

She also noticed that Herman's clothes were a bit strange. The first day they'd met, his ensemble consisted of a size 56 jacket and mismatched, high-water trousers. When he'd entered the store, the overall air quality had dipped considerably and Mrs. Moorhead, after a desperate attempt to maintain a gracious smile, quickly feigned a drippy nose so she could hold a kerchief to her delicate face.

Herman talked big and, quite honestly, too loudly as he ignored other customers and pontificated about the details of his financial strength. He excitedly explained how he and his wife Agnes had inherited money from her wealthy family. His father-in-law had sold a magnificently profitable business in New York and then suddenly passed away. Herman now had plans for the store, and, after some diligent consultation with their attorney, the Moorheads agreed to sell.

They completed the paperwork, and with well wishes, the keys were presented to Herman. He began his adventure the following week and did his best to succeed over the ensuing months, but after a couple of years he was forced to admit that retail was not his strength. The wanderlust took over and he began to plan his next big venture.

The inspiration for the idea came to him one night after going to bed with a headache. Suffering from an overdose of bicarbonates, he dreamed big dreams and awoke with the conviction that he was to pack up his things and head west with his family. His first go-around in trying to sell the idea to Agnes fell flat. Since he didn't receive much support for it, he continued making plans in secret.

Surprising no one, he suddenly sold the store in the spring of 1869 and invested in a covered wagon and oxen, telling his family they were "embarking on a great adventure," and leaving soon for Montana. After a few days of tearful conversations, Agnes, who could be characterized as a Casper Milquetoast, fell prey to Herman's determination. She told him only that the cabinet was at the top of her list of items to take.

Herman knew better than to press his luck and agreed to take it. He chose the first of April to leave Charles Town. No one at the time was quick enough to grasp the irony of the kinship between the chosen day and the fool who had selected it.

On the appointed day, Herman and their two boys hooked up the oxen and checked the load for the last time. In his delusional fantasy, the self-appointed "Monarch of Montana" climbed into the seat next to his royal wife as the boys scrambled into the back of the wagon, assuming their role as heirs to the throne.

They planned to sign on with a wagon train heading out from Independence, Mo. on what had become known as The Oregon Trail. Herman was impulsive and impatient, proven by his short term as a store proprietor. When he learned there would be a three-week wait to depart, he announced, with certain bravado, that they would strike out on their own. This was done against the advice of others.

Traveling through Kansas and Nebraska, they reached Wyoming by late June. Agnes never adjusted to the harsh, indelicate lifestyle. Much of her quiet time was spent wiping tears from her eyes as she longed for a U-turn. Herman and the boys played the part of the Great Hunters. They kept an alert watch for wildlife during the day and were able to shoot enough to feed the family. It should be noted, however, that the amount of ammunition needed to accomplish a successful kill averaged about double what it should have.

They traveled well with one exception. A major problem existed because of Herman's inexperience. The wagon he had purchased was actually a freight wagon, seemingly a good choice, but in fact, too heavy for the oxen to sustain their strength on a daily basis. By the time they reached Wyoming it had become apparent that the burden was too much for the animals. Herman was left with no option but to somehow lighten their load.

Herman felt one of the obvious choices was the cabinet—the heaviest item they carried. Bedding down for the night, he finally succeeded in getting Agnes to stop weeping and acknowledge that it must be sacrificed. As Agnes fell asleep that night, she tried to push thoughts of resentment and revenge out of her mind. But the logic of identifying the heaviest item on board kept pressing in upon her. The math was clear: the cabinet weighed less than 75 pounds and Herman topped 300.

Near dark, Herman and the boys finally carried Agnes' prized possessions away from camp, out of sight of the trail, and laid them under the shelter of a large tree.

Their last-minute choice to hide their discarded belongings under a tree was the inevitable salvation for the cabinet. As fate would have it however, a critical error was made by their choice to travel alone. They bedded down for the night, not knowing it would be their last.

A Real Tragedy

At dawn the next morning their camp was attacked by Indians who ambushed them as they lay in their bedding. With no one on watch, an onslaught of spears and flaming arrows ravished the camp. The entire family and the oxen were killed and the wagon burned. During the mayhem around the campfire, a wayward arrow sailed off target and lodged in the end of the hidden cabinet. Because of its weight, the cabinet had settled down into the wet grass overnight, and the arrow's flame failed to ignite it.

In a matter of minutes the attack was over. Having accomplished their raid, the Indians rode off, leaving the dreams of Herman and the travails of Agnes shrouded in the silence of the open prairie. The cabinet remained under the tree through the winter, withstanding blowing sand and drifting snow.

The following year a new group of travelers stopped for the night and discovered the remnants of a burned wagon and two oxen skeletons that, by then, had been picked clean by vultures. One family in the group, the Hartungs, also found the Johnson's scattered remains.

While the work of digging the graves took place, the Hartung's youngest boy, Markus, wandered into the trees and stumbled upon the cabinet. Having just dug the graves, the weight of emotion lay heavy on Robert and Darlene's hearts, and, at first, the boys' shouts seemed intrusive. But after seeing the cabinet they realized it represented all that remained of the settlers' dreams. The family agreed it could not be left behind, so Markus and his brothers teamed up to carry it back to their wagon.

That year, after traveling through Nebraska and Wyoming, the Hartungs had found the Johnson's camp. It had a profound impact on them as they later pushed ahead in tedious days of travel. They resolved to be tenaciously watchful, praying for safety for themselves and other families in the wagon train they had grown to love. Their westward route continued through Wyoming until the day they said goodbye to their friends and headed north toward Montana.

A New Home and New Families

The Hartungs chose to settle in Montana's Gallatin Valley, three miles northwest of Bozeman. For the remainder of that summer and into the fall, Robert worked to renovate an old barn where they would live. The snows came in early October and, by then, Robert and the boys had enclosed enough of the interior to have a snug place to ride out the winter.

Robert divided the building in two—a generous portion for themselves with enough room in the other portion for sheltering the livestock through the winter. With few furnishings, the house seemed spacious. The oldest boy, Zeb, built a ladder out of young lodgepole pines. It was tall enough to reach the loft that served as a second-story bedroom for the boys.

When the subject of the cabinet came up, it was agreed there was a greater need for it in the livestock area than in the living area. Robert built sawhorse-style legs for it, and, once completed, it served as a place for tools and horse tack. The cabinet remained there through that winter and subsequent years, gathering its share of dust and dents as anything in a barn does. This period represented the maturing years for the cabinet, far different than the genteel life it had enjoyed in the Moorhead's general store.

As the years passed, the boys grew into men and Robert's hard life as a farmer finally wore him down. He passed away working in the field at age 65. Darlene and the boys gathered with friends to bury him on a knoll near the east end of the ranch. Darlene moved to a small house in Bozeman and enjoyed her remaining years. The farm was passed on to Zeb, the oldest, but it was agreed that Markus would get the cabinet, since he had been the one who'd originally found it.

In time, he married his school chum, Jennie. He had grown up with her, working on their studies and playing together outside their one-room schoolhouse. Jennie admitted later that she'd had her eye on Markus during their school years, but he joked throughout their marriage that she had actually fallen in love with the cabinet.

Jennie bore him three boys and a girl. They lived and loved on a farm about 20 miles north of Zeb's ranch. Markus worked the land and raised wheat while Jennie worked hard raising the children and keeping the home fires burning.

World War I passed and the country fell on hard times. The Depression had an impact on the nation's economy and Markus had to sell much of the farm, and many of their belongings, just to keep food on the table. By then the cabinet had been in their family for many years, but it was one of the items that had to be given up at the Depression farm sale.

An Unfortunate Turn of Events

Among those attending the sale was a man from Oregon named Jesse Ohlgren. Jesse was in Montana on a fishing vacation and planned to return to his job at the Kalapooya Lumber Mill.

He was excited that he'd made the winning bid on the cabinet. The following day he headed for home, carrying it in the back of his pickup, a dependable Ford that was his pride and joy. He knew just how he would use the cabinet.

As he made his way through the Idaho panhandle, he daydreamed about his prized possession and, in the monotony of the hot day, dozed off. He was awakened suddenly when the truck lurched to the left after hitting the gravel on the shoulder of the road. He reacted by jerking the wheel to the right but the lightweight pickup rolled and he felt himself going upside down. The vehicle tumbled down an embankment and landed in a large patch of gooseberry bushes.

Jesse's head hit the windshield and he was knocked unconscious, but the pickup was mercifully saved from much damage by the fact that it landed in the flexible, loosey-goosey stalks of the bushes.

The cabinet had been wrapped in a blanket, but not tied to the truck bed, so when the truck rolled, the cabinet sailed skyward then clattered indignantly to a stop at the side of the road. Meanwhile, Jesse remained unconscious, out of sight of the roadway, and thereby invisible to anyone who might come along.

At the sight of a mysterious-looking box in the road, a passerby stopped and was delighted to find this gift from heaven—a fine piece of furniture swaddled in cloth like a newborn baby. He thought that it would make a lovely gift for his new bride. Looking around, there was no one in sight who might lay claim to it. He loaded it into the trunk of his Chevrolet sedan without closing the lid and drove off.

Meanwhile, Jesse woke up with a headache, but thankfully no broken bones. When he gathered his wits enough to determine what had happened, he looked for a way to get out of his predicament. He was not happy about the dents in his Ford or the disappearance of his new purchase.

After searching several minutes, he knew there were not many places it could have gone, except into someone else's possession. He waited a while until another vehicle came along and flagged it down. He was blessed to find an attractive, talkative gal who was both friendly and concerned about his plight. He immediately fell under the charm of this angel of mercy and proceeded to babble at length about his misfortune.

He soon realized the situation was not without its problems. Ms. Angel Eyes would be of little help in dragging his pickup back onto the road. She did, however, offer to drive him to her house where her husband, Norman, could provide the proper equipment and muscle to get him back on the highway.

Three hours later, they were able to do just that. He thanked Norman for his help and offered him money. Jesse hurried off, glad to be heading west again, but hungry and in need of a place to spend the night.

Just before dusk, he drove into the mining town of Wallace and spotted a restaurant called Josie's Café. It was a welcome sight. About the time Jesse found a parking place, he spotted a Chevrolet sedan next to him. As he moved around it, he noticed a bulky box hanging out of the trunk. To his amazement, he realized it was his cabinet!

He quickly tried to gather his thoughts. Being the gentleman that he was, he pushed aside thoughts of violence—smashing out the car windows, or entering the café and overturning Chevy Man's table in a grand show of abject disgust.

Jesse chose the only solution that would ensure getting his cabinet back. He concluded that two disappearing acts were a good way to end the day, and simply grabbed the cabinet, placed it into his pickup bed and drove away.

Safely on the road, he had a good time laughing as he drove. He temporarily forgot how hungry he was until 15 miles down the road when the town of Silverton came into view. He stopped there, making sure he parked away from the highway and out of view.

A few days later, Jesse arrived in Eugene, tired, but happy to be home. After work that day, he cleaned out enough space in his area to set up the cabinet. He enjoyed his new companion and felt life was good. But unknown to him, the economic downturn that contributed to the Hartung's loss of their farm was also at work in the timber business. After a few months, the mill was closed. The cabinet was packed up with other furnishings from the mill and stored in a holding warehouse.

The Shadier Side of Things

Before prohibition ended in 1933, there was both a thriving business in making bootleg whiskey and clandestine transportation of alcohol. A few months after Jesse's cabinet took residence in the warehouse, Benny, the security man, was asked to find something in which to safely ship a quantity of alcohol. The shipment was apparently a high priority for an important man at the Eugene railroad office, and a plan was needed to ensure success. The intended goal was for it to safely travel to Montana, in time for a wealthy friend's retirement celebration in the small town of Shelby.

The plan called for shipping the contraband by rail north to Seattle and then east on the Great Northern Railroad to Montana. Benny, who pocketed a healthy bonus for his trouble, stumbled upon the cabinet and thought it was the perfect shipping container. Three days later, a man arrived outside the warehouse door at 10 p.m., and Benny took 27 bottles into the warehouse.

Working quickly, he wrapped each of the bottles in several layers of newspaper, loading each drawer with tightly-packed, precious cargo. He then strapped the drawers tightly shut and bundled the cabinet in heavy canvas, again wrapping and tying it to create a solid shipping container. After filling out the shipping manifesto, he drove to the rail station and sent it on its way.

Arriving in Shelby, the cargo was unloaded and received without incident by members of the businessman's friends who were charged with setting up the party. The cabinet had done its job and all 27 bottles were intact.

The party was intended to honor Marvin Shoonbuckler, a third-generation banker who was considered the best banker in town. This was due in part because there was no other bank within 40 miles.

Marvin had been popular with the area farmers because he was willing to extend large amounts of credit to most of them with little or no collateral. Now they were worried that the next man on the job would want to tidy up the accounts.

A half hour into the party, bottle #15 of the 27 had been opened and everyone forgot about financial affairs. Marvin was now belting out songs at the top of his lungs and dancing with anyone who was not preoccupied. His shirttail hung out on one side and his tie was used as rope to lasso Daisy Fields for the next dance. Soon it was draped around Daisy's neck. She had been his longtime secretary and over the years had participated in other interesting escapades with Marvin.

About 1 a.m. the party wound down and the farmers drove home as best they could, dreading the thought of getting up in three hours to go to work.

The next morning the people who didn't have a hangover showed up to clean the bank before its 9 a.m. opening. By 9:10 there were a few customers waiting outside the locked front door, and by 10:20, a small crowd was getting unruly. They tested the doors multiple times only to find them still locked. Meanwhile, inside, as the cleanup crew finished their work, they assumed that the cabinet was considered merely a shipping box and hauled it away to the junk heap.

Finding My Family

The Great Northern Railroad station in Shelby was the very one where my childhood adventures had begun each summer. Prior to that time, my maternal grandfather had worked for the railroad on the lateral lines that serviced small towns with freight, supplementing the east-west Great Northern route.

My grandparents lived outside of Galata, 25 miles east of Shelby. Grandpa and Grandma raised five kids in a little farmhouse that sat in the middle of the flat, empty prairie. The week after the Shelby celebration, Grandpa had been directed to go to town and pick up railroad supplies. Driving through town, he spotted the cabinet in the railroad's junkyard. After obtaining permission, he loaded the cabinet into his truck and took it home.

Grandma was delighted with it and set about cleaning it up. She put it in the dining room and it remained there during the years my mother grew up.

When Mom left home to begin working, she hadn't finished high school, but traveled west where she'd heard there was work in Ellensburg, Washington. She worked as a waitress for a year before deciding to return home for a visit.

I recall her telling of her sadness as she neared home, coming over a rise in the landscape, looking for the house but seeing nothing. It was only then that she realized the house had burned to the ground.

She inquired in town (so small it was more like a neighborhood) and learned that her folks were living in a section house a mile west of town.

When the fire had started, it happened so quickly there was little time to save anything except an old pump organ and the cabinet, both pieces that were the dear to their hearts. Grandma and Grandpa died a few years after that, so with the section house vacated, it remained abandoned. When I discovered the cabinet a generation later, it was the best thing that could have happened. Had I not rescued it then, it may never have survived.

I found a short-legged table to set the cabinet on. In the years our kids were growing up, the cabinet served us in many ways. At Easter it was a great place to hide eggs. At Christmas we left the drawers slightly open and hung decorations from them.

As my writing career took on a bigger part of my life, I used the drawers to organize my manuscript drafts. Before computers I kept a massive collection of pencils, pens, erasers and typewriter ribbon in it. Lately, the top serves as a place to set our flat screen TV, and whenever I pass by the cabinet, I can't resist giving it a gentle touch to feel the silky finish and remember all of the stories that were told about it.

Sometimes I find myself misty-eyed when I think of those stories, but I'm so happy I got to play a part in them. And I am grateful for everything that happened because I responded to the call of that old, weathered door.

About the Author:

J. Steven Hunt's rural Montana upbringing encouraged his adventurous spirit and gave him an ongoing love for exploring expansive, open spaces around which many of his stories revolve. He is the author of *Love and Deception—One Family's Encounter with Dementia, Alex and the Airplane,* and *Stories of the Journey: The 75th Anniversary of Corban University,* as well as co-author of 11 DIY books on graphic design. Writing is just one of his creative expressions spanning his 50-year career in the arts. He lives in Oregon with his wife, Kathy, near their children and grandchildren.

3

The Blue Cardinal:

A Memoir of an Ocean Flight

R. D. Roberts

This is not good," I said to myself. Ice was on the wings of the airplane. It was time to look for a way out. I was seated beside a colorful aluminum door, white with a two-tone blue stripe, flying solo in a single engine Cessna Cardinal between Canada and Iceland. In the past few minutes, there had been enough ice built up on the wings to confirm that the first traces were not my imagination. I was looking at the real threat of growing ice. The presence of ice on the wings can ruin their ability to lift and without lifting, gravity takes over. Unless I did something soon enough, gravity would tug me to a cold wet grave.

Like most light airplanes, the Cessna Cardinal did not have a deicing system. I could not simply push a button to rid myself of the ice; I had to escape from it. To get free from ice, the pilot of a small airplane has four choices:

> - He can land at a nearby airport. I was flying over the Labrador Sea three hundred miles from the closest land. There were no nearby airports.

- A pilot can climb to a higher altitude to find air that is free from ice. However, I was already at my maximum altitude and could go no higher.

- He can turn around to find better weather. The weather behind me was getting bad. Turning around would thus do no good. By the time I headed back and flew three hours to land at Goose Bay, the weather would have turned downright nasty.

- A pilot can also descend. And that was my choice. I pushed forward on the control wheel to begin a descent with hopes of finding warmer air and started thinking about how I had managed, at 25 years old, to wind up alone over the ocean in an iced up single-engine airplane.

#

I have always been an airline pilot. I still have a photo of me, three years old, all dressed up in my uniform and holding my flight bag. All I needed was somebody to give me a job, an airliner, and a schedule. I was ready to go. This vision held tight for 25 years while I took care of a few details, little things like growing up and learning to fly.

I was 14 when I hit the lottery. My parents took over the operation of a small airport in Orange, Virginia. I immersed myself in flying. High school was an interruption as the airport became my universe. I breathed it all in, flew at every opportunity, and soaked in the pilots' stories. Pilots flew in from all over to drink coffee, eat a burger, and swap tales. I did not let them stop with merely telling a story. I pulled the details from them—the engine power settings, a flight's weather, and the minute techniques they had used to pull themselves from the jaws of disaster. They used salt and pepper shakers to set up the terrain and their hands to re-fly the maneuvers. With me asking so many questions, they probably flew their hands more than they flew their airplanes.

Some of the stories were my father's, a pilot who had operated in the bush back in the wild days of Alaska flying. Other stories were told by pilots who had flown B17s over Nazi Germany and by old clipper captains from Pan Am's flying boat days. The stories, not read from books, but told by the flesh and blood pilots who had lived them, kindled a fire in me to get out and join the adventure.

By the time I was 18, I had all the licenses and ratings needed to begin a flying career. Additionally, my time at the Orange County Airport endowed me with a legacy of rich oral history and I left, smitten with the romance of flight.

#

I had been over the ocean for three hours. I felt neither hunger nor thirst. With the wings icing up, I recognized the fear that had simpered in the background like a petulant adolescent since I had accepted the trip. The fear now growled in a loud grown-up voice. With fear nagging and my attention riveted on the flying, I was drained and felt old. The idea that I could die became real. It was not the post hoc fears I had known before—the after-fears born of the avoided car crash or a fall from a tree. Those were quick fears. Over the ocean, I bathed in fear's acid. It had many hours to etch away the immortality of my youth.

As the airplane descended, the air temperature began to warm up. That was good. But then, the air started to get bumpy. Really bumpy. Teeth jarring bumpy. The lower I went, the worse it got. There were two temporary fuel tanks in the cabin to give the airplane the range needed for the flight to Europe. The cables holding those tanks to the floor twanged like guitar strings. The tanks themselves, one beside me and a bigger one behind me, sounded like drums beating no rhythm. The aluminum tanks poinged and plonked. Worse than the noise, the fuel in the big tank slopped around, decreasing the airplane's stability. Turbulence and instability are a bad combination. Relieved of much of its normal downward push, the tail no longer made the airplane fly straight like an arrow. The airplane instead tended to wallow and pitch like a drunk.

Dust that had worked its way into the cracks and crevices of the airplane banged loose and floated up into the cold cabin air. I pushed my feet harder to keep my heavy boots from bouncing up and down on the rudder pedals. In the violent bumps, the instruments on the panel blurred. The turbulence was terrible. It seemed like the only thing that would not shake loose was the ice on the wings.

The airplane's magnetic compass was mounted at the top of the windshield. Seen through a little window, the compass indicator, called the compass card, danced around like a Frisbee in a terrier's mouth. I watched, captivated by the weird show. Then a big bump hit and the gyrating card took a bounce, jumped off its pivot pin, and wedged itself in the corner of the compass case.

Great. Now I did not have a compass.

I ground my teeth and my jaw ached.

#

An airline job remained elusive. Even though I had more than the required minimum flight experience, oil price spikes, a national economic recession, and the natural boom and bust cycle of airline pilot hiring closed all windows to getting hired by a major airline when in my twenties.

Instead of flying airliners, I gave flying lessons and flew as a charter pilot. One day, while looking through the latest Trade-A-Plane, a newspaper devoted to airplane classified advertising, I found this: "Seeking ferry pilots for worldwide aircraft delivery flights." I bit on the simple bait and called right away, before I had time to come to my senses. A week later, I was on my way to Europe in a single engine Piper Cherokee Archer with the ferry company's owner. She watched me fly and showed me the peculiarities of delivering a little airplane to Europe. After this one trip check-out, I would be on my own over the cold ocean.

Light airplanes are often flown to new owners around the world rather than shipped. It is much quicker to fly the airplanes. It only takes days to fly anywhere on the globe. Shipping can take months. Flying an airplane also reduces the chances of damage to the airframe as compared to putting it on a ship.

71

For shipping, an airplane must be taken apart and crated up. There are many opportunities for them to get bent. I was taking the Cessna Cardinal, a four-seat, one hundred thirty-mile per hour airplane, to Germany. The new owner would have his airplane in a few days. That is, he would have it if the airplane did not wind up in the ocean, where it would be a total loss. That might, however, be considered good. At the bottom of the sea the airplane would not be broken in shipment and in need of repair. Airplanes with a history of damage incur a value penalty.

"It's so dangerous. You can't do that. Why would you want to do that?" I heard this from several people who heard the news of my plans. It was indeed a valid observation, an admonishment to ignore, and a good question. Flying little airplanes over big oceans was dangerous. My choice to do it appeared crazy.

However, those flying stories from the Alaska bush and the air wars over Europe and the Pacific had buried themselves deep inside me. Since I first started flying, ten years earlier, I had always wanted to experience firsthand the limits of machine and self. I wanted to push across horizons, learn what I did not know, see what I had not seen, and feel what I had not felt. The Buddhist monk Pema Chodron wrote, "Nothing ever goes away until it has taught us what we need to know…" Flying across oceans was like that. A kind of destiny. Throwing myself into the mouth of adventure was a craving that never went away. The little ad in Trade-A-Plane was for me. It turned out I was the only person who had answered it.

#

During the descent, ice continued to accumulate as the Cardinal and I flew through various layers of clouds. The icing was light. Given enough time, though, even light icing causes a heavy concern. I would be nine more hours getting to Iceland. There is also the possibility--and Murphy's Law dictates it is a probability--that light icing will quickly get worse. Even at 25, I never assumed that any bad flying situation would get better. Pessimistic pilots, it seemed to me, had a better chance of living than did cheery optimists.

The ice and growing fatigue gave me tunnel vision. I did not even notice when the turbulence ended. I was surprised when I noticed the bumps were gone. There had been no attention getting bam-bam, one-two punch that often accompanies the end of the strong turbulence. It just ended. I looked around and found nothing had come loose on the airplane. Nothing had gotten bent or broken. The dust floating around in the cabin was my only reminder of the violent turbulence. I noticed, and have many times since, that aircraft manufacturers build remarkably strong airplanes.

With the end of the turbulence, the temperature shot up six degrees within a few hundred feet of altitude. "This is great," I thought. "Only four more degrees to go!" In a few minutes, the temperature would be above freezing and I would start seeing the ice shed from the wings. At first, there would be tiny flakes blowing off. Then, as the air got warmer, small patches of ice would leave the wings. When the air was well above freezing, large sheets would slide back and break up with a poof in the slipstream. It was a happy prospect, a dream. For the moment, things were looking good. The bumps were gone and the icing risk looked better. My only immediate concern was the loss of my compass.

The Cardinal had two heading instruments, the magnetic compass and a directional gyro, a "DG." The latter is a kind of a gyroscope with a compass rose. Since the takeoff, the DG had been wavering off its heading. Every 15 minutes or so I would have to reset it 15 degrees to line the DG up with the reliable magnetic compass. But the compass was now dead, its indicator card unmoving in its little window and wedged at a disturbing angle.

Therefore, instead of referencing the compass to correct the wayward gyro, I used the clock. Every five minutes, I moved the DG five degrees. I figured this would keep me on a fairly accurate heading. That is, it would keep me on a good heading if the gyro's ailment did not get worse.

Things being stable for the moment, my fear quieted. However, manifestations of fear are always changing, like a fire. Prior to the trip, fear had tried to warn me off: "You don't have to go. Taking the trip is dangerous. You might die in the arctic sea." The fear spoke to me and tried to reason. It proposed questions: "Do you really think you have what it takes to fly alone across the ocean? Your lack of experience might be the instrument of your own destruction." The fear appealed to my sense of compassion: "How can you expose your family to such worry? You should just beg off." Fear tried to save me from myself. It warned me to flee.

Then for a thousand miles after takeoff, while the airplane was still over solid ground, fear's voice continued but became louder: "Run away before it's too late. Just quit. Listen to reason. Land and walk away. You will feel ashamed, but you will be safe."

Once I was over the ocean, the warnings changed. Fear still gripped, still sang a chorus of self-doubt, still roiled and churned like a sickness within me, but its message was now different. Instead of telling me to run away, it told me that I had to fight. Fear yelled about my obvious questionable knowledge, judgment, and abilities, but it also squeezed and focused my mind so that I might come out alive.

Flight or fight. In the past few days, I had seen the mechanics of fear at work. However, there also seemed to be a transcendent quality. Fear seemed to move the spirit. Feeling the fear of real-time mortality seemed to clean the detritus from life, revealing, not beauty, but sublimity. It was a feeling akin to love, but without the radiance of well-being. Being in the whale's belly, though terrifying, seemed to put me in direct contact with life's central nerve.

However beneficent this might be, I sought relief from the voice of fear, which on this trip was a never silent demon. With everything stable for the time being, I made a radio call. I had not heard a word for over two hours.

"Anybody read Cessna 34220 on Common?" I asked on the VHF "party line" frequency. There was no answer. Several minutes later, I tried again. This time, someone called back.

"220 this is Northwest 30. Go ahead."

"Would you mind relaying a position report to Gander for us?" Even when flying solo, pilots employ the plural pronoun.

There was a moment's pause while the airline pilot grabbed paper and pen. "Sure. Go ahead."

I gave him my position information, much of it a rough guess since I did not have any precise navigation equipment working at the moment. However, a wag was good enough. At my altitude, I was flying below controlled airspace and there was no one around for hundreds of miles. Any airliners, like the Northwest DC-10, were at least four miles higher.

I thanked him for the relay and, wanting to gather clues about my heading, mentioned my lazy DG.

"Let's see … if you put the nose right on the sun … your heading would be three-zero-zero degrees."

"Okay, thanks. Do you have an estimate of the cloud tops?" I could not put the nose on the sun unless I could see it.

"Yeah, the tops look to be about three-three-zero." Thirty-three thousand feet. Even without ice, I could only hope to get to twelve thousand.

"Well, thanks, Northwest 30. You've been a help." And I meant it, even if his help was of no practical use to me. I just liked hearing his voice.

"Where you headed?" he asked.

"We should be in Reykjavik tonight and Stuttgart in a couple of days. You?"

"We're going to Minneapolis out of London. Have a good trip," he said.

"Thanks. You, too." I had not mentioned the icing, the recent turbulence, or made the heading issue seem more than an item of minor interest. Whining would not help. An airliner could do nothing for me. They could not reach out a hand and snatch me from the belly of my aluminum fish. The airliner flew in a different universe. En route over the ocean, real help was self-serve. But the talk made me feel better. What Jonah might have given for a radio.

"This is crazy," I thought again. Nuts. I was in the middle of the Labrador Sea. Beside me was a door that, on the ground, was so easy to operate. Pull a handle, open, and step out. I could step out and pound the ice off the wings. It was such a short step. I could see the wing right there! Here over the Labrador Sea, however, that step to the wing was three hundred and fifty miles long. I could not step out until I was on the ground somewhere. It would take me at least three hours to travel through the door to touch the wing.

If the ice should start to build up again or if an oil pump or some other critical engine part failed behind that single propeller, I could not stop and step out. I would be in the drink. Soon after that, I would likely be dead.

It was all crazy, but I had taken precautions and made good plans. There was a small life raft and emergency radio beacon stashed on top of the ferry tank. I wore a bright orange one-piece immersion survival suit, my legs stuffed into the suit's legs, the suit's arms and body folded over the back of my chair. I could not zip it all the way up and still fly. Imagine Gumby at the controls of an airplane. I could not just leave the suit in its bag, either. I had to wear it because the airplane cabin was too small in which to maneuver putting on a stiff, thick, neoprene suit.

After ditching, I would put my arms in the suit's arms, pull up the watertight zipper with my Gumby hands, grab my emergency gear, open the door, and step out into the sea. I would probably be underwater at first since the Cardinal was a high wing airplane. But in a moment, if I did not get snagged on something on the way, I might pop to the surface, grab the raft and pull its inflation lanyard, climb in, make sure the beacon was on, and sit like a bobbing buoy awaiting a rescue.

Yes, I had good gear and a good plan for survival, unless the impact, hypothermia, or drowning killed me. It was still crazy. I was in my right mind to be afraid.

But exactly what did I fear? Nature and mechanical parts do not harbor animosity. The sea is never angry. The sky is never brooding. The Cardinal had no feelings about flying over water. I had taken on this trip voluntarily. The risks to life were well known. I was not in conflict with the airplane or the sky. It was not man against nature. It was man against self. Ultimately, maybe it always is. The fearful demons and the dragons were all inside me. There was no external enemy or foe. Here, surrounded by trackless miles of air and water, my war with fear was contained within my own small mind and body.

"Enough of this existential gibberish," I thought. The fear and stress were, however, real and would never leave me. Even now, writing down the experience four decades later, the feelings again bubble up from some deep well. I grind my teeth as I write. The lines in a pilot's face do not all come from hours of squinting into the sun.

I needed to find out where I was. Although I could see nothing but layers of clouds, I felt quite sure that the DG, with my constant corrections, yielded a fair heading. Even so, doubt, fear's twin, lingered. I wanted confirmation and reassurance. I wanted to fix my position and know exactly where I was over the Labrador Sea.

Precise Loran C and GPS navigation devices were still years down the road. I did not have a sextant for celestial navigation; it would not have worked under the clouds, anyway. And besides, who ever heard of anyone flying alone in a Cessna taking a successful sextant shot?

For navigation, I was using dead reckoning. Having nothing to do with death, it is a system of deducing estimated position by figuring compass heading, wind drift, and elapsed time. It works remarkably well. A while after the Cardinal's flight, I dead reckoned across the North Atlantic, nonstop from Gander, Newfoundland to Shannon, Ireland. In two thousand miles, I drifted only forty miles off course, just a 2 percent error.

The Cardinal, though, had that pesky DG problem. My dead reckoning would be no more than suspicion until I began receiving the homing signal from the Prins Christian Sund radio beacon at the tip of Greenland. That is, if I was even headed toward the beacon. Maybe the DG had gotten worse and I was milling around, maybe in circles, out over the Labrador Sea, in which case I never would pick up the beacon's signal.

A nondirectional beacon, NDB, like the one at Prins Christian Sund, is nothing more than a radio station. A receiver in the airplane called an ADF is tuned in and a needle on the instrument panel points toward the station.

Well, it sort of points to the station. There is a lot of interference on NDB frequencies. Sun spots, auroras, astronomical radio wave spikes, engine ignition sparks, shoreline effect, precipitation static, and thunderstorms all seduce an ADF needle. A rock hard ADF needle is a rare thing. An ADF is not all that accurate.

Nevertheless, I began to tune the receiver to see if there were any useful signals coming through. I found nothing but the crash and hiss of background noise. One good NDB signal would give me a line of position. Comparing the line with my dead reckoned position would give me a rough fix. I would then know, within an unknown range of error, where I was.

Meanwhile, I continued the slow descent in search of warm air. There was no more ice accumulation, but the temperature stayed below freezing and the ice still clung to the wings. I went down to four thousand feet and then to thirty-five hundred. The temperature no longer took any of the big jumps like it had below the turbulent shear zone. At three thousand feet, the temperature was minus three degrees. I proceeded down to two thousand five hundred ...

On the ADF, I picked up a couple of choppy carrier wave Morse code signals. However, the signals were weak and the direction needle just swung to whatever galactic burst or snowflake produced a stronger milli-wattage. I was about to give up and concentrate on my diminishing altitude just as the needle gave a nod of commitment toward a signal. I listened, but found no Morse code identification. Instead, there was a voice. With a frequency near 500 kilohertz, this would not be an aviation beacon. It was a broadcast station. But where was it?

At two thousand feet, the temperature was up to minus two. It was almost enough. The clouds began to break up below and I began to see frothy white caps in the ocean. The surface wind was strong. Not a good day for ditching.

At one thousand five hundred feet, the thermometer stopped moving upward and the temperature remained stuck just below zero. I pressed the nose down to go a bit lower. The temperature got colder! It was not going to rise above freezing.

I no longer had hope that the air would warm up and melt the ice, but maybe it would not matter in the end. I thought of the old shrunken ice cubes I had seen in the freezer at home and remembered that ice sublimates. It evaporates. In a one hundred ten knot slipstream, sublimation does not take weeks like in a freezer, but it does not happen fast, either. Watching ice sublimate takes patience.

The ADF signal stayed strong. A radio station in some town or city sent out its chatter and tunes, the operator not knowing his signal was my lifeline. Maybe the station was somewhere in Europe. I had so much fuel that I did not care how far ahead the station was located. "Man!" I thought. "I could track this station almost all the way to the Soviet Union if I want to." I could just home in, cross the coast somewhere, pick up a reliable VOR navigation station and voilà! I would be in France! A quick hop over to Germany and I would be done! I would not have to worry about flying to Iceland. I could end my trip, and my worries, a full day early.

I picked up the map and searched for the radio station. About a quarter-way up the west coast of Greenland, I found "570-Radio Godthab." On the chart, it was just three inches away. The weather forecast for Greenland was good. Maybe I would follow the needle and just scoot over to Godthab, land, and do something about the compass. My fix showed I was about two and a half hours from Godthab and its three thousand feet of paved runway. Forget flying to France, Germany, or even Iceland. Landing in Godthab seemed like a good idea.

With a new plan and a new course, I thought it might be a good time for lunch. I was not hungry, my body still had no voice, but I figured I must need food. I fished into a brown bag and found one of the two ham and cheese sandwiches I had gotten from a machine back in Goose Bay. I found one of the three cans of Coke I had stashed next to the airplane's cold door. There was frost on the door's window. The can was cold and popped with a good snap when opened. I put the pop-top in the sandwich bag and took a long pull, the first drink I had had in hours. The carbonated liquid burned sweet, bubbly, and good down my throat. It was like a slap back into my body. I nibbled on the dry stale sandwich and took a bit of soda to moisten each bite.

"What is this?" I suddenly asked myself. Through the windshield, I saw a fleet of white boats. "Man, this is great!" I thought. "Fishing boats! Greenlandic fishing boats! Maybe they are out of Godthab itself!" I was excited and comforted.

Coca-Cola had just come up with a new advertising jingle. Giving up the idea that people standing on a hill singing and drinking cola would produce world peace, the company had lowered its sights. Drinking a Coke would produce a smile. The drink did taste good. However, my smile came, not from the soda, but from the view of the fleet of boats and their crews just ahead.

Then, with a pop like the bursting of one of the cola's bubbles, the happy picture ended. The soda can was dry. The sandwich was gone, and so were the boats filled with people. My fishing fleet became a field of ice bergs. Crushed and more alone than ever, I took a breath of resignation with no choice other than to press on. At least I had been happy during my meal.

Two more hours passed with my spirit in a stew of dejection and self-doubt. Then, on the horizon, was this another mirage, or were those real mountains? I watched for a while, expecting the new scene to fade. The mountains, however, grew more defined. Decorated with snow, their steep gray sides plunging almost vertical, they stood beautiful against the sea. Although Greenland's mountains are not the highest in the world, to me they were glorious, the best thing I had ever seen from an airplane. My thrill at the virginal scene was amplified by joy. I would soon be walking on land. Even though I had only been airborne for a few hours, it felt like I had been at sea for many days.

I soon landed, parked, and shut down the engine in one of the world's quietest towns. The propeller stopped spinning and so did I. I felt unplugged. I sat and stared out of the window with eyes that did not see. At some level, I realized that I was in Greenland. Greenland! Visiting Greenland! Visiting the world's second largest island was a surprise, a gift even. But I just sat there in a stupor, purging my fatigue. I had no impulse to look at the sights nor do anything other than vent the accumulated exertions from over the water.

With robotic moves, I finally unbuckled and opened the door. While flying, my moves had been small, the airplane cabin with its ferry tanks was tiny. It was like I had been sequestered in a Mercury capsule. Stepping out onto the airport ramp was the first big move I had made for six hours. I was stiff and sore. The fresh cool air of Godthab moistened my eyes and I began to see the foreign scenery. I imagined a human colony on another world. I saw stark institutional buildings, all sensibly designed to house the people and offices of Godthab. Fjords and mountains surrounded the town. There were icebergs in the harbor. They posed like national monuments in the fairway. Slowly through the thick mental fog, I began to know that I was "somewhere else."

Clawing out of the fatigue narcosis, I knew I needed to repair the compass. I was a long way from home, had a long way to go, and I was not going to delay the trip for want of a licensed mechanic … or a rest. As a boy, I had taken old airplane compasses apart. They were pretty simple. The biggest trick was trying to preserve as much of the compass fluid as possible. Breaking apart the Cardinal's compass case, being careful not to damage the gasket that keeps the joint from leaking, I found a screw had backed out. Its being loose made it possible for the compass card to leave its pin. I wondered how long it had been like that. Probably since the day it was installed new. It had waited years for an atmospheric martini shaker to put it to its failing test.

I put the compass back together, the seal secure, and the screws all back in place, but found that much of the fluid was gone. The compass card swung undampened by its missing stabilizing liquid. I asked the Inuit airport attendant, the only person I saw while in Greenland, about getting more compass fluid.

"None. Never seen none," he said.

From my days as a teenager knocking around the airport, I remembered seeing a bottle of compass fluid with the words "petroleum distillate" on the label.

"Well, then, can I have a small amount of jet fuel?" I asked.

His languages were Danish and Kalaallisut, with only a small amount of English. It took some time to communicate that I did not want him to fill the airplane with jet fuel. I only wanted an ounce or two of the Jet-A "petroleum distillate" to fill the compass case. Seeing me rip into the compass had no doubt convinced him I was crazy. I wonder if he would have stopped me if I had tried filling the Cessna's fuel tanks with gasoline engine-killing Jet-A kerosene.

The newly topped off compass worked and did not leak. I was bone tired, but still wanted to take off for Iceland right away. Canada's foul weather was heading east and I did not want to get stuck for who knew how long in Greenland.

The Cardinal was overloaded, permitted by the FAA to fly well over its design limit for the delivery flight to Europe. Even though we had burned off six hours of fuel, we still had 18 hours of fuel remaining on board. The airplane was very heavy for Godthab's three thousand feet of runway. The runways I had used earlier on the trip were all at least three times longer. There had been plenty of pavement for the overloaded Cessna. Godthab was a different story. The takeoff run took a very long time and I used almost all the runway's length. I had a close-up view of the far end of the runway as I crossed over it with only a few feet under the wheels.

The subsequent climb was also slow. If I turned on course right after takeoff, I would have immediately flown into terrain over four thousand feet high. With the airplane's poor climb performance, I initially had to head west, back over the Labrador Sea, opposite of where I wanted to go, and claw for forty miles to a safe altitude before turning east again towards the coast range. We would then fly over the icecap and tops of giant mountains that, in daylight, appear like islands piercing the two-mile thick ice blanket.

Through the dark night, I cruised blissfully ignorant above an unknown threat. What I thought of as my exhaustive flight planning had figured a trip only over the southern tip of Greenland. I had studied all the fjords, mountains, and reviewed the few airport facilities on that end of the island. I had not spent any time at all studying Greenland's high ice-crusted interior. The charts I carried had very little terrain information depicted. Some areas said, "No Survey." The charts were designed with the assumption that all flights would be made above eighteen thousand feet. Sometime later, I realized with belated terror that I had cruised at the same height as Mt. Forel, which lay only thirty miles north of my track across the ice cap. In my young and stupefied ignorance, I flew without concern for the shallow margin between my fragile aluminum shell and the ice and rock of Greenland.

For six hours, I flew over the ice cap and on over the Denmark Straight until I came to Iceland. It would have been good to see the airport and land visually, but Reykjavik's low clouds made an

Instrument Landing System approach necessary. Early in my flight training, I had learned the old wisdom to "always stay ahead of the airplane." To plan way ahead. Tired as I was and eager to be landed, I was so far ahead of the Cardinal's flight that, in my mind, I was already asleep in a hotel room. However, I was not there yet. So, I got the airplane all lined up on the localizer needle for the airport's south facing runway. When the glide path needle showed I was on proper angle for the runway, I pushed the nose over for the final approach. I felt the clean sheets and soft pillows, my eyelids already practicing for sleep. Then, for no apparent reason, both ILS instrument needles, the two indicators I needed to fly to the runway, slammed from side to side, and abruptly resigned, showing a red "OFF" flag.

For almost two days I had been continuously flying from the States. My fatigue felt like a separate entity. We were a trinity—the airplane, fatigue, and me. The few minutes required to break off the approach and come around for another try felt like a disaster. I grieved the delay. All I wanted was sleep. But once again, there was no choice but to keep flying the airplane. I pulled up and headed back over Faxa Bay to maneuver for another approach.

I heard another airplane, a Lake Buccaneer, on the radio. "Why is a woman out flying around in an amphibian airplane, in Iceland, in the middle of the night?" In my exhaustion the question counted as a cosmic mystery. However, the answer did not matter. It was the effect of her flight that hurt. The pilot took my place as first in line for landing, beat me to the Loftleider Hotel, and took the last hotel room.

A few minutes later, I stood at the hotel counter, grimy, cold, and exhausted. The young clerk saw a lost puppy on her doorstep. Her heart moved. She called several nearby hotels asking for a vacancy. All full. It looked like I would have to sleep in the airplane, which sat in sight like a cold coffin outside the lobby window, just beyond the airport fence. I picked up my bag.

"It is late," said the clerk. "You are so tired. I will be on duty alone until seven. If you promise not to say anything to anyone, I will let you sleep in the sauna." That is what she said. What I heard was, "You can sleep in the presidential suite."

"Thank you," I said. "Bless you" is what I meant.

She led me down to the hotel's basement. Finding a pillow and a pile of woolen blankets, we constructed a pallet on the sauna's wooden slats. She moved to the door and turned off the heater.

"Okay, you should be all good now. I will lock the door so no one can get in. I will unlock the door at six. You will be ready then, okay?"

I looked at my watch. It was 2 a.m. My head jerked up.

"Wait a minute. You're going to lock me in?" I said. There was no knob or lock on the inside of the carved blond pine sauna door. I would be in jail. I looked at the pallet. Its gravity overwhelmed good sense. It pulled me. "Okay. No problem. I don't want you to get in trouble. I will be ready at six. But please, if the hotel catches fire, will you promise to come down and let me out?"

"Of course," she said. But I had little confidence of her faithfulness under pressure. Nor did I experience joy at the prospect of dying in a burning sauna. How would that look? They would find a cremated corpse wrapped in a cocoon of burned blankets on a sauna bench. As my eyes closed, I contemplated such an ignoble end. "A weirdo's death," I thought as I drifted off. My demise in the sauna would be so different from the specter of my flight over the cold dark sea a few hours ago.

In the waking dream state of approaching sleep, I flew back over the water. Critical events from the flight flashed like cards in a deck, each one clear and real, the unconscious mind recalling and rehashing, projecting an endless line of what-ifs and should-have-dones. My mind folded the flight from Canada into the next day's 14-hour final leg to Germany. Recent history and the near future twisted together and many times the Cardinal flew through clouds and ice and got too close to mountains. My arms and legs twitched at the airplane's controls. Under closed lids, my moving eyes scanned the instruments ...

Then all the images receded as sleep cleaned it all away, for the rest of the short night at least, much as the sea washes away a sand castle.

About the Author:

At 14 years old, R. D. Roberts flew before he was licensed to drive. Today Roberts is an airline captain and continues to fly around the world. When not traveling he divides his time between the Pacific Northwest and Virginia.

4

The Gray Door
Del Riley

Early Years

Mother said, "Keep punching," as we drove away in a borrowed, eight-year-old 1921 Ford Model-T. My older sister Pat and I chimed in at the same time, "We are," with the batch of rising bread wedged in between us. Mother added, "Keep it up all the way to Grandma's house. I don't want to waste perfectly good bread."

I asked Mother how she was feeling. I was checking because she was about to have a baby. "I'm doing all right, Del," she replied. Dad had shared with me, but not my sisters, that Mother had problems having my sister, Pat, six years earlier. Then a baby boy had died one year before I was born. Mother had told me the story about my birth. Having no hospital locally, she had to travel 135 miles from Chinook to Great Falls, Montana, to a hospital that could handle a possible difficult birth. I was born almost exactly four years earlier in May, 1925, and was fine and healthy.

Dad was driving as fast as he dared from our two-story home, the Tommy Adams Place, outside of Chinook. It was several miles into town to Grandma's house. Grandma helped deliver babies for women in the area. Several hours later I had another younger sister. Mother named her Colleen. When I got to see her, I noticed she was different from the rest of us because she had blond hair and blue eyes. My sister Pat, who was two years older than me, had soft, big brown eyes and chestnut wavy hair. I had brown hair and blue eyes. My sister Joyce, two years younger, had light brown straight hair and blue eyes. After Colleen was born, Grandma baked the bread and Mother declared, "That was the best bread I've ever tasted."

That same year, I was sick with another horrible sore throat. Mother explained that a car was coming to fetch us to take us to a hospital for surgery to remove my tonsils. Pat cried, "I don't like that you'll be away, we've never been apart." I told Pat, "I don't care about the operation. I just want to go in a car. The only thing I have to ride is my tricycle round and round."

On the drive to the Chinook hospital, I was in the back seat nestled in blankets looking out the window. There were rolling prairies of wheat fields and barley that bumped up against ranges that Mother said were the Bear Paw Mountains and the Little Rockies. I knew what fields of wheat looked like. My Dad was a wheat farmer. About 1,250 people lived in Chinook and many had the last name of Riley because several of Dad's brothers and their families lived there.

It was a very hot summer in 1929 and farming was hard work. One day Dad announced, "I'm done with being a wheat farmer. The Canadian government wants people from the U.S. to utilize the farmland. I've heard from friends in Alberta about the great opportunities in dry-land farming. There's a farm called the Gardner Place at Frog Lake. It's near a small village called Heinsburg and we're moving there." Dad held an auction because we could only take a limited amount of belongings with us. The Canadian Pacific Railroad Company offered low prices to settlers to pack as much as possible into immigrant box cars. After the auction, he loaded seven horses and farm equipment plus some household items into two box cars.

With three young children and a baby only 4 months old, Mother said we couldn't go on the train with Dad. He helped load everyone, including Roy and Effie Harris and their two children, Russ and Millie, into their two-seat 1922 gray Model T car. Pat and I were thrilled to be going on an adventure. We drove out of Chinook, jammed in the Harris car sitting on upside down buckets and boxes and shouted good-bye to Dad. He had to go separately by rail with the horses and the things that were left after the auction.

We followed the Milk River which was a cloudy color. Mother explained the river started in the Rocky Mountains. The color came from the clay and silt. We saw strips of tall grasses and squatty trees that lined a creek or ditch but not very often. As we crossed the Canadian border at the small town of White Horse, there was a log house with a tall pole. At the top, waving in the breeze, was a red flag. It had blue and white crossed lines in the left corner and a shield with designs in the middle. Mother pointed out a wooden sign at the base of the pole that read, "Entering Canada." After our first long day on the road, we stayed in two roadside cabins overnight and paid 75 cents per family for the hard beds.

The next few days we followed the bumpy, dusty White Horse Trail winding around small hills, down gullies and across parched, wide open prairie. Sometimes tumbleweeds blew across the road. The big blowing dried weeds seemed bigger than our car. It was easy to spot deer and antelope grazing in the flat fields. That triggered excitement in the back seat and a game of 'who could spot the most animals in one day.' Russ Harris usually won because he was the tallest.

The dirt road was rocky and the tires blew out easily. Mr. Harris and Russ changed them often. It was very hot that August and the wind occasionally caused swirling dirt to become spinning tall columns. Mother called them dust devils. Mrs. Harris had a stash of Beeman's chewing gum in her satchel and created a game of 'who could find the newest thing' like a tree, hill, or car. We stared out the windows for hours looking and waiting but lost interest quickly as there seemed to be nothing but level, dry land. The White Horse Trail intersected with the Buffalo Trail. We drove on wooden bridges crossing rivers and streams and the countryside was dotted with random working farms, a few lakes and ponds. I got a piece of gum for spotting the first wooden bridge. Another tire blew out and as we stood on the side of the road we spotted several coyotes trying to catch prairie dogs. The coyotes were fast but the prairie dogs were quicker and had holes to dive into for safety. We laughed as one coyote came up with a muzzle full of dust and dirt. The girls squealed when a coyote won. I rooted for the little critters. It looked like they were winning.

We had gone about 150 miles when Millie Harris spotted a sign that read "Medicine Hat." I said, "Finally, some cars, people and stores." The town stretched along the South Saskatchewan River. We stopped at a mercantile and stocked up on groceries, got gasoline and continued on the Buffalo Trail. We had another 270 miles and several more days of traveling before reaching Vegreville where we'd meet Dad. Each night we found small huts or cottages along the road to stay in. We drove north and didn't see much except deserted farms and flat land. Mr. Harris explained that the Depression and harsh weather conditions forced many farmers to leave their homes and start a new life elsewhere. We went through the little village of Viking. When Mr. Harris announced we were close to the cut off to Highway 16 with only 20 more miles to go, his voice sounded a little higher. I figured he was excited like us. Mother told me a couple of times to sit still, but I couldn't; I was too wound up. After our one-week journey, we traveled 425 miles and were safely in Vegreville looking for the train station and Dad.

Mother checked the train schedule and found out Dad wasn't due for another two days. We said our good-byes to the Harris family as they continued on to Elk Point to stay with relatives. We were happy to discover they'd only be living about 15 miles from us when we arrived in Heinsburg. Mother checked us into a room on the second floor of a hotel, the first hotel I'd stayed in. I wandered out onto a small veranda made of black steel grating. Then I saw people walking below. I called to Pat to come out; she was up for anything I instigated. We stood on the steel balcony chewing the Black Jack gum. I looked at her, nodded my head, and at the same time we spit a wad of chewing gum on unsuspecting walkers adorned with pretty hats. I whispered to Pat, "Bull's-eye," and she giggled.

Dad arrived two days later and found a house until they could figure out how to get to Heinsburg. The train was too costly for the six of us, our horses and supplies, plus it only went that direction a few times a week. We lived briefly in a two-story house and Pat and I, while exploring the top floor, discovered empty boxes of Copenhagen snuff. We filled each one with sand and proceeded to eat it, pretending it was chewing tobacco. Mother caught us and told us if we ate sand we wouldn't ever be able to go to the toilet again. Scared, Pat and I went out into the yard and peeled down our pants, sat there and strained so we could poop. Mother looked out and saw our bottoms sticking up in the air. Pat and I got into a lot of mischief. She would glance at me with her soft brown eyes and knew exactly what I was thinking without me saying a word.

On to Heinsburg, Alberta

The following month, Dad packed everything onto horse-drawn wagons and we left Vegreville at sunrise. The countryside was sprinkled with little lakes, lots of birch, tamarack and fir trees, plus wildflowers and plenty of weeds. There was no road straight into Heinsburg, 55 miles away. The roads were rough and it would take us all day. We were on Range Road 65 about 15 miles when Mother told us all to watch for Township Road 534. I saw it first and Dad turned east and we rode 15 more miles. Mother then told us to keep our eyes open for Range Road 43A and when Pat spotted it, Dad turned north for our final leg of the trip. It felt like I had ants in my pants and was eager to be at our new home. We veered around a bend and between the trees we caught sight of the wide North Saskatchewan River which was down a steep, grassy hill. I saw my new hometown on the other side, up on another steep rise. I asked Dad how we were going to get across the wide river and he pointed to the ferry below. Going down the steep hill, across the river on the ferry, then up another steep hill was terrifying but thrilling at the same time. Our horses were huffing and puffing pulling the wagons and us down and back up the hills.

Dad discovered that the Gardner Place wasn't available so we stopped at the Cottage House, a two-room log cabin, and lived there through that first winter. The farm had a barn, well and an outhouse. The little building out back was not one my of favorite places and it was a dreadful trip in the winter after dark. I always heard coyotes and that, along with the cold, caused me to sprint at breakneck speeds. The Sears catalog was nailed to the wall to use for paper. I preferred the barn and all the neat animals.

Dad told me later that it was very poor planning on his part because he had no property to farm and no income that first winter. We lived around three lakes--Frog, Whitney and Laurier, and survived on fish and snowshoe rabbit. There was a smokehouse and Dad used whatever wood he could scrounge up to smoke the fish mostly using birch, fir and pine. The northern pike were bony but tasty. I really liked the smell and flavor of pine the best.

My Door

That spring, Dad announced that the Gardner Place at Frog Lake was finally vacant. It was time to move. After loading everything in the wagons and traveling several miles, we pulled up to the house. Mother and my sisters headed to our new two-story home but I made a beeline straight for the barn. The closed barn door seemed drab and blotchy. It reminded me of a cloudy sky or the color of the Milk River in Montana. I pushed open the gray, mud-splotched wooden barn door, anxious to discover what might be inside. I took two steps in and stopped. I spotted outdoor tools and bales of hay stacked along the walls. To the right were a few brown cows. On the other side were two big horses, all in their stalls. But a third smaller horse was standing in the middle of the floor staring right at me with his huge, dark brown eyes. I stared right back. From then on we were hardly ever apart. He was a reddish-brown bay horse with a black nose. He also had black tips on his ears and lower legs, with a black mane and tail. He wasn't as tall as the other horses so I named him Shorty. He was just the right size and perfect for me.

Everyday I loved brushing Shorty, especially his black, shiny thick mane. When I did, I told him everything that was happening, good or bad. Often he would nuzzle me and make funny noises. I knew he was talking to me. I brought him carrots that I would sneak from dinner. I didn't like carrots. When feeding the other animals, if he thought I was ignoring him he'd nudge me with his nose. More than once, I fell head over heels in the hay from the unexpected shove. He followed me around the barnyard like a puppy. Even when doing chores like rounding up Dad's cows, it was fun riding him. When I rode him it seemed like I was gliding on air or soaring in the clouds. If an animal could be a best friend, he was mine.

My favorite pastime was riding him bareback. I pretended to be a cowboy. I would get him running, slap him on the rump with the reins and he'd kick up his heels and he'd throw me off. One afternoon, some neighbor girls, Eileen and Ivadean Blair, were visiting my sisters. They were sitting on the fence as I raced across the yard on Shorty. I whacked him on the rump with the reins and apparently he didn't like it as much as I thought. He bucked higher than usual and I sailed straight up right over his head and landed belly first on the dusty ground right at the feet of the laughing audience. I could tell Shorty was laughing at me, too.

School of Hard Knocks and New Lessons Learned

My sister Pat was getting ready to start second grade at Frog Lake School. I informed my Mother one morning, "I want to be with Pat." Mother said, "Even though you aren't old enough, we are going to let you start school." This was probably a mistake because I was only five years old and just wanted to play. Our school was a one-room building with about 25 students, grades one through eight. We were lucky that school was only four blocks from home.

Miss Hall introduced herself the first day of school. She had an accent and was from England. She was short with brown hair that she wore in a big ball on top of her head. She didn't smile much and was very strict. She was not a bit bashful about banging us on the side of the head with a book when we messed up. She also used a large belt. A kid named Alfred had horrible bladder problems. He sat in the desk right in front of me. He was afraid of Miss Hall and didn't want to ask too often to go to the toilet. One day, he peed and it ran off his seat. I made a big deal of it, dramatically moving my feet out of the way. She came with the big book and whacked us both.

Every day Miss Hall came in, sat down at her desk, reached over and opened the small wooden drawer. She carefully took out her things to set on her desk, all without even looking inside. She'd be staring at us.

A family in the area butchered a cow. My classmate decided a funny thing would be to cut off the udder and four teats and bring it to school. He had the plan of putting it in her desk drawer. Someone, not me, opened the teacher's top drawer and then gently placed the bag inside. I was fidgety and on the edge of my seat. I was holding my breath and so was everybody else, it seemed. Right on time she sat down, opened the drawer and reached in, as always staring at us. But instead of touching her normal items like pencils and paper, she touched the cold rubbery bag. Her eyes bugged out and mouth dropped open. Just as she was about to say something, she readjusted herself and gathered her composure. She started pointing us out, every boy in

102

the class, whether we were involved or not. She knew exactly what house the "gift" had come from. He denied everything and we paid the price since she never could figure out who the guiltiest person really was. The oldest boys got the belt. The youngest ones got study hall.

One morning, Miss Hall explained the history of the Frog Lake massacre about 40 years earlier. White settlers from Europe had come to the area to live. They tried to show the Indians a better way of life. Cree Indian Chief Big Bear and his tribe had settled near Frog Lake. He had signed a treaty but was upset by what seemed to be unfair treatment. Wandering Spirit, the war chief of Big Bear's tribe, began to steal guns from neighbors. They were angry at Thomas Quinn, assigned as a representative of the Canadian government. The Cree were complaining that they were near starvation.

The massacre was led by Wandering Spirit. The band took Mr. Quinn hostage on April 2, 1885. Then they took more white settlers hostage and took control of the town. They gathered the settlers, including two priests, in the church, where Mass was in progress. After Mass concluded, the Cree ordered the prisoners to move to their camp a few miles away. Mr. Quinn refused so Wandering Spirit shot him in the head. Even though Chief Big Bear attempted to stop the shootings, Wandering Spirit's band killed another eight unarmed settlers.

Poor Alfred was so terrified he wet his pants, which wasn't unusual. Two desks down, my friend, Rhoda Evans, was whimpering and trying to be very quiet. Before Miss Hall's story, I was already a little afraid of the Indians but now I was terrified.

She continued saying that a Hudson Bay Company clerk, Mr. Cameron, went to the Hudson's Bay shop to fill an order that Mr. Quinn had given him before Mass. When the first shots were fired, Mr. Cameron escaped and made his way to a nearby Cree camp where the chief pledged to protect him. She finished by saying Wandering Spirit and five other warriors were convicted of murder and were hanged. Big Bear had supposedly opposed the attack but was charged with treason, convicted and was in jail for three years. It was clear how she felt about the Indians. When I got home, I told Dad what Miss Hall had told us about the massacre, and he said, "I think she told her own version and not really the truth."

At first I wasn't happy that Dad made us move again, this time to the Heins Place. He said the land had fewer rocks, a good well and was better overall. I knew it had a barn and I was taking Shorty with me, so I'd be all right. And I really liked Miss McBride, who was our teacher now. I was in second grade at Whitney Lake School.

Miss McBride was tall with sandy-colored, shoulder length hair that she let hang loose. When she smiled, her face lit up like sunshine. She smiled all the time. She had big hazel eyes and she was nifty. Around 25 students attended grades one through eight. School went until the end of June so walking in spring and early summer was easy. In the winter, I drove a small sleigh that Dad made. The neighbor kids who had skis would take a rope and I'd pull them behind our sleigh going home.

One day, Miss McBride said she had a story to share about the Frog Lake massacre. I remembered what I'd heard from Miss Hall a few years earlier and knew I never wanted to hear that scary story again. But Miss McBride told a different version. She explained that the Indians had lived on their land for hundreds of years. Then European white folks had come, taken over the Indians' land and made them move to smaller parcels. They wanted them to change their religious traditions to become Catholics. The white settlers killed the bison needlessly and brought in diseases like measles, chicken pox, flu and other horrible illnesses. With no natural immunity against these germs, natives died in huge numbers. She said, "The worst of the suffering was caused by germs, not by guns."

She said the Frog Lake massacre happened because the Indians were angry for the reasons she just explained. They started finding guns, ammunition and food supplies from the area. The Cree were extremely upset at the government's representative, Thomas Quinn, who treated them horribly and causing many of them to starve to death. People died at the massacre. The Indians paid for the mistakes. It was a familiar story to me but not as frightening as when Miss Hall told it.

Even though I thought I knew what was coming next, Miss McBride surprised us when she said she had heard a love story but couldn't confirm if it was true or not. She told us about a young man called Lawrence. He was in love and wanted to marry a Cree maiden. In the 1880s this was almost unheard of, especially since he was a Catholic. Miss McBride didn't know if Lawrence was his first or last name. Every time the couple met in a secret barn, they planned how they would run away and start a life together.

One night, the young Indian girl waited until her family was asleep then crawled through the newly dug small hole in the corner of her family's teepee. She was very afraid because if her family or tribal members discovered her mission, she would be put to death for being a traitor. The bright moonlight shining on the fresh snow twinkled like a million diamonds, helping her find the way through the darkness. No matter what the consequences, she knew in her heart she must go to her lover and warn him of the upcoming danger, even if it meant her death. She had made this journey many times before and had always returned before her family awoke in the morning. She pretended she was a frightened deer running across the frozen tundra as fast as she could. She felt the golden eyes of wolves and coyotes watching her.

The importance of her mission, and her love for the white man with big, blue eyes, drove her on through the cold. After about two hours of running, she arrived at the fort. She spotted several guards but managed to weave her way behind bushes and wagons before squeezing through the partially opened barn door. The warmth of animals would help while waiting for her lover. To her surprise, he was waiting with an affectionate embrace.

She told him exactly what she had overheard at the pow wow. When he learned from her that an uprising was to occur at the Frog Lake Catholic

Church on Sunday, he was at a loss about what to do. If he told the officials, they would insist on knowing where the information came from. His Indian love would be in terrible trouble not only from the white man but her tribe. They would know she had betrayed her own people. If he didn't give the warning and people were killed, they would have to live with that guilt and it would be unbearable. After agreeing on a plan, she ran as quickly as she could, returning home, unnoticed, just before daybreak.

Lawrence waited one day then rode 30 miles east to the authorities at the Northwest Mounted Police post at Onion Lake. He told them he had been a resident of the Frog Lake area his entire life and had known and observed the Indians. He said recently he'd noticed unrest with the Indians. He also observed some war parties out stealing guns and supplies. He believed there would be an uprising soon that would harm residents of Frog Lake. He suggested it would be wise to relocate the settlers for a while to see what happened. The Mounties quizzed him for a while but didn't agree with his assessment of the situation. They ignored him. Lawrence did not attend the Mass on Sunday morning, the day of the massacre.

She ended the story by saying that the governments of Canada and the United States continued to struggle with Indians, who were the first people on the land. I felt sorry for the Indians because they were here before us and were treated so badly.

This was the first time I realized that there were two sides to every story. I preferred the way

Miss McBride saw the world. She had a completely different way of teaching, the way she handled us boys and never hit us. One day during recess, I had to write "February" 50 times because I had left out the first "r." We had many plays and parties in school and one Christmas she gave all the boys skis. I had a lot of respect for her and wanted to do right for Miss McBride.

Prairie Life

The Heins Place was a little one-room house made of logs. At the edges of the big room were three beds and a heating stove in the center. Off to the side was a cook stove in the kitchen area with a large table. Dad built a one-bedroom addition for him and Mother.

Mother made straw tick mattresses for our bed. She sewed together four strong, empty 100-pound flour sacks to make a cover. I helped her as she stuffed each one with good, clean straw and packed it tightly. What she didn't take into account the first time was that the straw contained fleas or lice from animals. Before long I was scratching, then my sisters began itching. It was a painful ordeal removing the pesky bugs from our hair. She tried several homemade concoctions including lye soap and using a bone comb that didn't work. Then she tried a potion that smelled like gasoline that burned my scalp and caused a rash that lasted for days. But the bugs were gone.

Mother often said, "Del, go to the cellar and bring up some fish." The root cellar was another favorite place of mine. All summer Mother preserved potatoes and vegetables along with many types of berries and meats. She stored items in this dugout room directly beneath our kitchen. I was always going down there for something. The smells made my mouth water with the dill pickles brining in a 10-gallon crock, and another crock with butter. Knowing no one else was there, I popped a handful of dried blueberries in my mouth. They were my favorite berry. The potatoes in the darkness were eerie-looking, like giant spiders with the white sprouts looking like curvy legs. My sisters didn't like it down there--another reason I did.

The land was infested with gophers since it had been abandoned for some time. Dad made some snares and I put them around the holes. I stretched out on the grass, held really still, barely breathing, and waited. The first gopher popped its head out. I yanked the snare and caught one; it was like I'd won a prize! Dad learned that the government would pay a penny a tail for them. I saved the tails in an old box and I mailed them in. Snaring gophers was lots of fun and a moneymaker that helped purchase groceries.

Every family had big gardens in the summer. It's where our food came from throughout the winter. As the only boy, I seemed to get my share of outdoor work with Pat. We learned early to see the difference between a weed and a plant. There was much to do, with wood to carry and animals to fetch. I learned very young how to milk cows. Doing that each morning and night was my hardest job. I didn't like cleaning the barn either because the manure was heavy and there was a lot of it. The old straw had to be removed and new straw put down for their bedding. But at least I was with Shorty and he helped me through the hard days. He seemed to accept me no matter how I acted or what I did. I talked to all the farm animals but only Shorty answered with a snort, nudge or flick of his tail. It was endless work and I told Shorty one cold night, "I do not want to be a farmer."

Our Town

Our teacher, Miss McBride, told us some early history about Heinsburg which started in 1905. In 1913, John Heins established a post office and store at his home near Whitney Lake. The next year a ferry started five miles south. With the coming of the Canadian National Railroad late 1928, two grain elevators were built near the river. The town of Heinsburg moved to be closer to the railroad. We lived in what was called Old Town, or the original Heinsburg, about three miles from the newer Heinsburg. If we happened to be in town when the train arrived, it was exciting to watch the commotion of men unloading the merchandise onto dray wagons then delivering it to the merchants.

There was one main street and both sides were filled with stores and businesses. There were three general stores: The Red & White Store was owned by Mr. Gregor. Benny Kates and Mr. Fuller used their last names for their stores. Gregor's and Benny Kates's two stores were big, with everything one could imagine. They had paint, furniture, kitchen goods, clothing and candy. I was drawn to the smell created by open barrels of dill pickles and peanut butter, blended together with leather goods and the oiled floors. It made a strong, spicy smell.

There was one Chinese restaurant, a drug store, a harness store with leather goods, a church and one blacksmith. There were two grain elevators that were so tall they seemed to reach the sky. Farmers, including Dad, brought and stored the grain at harvest time, then sold and shipped it out on the train.

On one trip to town, Pat and I had a few coins. We were looking forward to spending them on Clove chewing gum. We raced into the Chartier Hotel towards their candy counter and stopped in our tracks. We stared at the ceiling as something strange was hanging from the center of the room. It was a rope with a rounded, clear glass piece attached. Someone flipped a switch on the wall and the round glass lit up. I wondered how they got the kerosene up the rope to the wick. A lady at the counter called it an electric light bulb.

Mr. Fuller, owner of one of the grocery stores, once asked Dad to haul some merchandise for him. Dad knew it was skullduggery and said no. Mr. Fuller, along with some others, moved all the items at night from his small store to an abandoned farm not far from the Indian reservation. Then somehow the store burned down. Everyone knew Mr. Fuller did it to collect the insurance money and he did collect. Then he started selling items to Indians. Mr. Fuller was too bold because someone reported him to the Royal Canadian Mounted Police. They came and arrested him and he was in jail for several years. Dad told me never to steal, lie or cheat.

Neighbors and Winters

The Lorenson and Blair families lived nearby. All of us kids entertained ourselves with games of Hide and Go Seek, Red Rover and Follow the Leader. Many times we made up new ones. In the freezing winter months, except for going to school and doing chores, we were inside most of the time and played card games and cribbage.

There were several neighbors from Germany and another from England, the Jenner family. Harry, the son, spoke proper English and always wore nice clothes. Some called him a dandy and said unkind things about him because he was not your average farm boy. But he was good and decent and even though older than me, I liked him.

Donald Lorenson was my best friend. We pulled a lot of shenanigans and promised each other never to tell a soul. He had six brothers and sisters, the oldest being Toots. I thought she had an odd name. Donald told me she shared the same first name as his mother, Hazel, so they called her Toots. I learned that Toots wasn't really related to them. She was staying with The Lorensons because her parents died. Her older brother Blaze was hunting 50 miles north at Cold Lake. She was 16 years old with curly auburn hair and eyes the same color as Shorty's. She was like an older sister to all the Lorenson kids and us, too. We all loved her. I realized I liked girls with brown eyes.

That winter her brother was killed in a hunting accident. Mr. Lorenson couldn't take Toots to her brother's funeral but Dad had time. He took the Lorenson's team of horses and a buggy with a small sleigh, and drove as fast as they could to Cold Lake. I felt so sorry for her because she had no parents and then no brother. Mr. Lorenson told her she would live permanently with them. She was very sad the rest of that winter. Mr. Lorenson had a beautiful sorrel, an ex-race horse, that wasn't worth much. He gave the horse to Toots. I could tell it helped her a lot; now she had something of her very own. She made a name for herself around the area racing that horse. Mr. Lorenson developed a little business delivering eggs and milk to town about two miles away. We'd see her ride by like a shot on her way to town to deliver fresh dairy.

Later that winter we were running low on hay for our animals. Dad and I slid open the barn door to take out the team of horses. Shorty was lucky to be staying home. Instantly the temperature from the warmth of the barn to the outside dropped below zero. This wasn't unusual for the time of year and something I never got used to. After hooking the hayrack to the sleigh and climbing onto the hard seat, we wrapped ourselves in layers of rabbit robes. Dad had traded items with the Indians for the robes that were made from many Snowshoe rabbit pelts sown together. We were heading east 18 miles to the Blackfoot Indian Reservation. He knew the Indians had stockpiled hay. It would be a slow trip both ways. We couldn't trot or run the horses for fear they would suffer from frozen lung. Dad put a shield over their noses to help filter out the cold. Our horses were invaluable and would be impossible to replace.

On our journey Dad told me how he became acquainted with some of the Indians, especially Chief Joe Bum, Frying Pan Bum and Joe Pecho. Because he had a rapport with them and they trusted him, they often gave Dad the best deals. In the winter they'd come with baskets of raspberries, strawberries, blueberries, gooseberries, Juneberries, which were like little pulpy blueberries but not good-tasting, and tart chokecherries, plus lots of fish. The Indians always needed salt, sugar and flour. We didn't have much but Dad felt it was important to trade a certain amount with them.

After several hours, we arrived at Chief Joe Bum's home, where he and his brother, Frying Pan Bum, lived together with their families. The house was a large wood frame covered with canvas, animal skins and some wood. The Indians were great hunters. Animal hides were plentiful so their clothing was mostly leather. They made their own moccasins and made them for us also. An Indian lady took the measurements of our feet with just a piece of string. Dad said, "We are poor but these people are poorer." When we arrived back home and Mother had a large pot of rabbit stew ready for us, I felt very lucky.

The lakes, ponds and river froze several feet thick every winter. When the river froze, entertainment was the "ice breakup." A big board was posted in town that listed times and dates. Everyone bought a guess. In the spring when the river started breaking, whoever had the closest time and date won a large pot of money; Dad never won.

Often we'd cut three or four foot slabs of ice and store them in our ice house. Then we'd stack and cover them with sawdust to keep them through the summer. We got the sawdust from Mr. Frazer, who had a little sawmill on the edge of Whitney Lake. He was a nice man, and his wife was an Indian, which was a little unusual. We stayed with them for two weeks when Mother went to the hospital in Elk Point. She was pregnant but had a miscarriage. Even though they whispered, I heard them say they didn't expect her to live long enough to reach the hospital. Pat and I were old enough to know what this meant. We were heartbroken for days but thrilled and relieved when Mother was better and returned home to us.

High Jinks and Shenanigans

"I'll be back in a little while," I shouted to Mother. She was lying on a blanket under a big tamarack tree. I was at Whitney Lake with my family for a picnic with townsfolk on a summer Sunday afternoon. We were finished with dinner. I was stuffed full of roasted chicken, potato salad, coleslaw, sandwiches of sliced ham, beans, dill pickles and my favorite, blueberry pie. I didn't want to take a nap like Mother and sisters, so went out to do some exploring.

I found a birch tree in a sandy area of the lake. I pulled out my pocket knife and carved my initials "DWR." Then something glistening and bright caught my attention. It was to the right at a little inlet of the lake. I wandered over and sure enough, there was something shiny tucked down in the damp cool moss. But I still couldn't tell what it was. I reached down and pulled out a bottle. When I glanced around I spotted many more bottles. It dawned on me that this was something my Dad should know about. I ran back to the picnic and showed him my one-bottle treasure. He took one look at it and asked, "Where did you get this?" I told him and Dad said, "I think my son has discovered Old Berg-the-bootlegger's stash of moonshine." Men patted me on the back and asked me to show them where it was. It became a game of Follow-the-Leader, as all the men were following me. I took them right to the spot of hidden booty and the men pulled out every last one of the bottles. It seemed that Old Berg hid his homemade moonshine in the cool moss and let it age before he sold it.

I heard a ruckus and the next thing I knew every man, including Dad, was drinking moonshine. Then all kinds of crazy things started happening. One guy picked up the rear end of a Model T showing how strong he was. One man climbed a tree making noises like a monkey. Men were wrestling all over the place. The nice calm party turned into some kind of craziness. It was clear my Mother wasn't happy and asked, "What happened here to cause such wild behavior?" After my explanation, I whispered to Mother, "I wish I hadn't found that moonshine; I don't like what it does to the men, especially Dad."

Living on a farm, it was common for me to see calves, puppies and kittens born. I was about eight when my parents decided I should know even more about the birds and the bees. Dad said he and I were going to visit the Andersons. We walked a couple of miles as Dad was leading our cow Dolly along when I asked him, "Why are we taking Dolly to the Anderson's?" Dad simply replied, "Dolly is in heat." I actually knew something about the birds and the bees but I didn't know what the word "heat" meant. We arrived and the Anderson kid and I thought the behavior with Dolly and the bull was a little strange. But when it was over, Dad and I turned around, walked back home and put Dolly back into the barn. We went into the house where Mother was at the stove ironing Dad's only white shirt and she said, "It is so hot in here, I can't stand the heat." I turned to Dad and said, "Oh, looks like another trip to the Anderson's." My parents laughed and I didn't know why.

When Mother ironed Dad's only white shirt, it meant one thing. There was a dance coming up soon and we'd all be going. On a hanger against the wall was Dad's blue suede suit. My parents liked to dance and there were often parties at Frog Lake or Heinsburg Halls. We got all decked out, bundled up in rabbit robes, loaded in the wagon and headed for the dance. Dad and Mother could really waltz. People backed away and let them have the dance floor. Mother and Ed Lorenson lined up for the Fox trot and the polka with music from the Heinsburg Band, started by Harry Jenner. They played cowboy music like "Red River Valley." After a while, several kids and I left the adults and went into a back room. There was a big reel turning, projecting moving pictures on the wall and making a strange grinding sound. The moving pictures showed men dressed in western clothing and they were fighting. One hit the other and knocked him backwards into the water tank. I said he must have really gotten hurt and my friends laughed. The picture was called "The Big Trail." The main man was named John Wayne. I really liked this new entertainment that Toots called a "movie."

The dance went late in the evening. I got tired and fell asleep. Mother was shaking me awake and said they had looked high and low for me. They couldn't find me and thought I disappeared and died in the freezing cold. They discovered me asleep under several layers of women's warm, soft rabbit coats. That became my favorite place to sleep and they learned to look for me first in a pile of coats. Sometimes I was happy about these dances because they were fun to watch. But also I was sad because Old Berg, the bootlegger, would be nearby selling moonshine. The men would make trips out to buy pints and the longer the evening went on, the more they drank, including my Dad. Moonshine did strange things to him and he'd fight at the drop of the hat. My parents argued a lot, mostly over his drinking.

One summer day, Dad announced it was time for our yearly trip to see the Emery family. Our friends from the States now lived at Cold Lake. We loaded the wagon, hitched up our horses, Blackie and George, and headed north. After a slow day, that evening we spread our blankets on the side of the trail. Mother cooked rabbit stew in a pot over a fire. We huddled together looking at what seemed like a millions stars. Dad told us a story about the one-handed Indian hiding in the woods with a tomahawk. Mother scolded him for scaring us. I had a hard time sleeping but it was also because I was excited about seeing my good buddy, Andy. He was eight years old like me. His father was named Del. It was keen that we shared the same first name.

While Andy and I were playing one morning, we spotted our dads looking around nervously. They put something in a bucket and lowered it into the well. They didn't know anyone was watching. After they went to the field to work, we ran over to see what they stashed in the bucket. Andy grabbed the rope, hoisted it up and we found several brown bottles of something liquid. "You try it first," Andy told me. I took a little sip and said, "It's not good but it's not bad." We each enjoyed a cool bottle not knowing what we were drinking. It didn't take long before we were both throwing up and unable to walk. I heard Mother's voice like she was miles away asking, "Del, can you hear me?" I didn't open my eyes but nodded my head, which hurt a lot. Later, I heard my sister Pat whisper, "Are Del and Andy drunk?" Mother replied, "Disgustingly drunk." Two days later, after we fully recovered, both mothers told us in detail what had happened. And they repeated the story often that week. I told Andy, "I will never drink moonshine or that stuff ever again." He agreed.

Mother always carried pieces of lye soap in her apron or dress pocket. Often if we were near any kind of water, she would say, "It's bath time." Dad and I would go in first. Then Mother and my sisters went in. Many times this was easier than at home where we'd carry buckets of water that she'd have to heat on the stove and pour into a big iron tub.

After Andy and I recovered from the drinking binge, Mother told us to get cleaned and take a bath. She handed us the soap and we headed for the lake. It was called Cold Lake for a good reason. Since it was just the two of us, we stripped off our clothes and went skinny dipping. Andy looked different than my sisters. I hadn't been around boys my age in the nude and was surprised when we got out of the cold water. Andy came running out shivering and his parts were shriveled up, almost beyond recognition. Looking at my friend as he walked towards me I noticed what appeared to be a red button where something else normally was located. I thought something was wrong with Andy but I didn't say anything or tell him he seemed to be short of something. I decided not to look down for fear I had a red button like Andy.

Trouble Brewing

The summer of 1935 was the hottest on record. This was followed by the coldest winter in 1936. Temperatures in Canada were 20 degrees below normal and Mother wrapped us in many layers of clothing to go outdoors.

One day, we were surprised that Miss McBride arrived to stay with us. She explained that Dad had taken Mother on the train to Elk Point because she lost a baby and was bleeding badly. I felt the same dread and worry as I did when this happened to Mother before. I had nightmares that Mother wouldn't return and had an upset stomach for days. One day she came home, pale and worn out. But she survived again and that's all we cared about. Pat and I watched over her and did extra chores to make it a little easier for her.

Times were really hard. The Depression continued and people had no money. The wind was blowing dust everywhere which people called the Dust Bowl but on the Canadian prairies. After the winter cold wave, that spring it appeared that my folks were splitting up. Mother took my sisters on the train and went 320 miles southeast to Calgary. They stayed with her mother and Scotty on their prospering dairy farm. I was unhappy because she didn't take me with them. My grandfather died before I was born so Scotty was the only Grandpa I knew. Scotty was from Scotland and he and Grandma never married but he treated us like his grandchildren.

I stayed with Dad on the farm. I was so lonely for my sisters and Mother. Dad drank a lot. I spent a lot of time in the barn with Shorty. He and my buddy Donald helped get me through the most miserable summer of my life. Dad received a letter from Mother saying she and Colleen were coming back. I thought that was great news. They returned and my parents were determining whether they should stay together. They decided they would continue to try to keep the family together but to sell out and return to the States. I didn't want to move again or leave Heinsburg, especially Shorty.

Dad, Mother, Colleen and I rode the train to Calgary where my other two sisters were. I was so glad to see Pat and Joyce and they missed me, too. Scotty's farm had about 30 cows and he let me help milk them. Scotty had bright red hair and his blue eyes seemed to twinkle when he thought something was funny. He offered Dad the opportunity to go in with him. He told Dad that with his help, they could expand the farm. They had plenty of room for us and eventually Dad would have part ownership. We all wanted to stay but Dad didn't want to do it. I didn't understand why because it seemed like a real break for us plus I loved Scotty and he cared about us.

We returned by train and my folks held an auction and sold the farm equipment and many household items. I went to the barn and told Shorty that we were leaving. I cried as he looked at me with his big brown eyes. It seemed he knew what was coming by all he'd seen over the past couple of years in that barn. With the little money the auction brought in, Dad bought an old 1923 Dodge car. He converted it into a pickup and packed all our belongings in that old truck.

I pushed this weathered barn door closed for a final time. The gray door at the Gardner Place and this barn door generated many fond memories and was a place of escape for me the past several years. We waved good-bye to the Lorenson family, who all stood in their front yard bidding us farewell. But the hardest part for me was leaving Shorty.

So Long, Canada

We drove through Heinsburg, crossed the river on the ferry to Vegreville and southwest to Edmonton. The 150-mile ride was very quiet and it was a sad trip. I already missed my friends but mostly Shorty.

In Edmonton, we stayed with friends and went to a movie one night. It was the first 3-D movie I'd seen. An Indian walked on stage and threw the hatchet right at me. I flinched to get out of the way. It was funny to everyone but me. We rode in a car around town. It was noisy because of horns, buses and trolleys and I'd never seen so many people in one place. I saw street lamps glowing because of electricity. I learned about a telephone and radio. All I wanted to do was go back home to Shorty. I was 11 and seeing many new things that I wasn't sure I liked.

We headed south for the States but were stopped at the border in Coutts. Dad couldn't get across because he didn't have the paperwork to prove he was an American citizen. He was flat broke. This didn't help my parents' marriage. Aunt Katie and Uncle Jim came up and brought us groceries. Mother, my sisters and I could easily go back and forth across the border to the little town of Sweet Grass, Montana. We attended school until it burned down. We stayed all winter because it took that long for the paperwork allowing Dad a visa to come across as a noncitizen. Because of the Depression and jobs in short supply, the government had a strict stipulation about immigration into the States. They wouldn't admit people who might end up on welfare. Uncle Jim worked in the oil fields. He lived in Oilmont, not far from Shelby, and 20 miles from Coutts. He was doing well and lined up a job for Dad as a carpenter in Shelby, constructing a city building for $1 an hour. That promised job was what got Dad across the border with the work visa. We lived in Shelby, but not for long. Dad hurt his hand and got a small settlement. We left there that same summer. I had lived in seven places by age 12. I told myself when I grew up I would get a good job and I wouldn't ever move again.

After leaving Canada, Del's family continued a vagabond lifestyle for a year or two living in Zillah, Selah, Yakima and Vancouver, Washington. He attended high school in Yakima, Washington and his senior year in Silverton, Oregon in 1943. His parents divorced. He served with the Army's 10th Mountain Division in Italy in World War II and was seriously injured in 1945. He returned to Silverton, Oregon and later moved to Salem. He married and settled permanently in Albany, Oregon, in 1953, where he and wife Patty had three children. They have 10 grandchildren and 14 great grandchildren. He was Linn County Clerk for decades and is known as the father of vote-by-mail for the State of Oregon. He is still active in church and civic organizations, and is the patriarch of dozens of nieces and nephews. Two sisters have passed; younger sister Joyce lives in California. He learned numerous lessons while growing up and many decisions made throughout his life had roots starting with his childhood in Heinsburg.

Postscript:

In 1967, with his wife and three children, Del returned to Chinook, Montana, on the way to Heinsburg. He was relieved to find his memories accurate when:

- He found the Tommy Adams Place in Chinook, where he had ridden his tricycle round and round when he was four years old.

- He found the birch tree on the shore at Whitney Lake where he had carved "DWR."

- In Heinsburg, he saw the two Blair sisters who had witnessed him getting bucked off his favorite horse, Shorty. They remembered it vividly.

124

- Because of his nagging World War II injury, he drove 23 miles to the hospital in Elk Point, where classmate Rhoda Evans was working. She recognized him immediately.

- He and Donald Lorenson were reunited and stay in contact to this day.

He and his family camped in their 15-foot travel trailer on the lawn on Harry and Toots Jenner's home. The Jenners continued to use an outhouse for a toilet but had running water and electricity in their home. Toots made the Riley family a fresh raspberry pie that they still talk about. Harry Jenner went all over town telling residents that Del Riley was in town. Harry told Del that Gerald Lawrence, who operated the grain elevator, was the great grandson of Mr. Lawrence, who evaded the Frog Lake Massacre 82 years earlier because his love, his Indian maiden, told him ahead of time what was going to happen.

Returning in 1978 for the 50-year anniversary celebration of the Canadian National Railroad coming to Heinsburg, Del was asked to ride on a special float in the anniversary parade. Who should he be reunited with but his favorite teacher, Miss McBride.

This story is inspired by true events as told to the writer, his daughter, Deleen Wills.

5

The Emerald Door
NiCole Anderson

It was well into fall and on the way to winter in the Great Northwest and my wanderlust was growing by the day. I was in need of an escape... an oasis...an adventure! It had been far too long.

A friend told me of a place in the woods deep in the heart of the Cascades, only known by word-of-mouth and a well-kept secret. Not much was told as you had to be an adventurer at heart and not afraid of the unknown. All that was said was, "You'll never forget it" and the location. She handed me an envelope. It was ivory linen and printed on the front in beautiful calligraphy was *"Golden Rule 1 of 5: You can't tell anyone what you find, only pass along the map."* Not being fond of rules, let alone four unknown rules, I hesitated accepting the map, but the spark and expression on her face squashed all doubt; this was something I simply had to do!

With two more days of work before my vacation, I had plenty of time to consider whether this would be a smart move for me. Did I really dare venture into the woods alone with nothing but a map and a promise of adventure? What would my friends say if I told them? What would my Dad say? All of these voices were going through my head and my confidence was beginning to waiver but my uneasy spirit was dying for a little excitement.

I had explored many of the local hikes in the area throughout the summer, but only for one-day hikes and climbs. They were the ones that were known and well-traveled by many others. For this trail you needed a map to get there, not GPS, a MAP! I had used maps before but was out of practice as the "map feature" on my iPhone was a staple for any adventure. It would not help me anyway in this particular instance as one of the draws was that there was no phone service. I was even more nervous that I had to use a compass as there were no groomed paths or signs and the trails were vague. Oh well, that just makes for an even greater adventure and who knows what you'll find when the path is not clearly defined.

Never wanting to back down from a challenge, I decided to set off and find out what would await me there. I packed a bag with a few essentials and got ready to go on my next great adventure! Carefully opening the envelope, I pulled out a hand drawn map and another ivory linen envelope with *"Golden Rule #2"* on the front.

Work was done, my bag was packed, and the road was before me. All I had to do was walk through the door. Was it a smart move? Probably not, but my curiosity was killing me and I had to see what I would find where "X" marked the spot! I grabbed my bag, jumped in the car, and set off for what promised to be, if nothing else, a great hike and opportunity for a photo safari.

It was the perfect fall day, sunny and 65 degrees with a light breeze that enhanced the clean mountain air. I found the trailhead with little effort, parked my car, grabbed my map and pack and set out before I lost my nerve. The trail was not groomed or paved like other public trails but had a natural perfect beauty that actually drew me in and removed all doubt and fear.

I decided to pay attention to every detail and enjoy each moment of my experience rather than focusing on the destination and missing the journey, something I'm not very good at doing. The fall colors were a rich tangerine, gold and wine. The quiet was disturbed only by the rustling of leaves as the breeze softly moved them and occasionally displaced one so it gently floated onto the trail. The sound of nature was subtle but present.

I knew some time had passed but I wasn't tired. The trail was on a very slight incline with an occasional switchback. As I checked my fitness tracker, I was surprised to see I had already gone 3.3 miles. The destination was only six miles in so I was halfway there. I had been so focused on the creation surrounding me that all the voices of doubt had diminished with only an occasional moment of anxiety at the uncertainty of what lay before me. I knew that the person who entrusted me with this opportunity would not put me in harm's way, so I pressed on with anticipation.

The trail was getting tougher to traverse as there had been a recent storm and several trees had fallen. Fortunately, they were small enough to simply walk over and the trail was well marked by those who had come before me.

The second rule was to come up with something to leave behind that would last, but not disturb nature, and add it to the map for the next person. Because I love a little sparkle, I chose a pink geode to place four and a half miles in. As soon as I reached the exact distance, I looked for the perfect spot to place my contribution. On the right side of the path was a stream bubbling out of the rock near a young red leaf maple that had been planted not long before I was chosen. A tiny hand-tied bridge made from sticks and hemp was laid over the stream. The addition of my enchantingly colorful crystal made for a miniature Asian garden. Some of the other clues were subtle but precisely marked on the map— a carved stick, a unique plant or stone strategically placed. I was definitely on the right track. At this point I decided to stop and appreciate the scene before me and have a light snack and some water. I tried to relax and soak it in but with only a mile and a half to go, the excitement of the unknown destination was building. I found that my pace was quickening rather than slowing with fatigue, as was my usual MO on a hike of this distance.

With only a quarter mile to go, I found myself at what appeared to be a dead end. I checked the map to see if there was something I missed. I read, "The path is narrow but sure, go straight ahead between the twin trees and your destination will soon be in sight." In faith, I stepped over a log and through two white birch trees that appeared to be the same diameter and height. After a few yards, I could see the peak of a roof in the distance. I was almost there.

I could now see the final destination. It was a small stone cottage with smoke rising from the chimney. The sun was setting and the light shimmered on the lazy river that ran in front of the beautiful structure. The vivid sunset blend of orange, fuchsia and violet colors complemented the stunning fall foliage surrounding the little house and lining the banks of the river. Yet all this paled as I approached the spectacular door that drew me in. It both intimidated and welcomed me at the same time. The door was weathered wood with antique emerald glass framed in perfectly polished copper. Someone spent a great deal of time caring for this feature to ensure that there was no patina or discoloration of any kind. On the wall next to the door was a sign: "Welcome adventurer! You have arrived at your destination. Make yourself at home."

Upon closer inspection, I noticed another ivory linen envelope carefully tucked into the copper scrollwork of the door. *"Golden Rule #3"* was etched across the front. I knew I was in the right place. I opened the note and read, *"As you cross the threshold of this beautiful door, leave all worries, troubles, cares, guilt, obligations or any other negative emotion behind. Simply LOVE yourself."*

I was starting to understand why my friend had picked me to be the next chosen guest of this special place. I had been quite skilled at these negative emotions as of late and even now fear started to creep into my thoughts as the cynical part of me wondered about my safety here alone in the mountains. I quickly remembered my friend and the fact that she would never put me in danger and opened the door. Walking over the threshold with feelings of anticipation, I closed the heavy door to the world outside.

As I entered, the first thing I saw was an incredible stone wall with a gas fireplace. The flames rose through aqua-colored fire glass. Next to it was a beautiful natural sunken spa and a wall of windows looking out over the river and woods. It was warm and inviting and if that wasn't enough, the smell of freshly baked cornbread filled the room. I set down my pack and started to explore. The room was open with a small kitchen off to the left. There was an island with a sink and a rustic bar. Just past the island I could see a crockpot and the pan of cornbread on the counter. Whoever had created this oasis had thought of everything. The refrigerator was stocked and dinner was served. How did they know when I would arrive? Who would do this for a stranger? The questions just kept coming until I looked at the Golden Rule I still held in my hand and decided that I would indeed try my best to follow its direction. I opened the lid and found a steaming pot of clam chowder and realized how famished I was. I had taken my time and enjoyed the journey using the time to practice with my camera, something I didn't do very often these days. Other than my short break and snack at my map marker, I forgot about food. I had packed a couple cans of soup and planned to hike out for a meal or two and some supplies after I unraveled the mystery. Clearly that would not be necessary.

On the counter was a wooden tray that held a china bowl, plate, and silverware carefully wrapped in a linen napkin. As if this wasn't enough, there was a crystal Riedel wine glass and a 2012 Willamette Valley Pinot Noir waiting for my arrival. I opened the wine, dished my plate and made myself at home on the overstuffed red brocade chaise lounge next to the fireplace. The food was delicious, the wine bold with a hint of spice. I felt like a princess. I finished my meal and put everything away. I continued to explore this enchanting cottage.

To the right of the door was a wrought iron spiral staircase going up to a loft. The iron scrollwork resembled a magical vine ascending to heaven. In the loft, I found an open room with a canopy bed, and a partial bath. The bed had an antique brass headboard with 300-thread count sheets, a fluffy down comforter and a plethora of pillows in all shapes and sizes.

The canopy over the bed was draped in golden chiffon and lit with tiny white lights. In the corner, behind a sheer curtain that was tied back with gold tassels, was a beautiful brass claw foot tub. There were two, four-foot candle stands and a variety of candles around the room. An antique hutch, made into a sink base, sat in the corner. It had a ceramic wash bowl and the water flowed from a faucet that looked like an antique hand pump. Although all this was pulling me in, I decided it was too early for bed and opted to go and indulge in another glass of wine and the spa below.

The water was an ideal 103 degrees with gentle jets. There was a familiarity to the fragrance emanating from the water. Through the wall of windows, I had a perfect vantage point of the clear night sky bursting with stars. The warm water melted away all remaining cares and I couldn't remember ever feeling this relaxed. I emptied my mind and rested completely in the peace and silence.

My eyes were getting heavy, so I decided to go upstairs and put myself to bed. I curled up, embraced in down warmth and drifted into a sound, deep sleep. I don't think I moved a muscle until the sun began to rise and fill the cottage with a soft glow…the perfect enticement to start the day and discover. The smell of coffee that I had set to brew the night before was the final key to convince me to leave this comfy, warm bed and venture downstairs.

I made some breakfast, poured a cup of coffee and settled down in the cozy nook in the corner. As I drank my coffee, I noticed the book on the table. Notes from other guests resided on the pages of this rustic handmade journal—a place to share experiences that must remain locked within these walls before returning to the real world. I read a few of the entries and when I set the book down to get more coffee, it opened to the next blank page and an ivory linen envelope with *Golden Rule #4* sat before me.

"Enjoy the cottage but don't lose your sense of adventure. Complete three challenges:

1- Hike to the top of the mountain to see what's there.

2- Go up river for a natural wonder.

3- Find the buried treasure using this map."

Feeling well rested, I decided that climbing the mountain was the challenge I would take on first.

I got ready, grabbed my camera and set out. It was a fairly steep incline but only moderately difficult. The fall colors were breathtaking with the constant splash of green, of course, as this is the Evergreen State.

The trail was not well traveled so I noticed more of nature's creatures than on the public trails. The songs of birds filled the air. A squirrel climbed a tree and curiously checked to see what I was doing on his turf. A pair of young deer, still sporting a few spots, stopped grazing in a meadow to determine if my camera was posing any danger or if they might continue their breakfast. An eagle flew overhead toward the river to see what he might find for his morning meal. The composition was endless and I was grateful for the fully charged battery and 16GB memory card that was filling up quickly. Finding the monopod walking stick/camera mount well worth the purchase, I decided to shoot at will and decide later what would be worth keeping. I had my work cut out for me.

After going three miles and ascending about 1,300 feet, I found myself looking at rock formations that would require all my attention for the completion of this journey. I shot off a few more quick pics, packed my camera and walking stick into my backpack, put on my gloves and went for it. It wasn't super steep but being alone, I used extra care to avoid injury that might keep me from returning to my private oasis. Almost to the top, I paused and looked out over the valley below. Off in the distance was Mt. Rainier. The mountain was "out" and this majestic behemoth rising above the valley before it commanded attention. With just a few more feet to my destination, I noticed the faint fall of snow around me. There was just enough to be delightful but not enough to cause concern. The sun shone bright and the tiny flakes melted as fast as they hit the rocks. I was at the top now and the view was more than I could imagine. There was a glacier pool that fed a stream and must have formed a waterfall. I could not see it but could hear the water as it hit the rocks on the way down the other side of the mountain. I pulled out the blanket I brought, made myself comfortable, and retrieved my camera and a small journal to jot down some notes. I didn't want to forget anything! I relaxed and celebrated the creation surrounding me.

Feeling the accomplishment of the climb, it was time to go back and soak my muscles in anticipation of the possibilities that might await me. I knew my shins would want a little extra attention tonight. Carefully packing my things, I set off for the tiny cottage by the river. The descent was trickier as some of the snow was sticking now and made the rocks slippery. Once at the base, I breathed a sigh of relief and realized that I had been holding my breath most of the way down. The snow had stopped and the trail was easy after that. I had left trail markers as I did not trust my sense of direction. I was grateful for the easily followed, thoughtless trip back and for the opportunity to not think, just walk.

When I arrived at the amazing emerald and copper door of the cottage, I stopped for a moment to admire the skillfully crafted metal and glass. I saw it when I arrived but had I really looked at this door that welcomed me in or did I let the anticipation of discovery overshadow its splendor? I entered the room and made myself comfortable. There was nothing that I had to do, no obligation, no chores. I could do whatever I wanted. I was going to cook! Really cook, not just throw something together as fast as possible that would sustain me. I had seen some salmon and fresh veggies. The kitchen was well stocked with spices and infused oils, pretty much anything you might need; it was time to create a culinary masterpiece. I noticed the Bon Appétit magazines on a shelf and started browsing recipes. I found one that hit the spot: salmon with balsamic roasted asparagus and mushrooms.

I poured a glass of Pinot, set the stereo to play a nice blend of Rachmaninoff, Tchaikovsky and Bach, and started cooking. I had forgotten how I loved to cook when I had the time. Let's be honest, I just stopped making the time. Why did I allow stuff to squash my joy? When did I decide to let life be just obligations? Maybe that was really the point of all this. With no distractions, I can do what I love rather than what I think I should.

Picking the perfect pairing from the wine rack proved to be challenging as there was a nice Rosé to tempt me but decided to stick with Pinot since I had cooked cedar-plank grilled salmon. I took a seat at the comfy nook in the corner and enjoyed every bite of this carefully prepared meal. I still couldn't believe some benevolent soul would create this amazing oasis and share it with others. My thoughts went to figuring out who would I bestow with this gift? Who needed this most? Who was daring enough to accept this challenge? As I took my last tasty bite, I found myself completely satisfied with a sense of accomplishment and turned to see what I would do now.

I decided once again to indulge in the amazing water feature in the middle of the room. The spa was framed in river rock, delicately lit with an aqua blue light and scented with jasmine and bergamot. I turned on the jets and as they melted away all remaining muscle tension from the day's exploration, my gaze went to the clear sky full of stars. It was bliss and this would come to be my happy place when, I would like to say if, I returned to the real world. As I looked to the stars I realized that possibilities were endless. I determined that while in a frame of mind that opened my imagination to limitless ideas, I should come up with a bucket list.

I was finding this quite a challenge and turned my thoughts to how blessed I have been so far in this life. Memories started pouring in: Trapeze lessons in the Emerald City (Seattle), zip lining in Puerto Vallarta and Mahogany Bay Isla Roatan, swimming with dolphins in Grand Cayman, cave tubing in Belize, standing 1,823 feet and 148 floors up on the observation floor of the Burj Khalifa in Dubai, exploring the splendor of the Sheikh Zayed Grand Mosque in Abu Dhabi, admiring the craftsmanship of the ancient remains of the Acropolis in Athens, enjoying the beauty of the Sultan's Summer Palace and St. Sophia Church in Istanbul, and indulging in the opulence of the Queen Elizabeth cruise ship.

What additions should I put on a list? They needed to be imaginative but still doable. I would do myself no favors by creating something that I could only dream about and never achieve. The last thing I needed was to set myself up to be constantly dreaming and discontent with life. Here we go:

#1 – Skiing in Whistler.

#2 – Paragliding in the Cascades.

#3 – Contribute to a published book.

#4 – See the Northern Lights in Iceland.

#5 – Take a romantic river cruise on the Danube from Budapest to Germany.

#6 – Explore my favorite place on earth, Disneyland, but this time in Paris.

#7 – Safari in Botswana.

I was starting to feel like a prune, so I wrapped myself in the plush bath sheet and sat by the fire so I could write it all down before sleep wiped the thoughts from my mind. It was getting late so I retreated to the loft, submerged my warm relaxed body in down and pillows, and drifted into another blissful sound sleep. Heaven!

I once again awoke to the warmth of the sun painting the walls with color. Looking over the railing at the river, I spotted twin deer just in front of the deck searching the riverbank for a patch of grass or a tasty snack. Looking closer at the quiet, undisturbed scene, I could see a squirrel, birds and the occasional splash from a fish. I just took it in trying to embed the picture in my brain so it would never fade from memory.

Trying to decide what the challenge-of-the-day would be, I made some breakfast and coffee and again started reading the journal on the table. It was filled with grateful thoughts, exciting stories, and insightful light-bulb moments from a variety of people who had taken the time to self-reflect and share. One story caught my attention and I knew what I wanted to do today. I got dressed, packed a lunch and set out.

I had only seen one small section of the river. The picture windows, framed by the walls of the cottage, formed a picture resembling a Thomas Kinkade painting. Today I would explore the banks of the river and perhaps the source. With camera in hand, I made my way up river. The water level was still low from the lack of rain over the summer but was starting to increase with the recent storms. The autumn leaves were starting to diminish and fell one by one anticipating winter. The chill in the air was much cooler and I was happy I brought my battery-heated jacket. The walk was beautiful and scenic but not too strenuous.

Today I would enjoy a soul searching walk through the forest, not exercise. Around the bend of the river there was an old log that formed a kind of throne. I imagined a fairy princess sitting on her throne as she presided over her unseen world of nymphs, elves, and other mystical creatures. I had gone a few miles and thought this might be a perfect venue for a bite to eat and if I sat quiet and still, perhaps some photo ops of curious woodland creatures. Who knows what one might see if eyes and ears are the only senses one uses?

As I watched the river, I noticed some movement along the bank where there was a collection of branches and logs. I could just make out the flat tail of a beaver. I watched him as he skillfully worked on his winter home. It was incredible how instinct bestowed by God was made evident in this creation. I soon realized that he was not alone as one mischievous little kit came up on shore to explore. The pictures would prove to be priceless. Of all my adventures, this week so close to home, would provide memories that would be tough to overshadow. It wasn't simply seeing the majesty of creation before me that I have never fully appreciated, but also because of self-reflection that only comes when you allow yourself to dismiss denial and look inside for the one worthy of the love of a Savior.

I pulled out the ivory envelope marked *Golden Rule #3* and read it again. I had kept it close and read it often when any negativity began to surface. Maybe I would consider a tattoo after all. When asked, I always said that there was nothing I liked enough to make permanent. This might be the exception. The sound of the paper disturbed the creatures I had enjoyed watching busily at work and they retreated inside their primitive structure. I packed up and continued walking up river.

I could just make out the sound of running water. It would not be long now. As I made my way around the next bend I could see it. The glacier pool I had seen the day before dropped over the side of the mountain out of sight like nature's infinity pool. This formed one of the most beautiful waterfalls I had been privileged to witness. It fell approximately 175 feet but was redirected by two rock shelves that made it appear like a giant water feature carefully sculptured for full effect. There were ferns coming out of the rocks drinking in the cool, clean water and it looked like a painting. It had been a full day and the moon was peeking through as the sun started its descent. Not wanting to try to find my way back in the dark, I tore myself away and headed back to the cottage.

There once again was the beautiful door that held such wonder, comfort and peace beyond the threshold. I could not wait to relax inside and write down my experiences from the day. I lit the candles surrounding the beautiful, elegantly crafted claw foot tub. On the vanity was an antique mirrored tray with a collection of bath salts, handmade soap, and moisturizers. The blend of aromas was intoxicating and made me feel like I was in a tropical garden. As I relaxed in the warm fragrant water, I thought about the day and the things I had witnessed. Realizing I was starving, I wrapped up in the plush robe and went downstairs for a bite. The journal on the table caught my eye and I again began to read about the many adventures shared by those before me. I got so caught up in reading that it was hard to stop long enough to add to the beautifully crafted pages. I wrote down what I could before my eyes began to droop and headed off to bed.

I awoke the next morning to see an eerie mist coming off the river. It was thick and made it impossible to see anything outside the cottage. Unless it burned off, I would not be venturing out today. It was an opportunity to sit, read, think and relax. As uneasy thoughts started to invade my mind, I pulled out the envelope I had been carrying around and tried to chase away the negative emotions. The warm spa and cozy fire melted away all anxiety. I started imagining what curious magical creatures might be hiding in the mist and found myself smiling at the delightful scene dancing around my imagination. This was heavenly. I never liked being alone but was quickly discovering the benefits of no distractions from people or things. As I watched, small white flakes began to fall and disperse the mist floating across the river and melt as they hit the water. The bank, however, was turning white before my eyes. I wondered if I should leave, just in case, but decided that being stuck in paradise would be just fine.

As I watched the remaining patches of mist hover over the water, I pulled out the map that was included with Rule #4 and started studying the path that would lead me to some unknown treasure. The snow continued to fall, so finding the markers could prove to be difficult so I set it down and put on some warm clothes to go play in the snow. It was a perfect white blanket now, untouched and inviting. Finding a perfect spot off to the side of the deck that would still be visible from inside, I lay down and began moving my arms and legs in an attempt to create the perfect snow angel. I felt like a kid with no cares or worries and delighted in the feeling of snow hitting my face. The clean fresh snow tasted like a frozen treat. Now for the tricky part—getting up with the least damage to my childish creation.

Grabbing my camera, I started shooting the scene before me. It was like an entirely different location now. I changed my focus, no pun intended, to view everything as if it were a picture. Being out of practice, I tried to remember how I used to look at the world, seeing the art in the detail that is lost to a quick overview full of distractions. I noticed the branch with a slight accumulation of snow that was melting in the sun that now peeked through the clouds. The water glistened as it fell from a remaining leaf——a picture perfect combination of effects for my composition. There was a tiny green fern desperately reaching out to the sun through the cold white coat slowly enveloping its existence. It seemed to say, "Summer is over, it's time to sleep."

I was totally immersed in the moment when an overwhelming wash of panic brought me back to reality. If this kept up how would I find my way out? I recounted the markers on the map, thinking through what I would be able to make out through the snow. Were there enough visible points to get off this mountain? The snow had stopped falling so I headed inside to look at the map. As I reached for the handle of the beautiful door, I reminded myself of Rule #3, the fact that I was in no hurry and there were plenty of supplies, and the wave of panic dissipated. I also remembered that my benevolent benefactor knew I was there, as did my friend. Time to stop worrying and get back to the peace I had found in this moment of natural beauty that I was so fortunate to be allowed to witness. I crossed the threshold and ascended the spiral staircase to look out from the loft at the postcard moment before me. Had time stopped? It was so still except for the remaining patches of mist gliding over the water.

After dinner I attempted to figure out the telescope by the window to see what constellations I could remember. Looking through the books on the shelf, I found one with a guide to local constellations by the season. The sky was so clear now that the stars seemed close enough to touch. I could easily make out the North Star and the Big Dipper but without my Sky Map app, I struggled to make out any others. I decided to simply appreciate the splendor and relax in the warm fragrant water, leaving the astronomy to others. The clear sky also reminded me that the snow would not be stopping me from leaving this little piece of heaven and I would soon have to return to the real world. I allowed this thought to invade my mind for only a moment and forced my thoughts back to the present and memories of the day and all I had experienced here, including the magnificent door that protected the entrance of this sweet cottage. I would sleep well tonight.

It was bittersweet as the sun once again woke me with color and warmth. Today I would go on one final adventure, then head back to my life. I hoped I would take the lessons learned here back with me and not allow myself to forget to take time to do the things that I love and to value myself. As I drank my coffee, I studied the treasure map and made one last entry in the journal on the table, "Words cannot express my gratitude for the kindness and generosity of the person who made this experience possible. Thank you!"

Finding only a note telling me not to fret in the cabinet where one might see cleaning products, I attempted to straighten up as best as I could to leave things as I found them. Then grabbing my things and taking one last look around, I closed the emerald door behind me and went in search of my treasure. The map was easy to follow and intended to directly accomplish the task. "Take 20 paces from the threshold, left at the bolder for 30 paces, walk toward the river and you will see the perfect place for a wish."

As I walked contemplating the wish I would make, I saw a handcrafted wooden well that stood three feet tall filled with flowers. In the base was a miniature door that resembled the cottage door that had welcomed me in and shut out the world for this brief moment in time. As I opened the tiny emerald glass hatch framed with copper, I saw a green velvet box with an ivory linen note card.

Golden Rule #5: "Always remember your worth and what is important. Take time to reflect, do what you love and make each day an adventure. Pass the map on to someone who needs it most."

Opening the tiny box, I found a delicate copper bracelet embellished with emerald beads to remind me of the kindness and generosity of this benevolent benefactor, and the lessons I had learned.

Taking one last look around, I tried to take in every detail. The cottage, river, trees, the general serenity of the whole and of course, the door! I knew once I left it would feel like a dream. With a sigh, I pulled out the map and started down the mountain. As I walked, my thoughts went to the choice at hand: Who would I bestow with this incredible gift? Who needed it most? Who was adventurous enough to accept the challenge? I knew exactly who I would choose and couldn't wait to pass on the map!

I adjusted my pack and started walking. Looking at the bracelet on my wrist, I determined to go home and start living with a renewed outlook and purpose. When life gave me negativity, I would picture the perfectly polished copper door with emerald glass and choose to keep an optimistic outlook and really LIVE each day.

About the Author:

NiCole Anderson is an adventurer at heart. After living in seven states and Madrid, Spain, she settled in the Pacific NW and started exploring. She enjoys travel, outdoor sports and crafting beautiful things.

Never wanting to back down from a challenge, when asked to contribute to this project, she found inspiration in the beautiful mountains of the Cascades, Olympic Peninsula and Pacific Coast and a new passion: writing.

NiCole is a daughter, sister, mom, nana and friend. She has a large supportive family living all over the world who also love adventure. With such a wonderful family including two amazing daughters, one terrific grandson and incredible supportive friends, she considers herself truly blessed.

6

The Faded Red Door
Merry-Go-Round & Found
Rebecca L. Hillyer

It felt like a Monday, but it was a Wednesday.
I had just left the courtroom feeling defeated—again.
Every time I appeared in front of Judge Ramirez he
did everything in his power to make me look and feel
like a fool. Not just any fool mind you; he made me
feel like I was committing malpractice. I knew why
Judge Ramirez hated me. Many years ago, when Judge
Ramirez was a young lawyer working for the Attorney
General's office, fresh out of law school, we opposed
each other in front of Judge Smith. Old Judge Smith
was the longest sitting circuit judge in the state. Judge
Smith often sat on the bench hearing cases while
reading the local newspaper. It was always fun to see
the shock on the face of attorneys who were
appearing in his courtroom for the first time. Mr.
Ramirez was arguing his case against me and Judge
Smith ignored him. He restated his case a second time
with the same result, then a third time at the top of
his lungs as if Judge Smith couldn't hear him. I knew
better than to respond to Mr. Ramirez and just
watched the interaction knowing he was going to get
a stern reprimand. After the third argument, Judge
Smith lowered the boom and made Mr. Ramirez look

and feel pretty stupid. In my mind I thanked the Judge for doing my job. Five years later when Mr. Ramirez was appointed to the bench he always made a point of paying me back.

While walking down the courthouse steps, I decided I needed a treat. Now, when I say treat, I am usually talking about some high calorie snack. It was late morning so I headed to the local coffee shop that has great French pastries. By 11 a.m. the shop was completely empty. Instantly I was recognized by the manager as a regular. I guess she could tell from my appearance that I had a miserable morning. She rushed out from behind the counter and offered me the newspaper. Unfortunately, all the earlier patrons had riffled through the shop's newspapers leaving only the classified ads from the Oregonian. After offering me the paper she sheepishly said she could only find the classified section. I grabbed the paper, muttered something about how it was my favorite part of the paper, thanked her and quickly ordered a cup of coffee and a cinnamon roll.

It was honestly the truth—the classified section was my favorite part of the paper. I had certain sections I looked through: antiques, sport cars, sailboats, etc. My coffee and roll came quickly and I dug right in. After a satisfying piece or two of the delicious, gooey roll were devoured, I folded the paper into a manageable size and started looking for my first section—Antiques. I started reading down the narrow columns for something interesting. Then I found it. There was an antique carousel horse for sale for $3,500. "No way," I thought. These ads break on Sunday and all the good stuff is sold long before

Wednesday. Not sure why but I quickly tore out the
ad and put it in my Day Timer. I downed my coffee
and finished off the roll while hunting through the
ads. After I finished, I quickly paid the bill, left a nice
tip for the manager's kindness, and hurried back to
the office.

As I parked the car and walked into the office
I could feel the caffeine and sugar rush. For a
moment I regretted my little splurge. Once in the
office I was bombarded with the usual phone
messages, clients waiting for appointments, and mail.
The instant of regret was gone as I dove into my
work load. Despite the occasional court appearance
with Judge Ramirez, I loved being a lawyer and found
it very rewarding. I always thought that if I ever left
the practice of law it would be because of Judge
Ramirez. Many years later, a bout of breast cancer
proved me wrong.

It was nearly 3 p.m. before I recalled the ad
for the carousel horse in my Day Timer. When I
found it between the pages, I grabbed some tape and
taped it to that day's page. I started an internal battle.
Should I waste my time calling only to be told I was
right that the horse sold last Sunday, or should I take
a chance? I then recalled a time when I was in my
teens. On Saturdays my Mother and I would go
"junking." That consisted of driving from Salem to
Aurora on old Highway 99E and hitting all the
antique stores (some more junk shops than antiques)
on one side of the road and then hitting the other side
of the road on the way back home. I always came
back with something fun like an antique Coke sign or
rickety chair. These trips usually took all day, included

lunch and a take-home pizza for dinner, if I was lucky!

I had been crazy about horses my whole life. My father loved horses so I always thought I inherited that trait. I earned my money babysitting neighbor kids and saved it. When I was 12 years old I had saved enough to buy my first horse, named Dolly. Dolly was a light bay mare with no papers, probably a combination of Quarter Horse and Morgan. She knew more about being a horse than I knew about being a rider; as a result, Dolly always got the best of me. I owned a total of nine horses before my riding career was cut short in my last year of law school, by a semi truck that missed a stop sign.

The car accident left my Ford F-250 broken in half and me in the hospital. My back was badly injured. I was told by my doctor that there were two activities I could not do in the future—motorcross and horseback riding. Apparently both these activities put extra strain on an individual's back. I was heartbroken that I couldn't care for my horse or ride her again. My horse's name was Julie; she was a black Quarter Horse with only a few white hairs on her forehead and was a blast to ride. Julie was my dream horse and family. I had her for 6 years. Ultimately, I sold Julie to a good friend who kept her until the day she died. This way I was able to visit Julie, but of course it was never the same as owning her and caring for her every day.

Since I loved both horses and antiques, it made perfect sense that I would want an antique carousel horse. Just think, a horse that could live in your house forever and never need to be fed. On one of our junking trips, my mother and I went to the usual shops up one side of 99E and down the other. When we spied a new shop in Brooks, Oregon, the first small town on our route, we thought it looked particularly shabby. It had a chipped red door making it look more like a barn than a shop. Although neither of us said a word to each other, we both wondered if it would be safe to enter. I carefully opened the door. The door squeaked like a door on a Halloween haunted house. I looked back to see if my mother was still following.

Inside, to our great surprise, the place was full was wonderful treasures. It took me only a moment to see dozens of carousel horses hanging high from the open rafters. These horses were all painted bright Chinese red with black manes and tails. I stopped in my tracks and just spun around looking up at all the different horses. The horses were different sizes and looked like they were jumping through the air at all different angles—it was pure magic to me. The shopkeeper approached us and explained that he had recently purchased an entire carousel in the midwest, sold the carousel, and brought the horses here. I was immediately saddened to hear that another carousel had met its demise. Old carousels were being purchased and broken up because the animals were much more valuable as antiques for collectors than giving children 50-cent rides. When I asked how much they cost, I was told they were all $2,500 each—take your pick. Well, when you are a 16 year-old kid with a real horse to feed, $2,500 might as well be a million.

153

And so the story went on for many years.
When I finally could afford $2,500 for a carousel
horse, they were $5,000 and when I could afford
$5,000 they were $10,000. By the time I was 35 years
old, I figured I would never own a genuine antique
carousel horse. That is why when I saw the ad in the
paper I thought it could not be true, and if it was true,
surely the carousel horse was gone.

Since I missed having a real horse, the
carousel horse would be the next best thing. O.K.,
that was it, I was going to call. I would never forgive
myself if I didn't. I quickly dialed the phone number.
I was expecting that no one would answer because
they would be at work and I would get nothing but an
answering machine saying the carousel horse had
been sold. On the third ring a women answered,
"Hello, this is Mrs. Nordstrom." She sounded very
kind and when I asked if she still had the horse she
said "YES!" I was so caught by surprise I didn't know
what to say. Mrs. Nordstrom had to ask me if I was
still on the phone. I quickly responded with a series of
questions, at that moment being a trial attorney really
paid off. Mrs. Nordstrom had a little history card
about the carousel horse she was given when she
purchased him. I quickly learned that while I had
wanted one of these horses for years, I knew very
little about them. It turned out she and her husband
had two horses and were planning to keep one and
sell one. The one question I was hesitating to ask was
about the horse's condition. Since the horse was so
inexpensive (for an antique carousel horse) I was
afraid my dream would shatter if the horse was
missing legs or otherwise broken. After a pause she
said, "No, the horse is in good condition," like she

was surprised I would ask. And lastly, she added that it came with a heavy brass pole.

I thought this was too good to be true so I should move on it—now! I asked Mrs. Nordstrom if I could come and see the horse. She responded that her husband was out of town and wouldn't return until Friday and she didn't want anyone to come to the house until his return. I then explained that I was worried she would sell the carousel horse to another buyer if I waited until Friday. The woman chuckled and said I was the first to call about the horse. Mrs. Nordstrom went on to say she was old-fashioned and that since I was the first to call I would get the first chance to purchase the horse. I immediately thought to myself, "People like her really do exist!" I then asked if I could come to see the horse Friday after work and she said that would be just fine.

Waiting from Wednesday afternoon until Friday evening was like a child waiting for Christmas. The days dragged by. I called an artist friend, Carol, who had volunteered on a community project to build a carousel and carve all new carousel animals, to talk about my new endeavor to purchase an antique carousel horse. I just knew Carol would have some advice about the purchase. When I told Carol about the ad and the carousel horse, the first words out of her mouth were, "What's wrong with it?" She quickly explained what she meant by saying that if its legs are missing there are people who can carve new legs for it. When I explained the horse is supposedly in good condition she exclaimed, "You can't buy the beech wood to carve a new carousel horse for $3,500!" Carol said, "You'd better hurry and get up there and buy it." I explained about the lady's husband being out of town and asking me to wait until he returned and that she was giving me first dibs. Carol then suggested I should purchase this carousel horse no matter what it looks like. That made me think—What does the horse look like? I never asked for a description.

Friday finally came. I left work early and my mother asked to come with me. Being a lover of antiques she wanted to see what this woman's house looked like and how many other treasures were there to see. First stop was my credit union. I had planned to get a cashier's check for $3,500 so if I liked the horse I could bring it home that evening. Not leaving anything to chance, I asked the teller if I could call the woman to make sure her name was spelled correctly. I told Mrs. Nordstrom I was at the bank and asked how she wanted the check made out and how she spelled her last name. She politely said, "Yes, Dorothy Nordstrom and Nordstrom is spelled just like the department store, but no relation." For a moment I thought about how many checks I had written to Nordstrom's over the years. Way more than $3,500! For a minute Mrs. Nordstrom sounded distressed on the phone saying, "But what if you do not like the carousel horse after you have the cashier's check in my name?" I explained that I had already asked the bank teller and she said I could bring the cashier's check back and deposit it back into my account. Mrs. Nordstrom seemed satisfied with my answer. I told her I would call and get directions once I got home.

Mother and I managed to be squarely in the middle of Friday afternoon traffic on our way to

Portland. Normally the traffic makes me crazy, but not today; I was on a mission. After a wrong turn or two we made it to the Nordstrom's home. It was a large older home, very grand in appearance and sitting very near the Sandy River. There were no cars or any signs that anyone was home. I rang the doorbell and waited. No one came. "Oh no!" I thought, "This is all a big joke; the carousel horse was too good to be true." "Stop it," I told myself. Mrs. Nordstrom seemed much too nice to be involved with pranksters. I rang the doorbell again and waited. Mother threw me a glance that said, "Are you sure this is the right place?" Finally a small, bent-over woman answered the door. After seeing her, I felt guilty about ringing the doorbell twice. I introduced myself and my mother and we entered the house.

The house was even grander inside than out. The high gloss furniture, marble floors and crystal chandeliers made us feel like we just walked into a 5-star hotel instead of a home. Mr. Nordstrom came rushing to meet us. Not far into the living room there was the most beautiful antique carousel horse I had ever seen. It was stripped of all paint and suspended on a brass pole from floor to ceiling. It was on the small side with multicolored jewels on its carved bridle and saddle. It was love at first sight.

I immediately started commenting on what a lovely carousel horse it was, even more beautiful than I dared to dream. Mrs. Nordstrom smiled and said, "Yes, this horse was carved by a company called Parker—very collectible." This was the carousel horse they were keeping. I felt a little embarrassed about my comment and obvious assumption. Mrs. Nordstrom must have sensed how I was feeling and quickly showed us into the family room area toward the back of the house. Also sitting on a brass pole floor to ceiling was a very different carousel horse. This horse was larger with less detailed carving and was painted white with a bright orange and blue bridle and saddle. He had spaces where jewels once sat. Mrs. Nordstrom explained that this horse was a 1911 Herschell-Spillman. She continued to share details that this horse would have been on the outside row of a traveling carousel since it is larger with glass jewels on the bridle and around the saddle, but the jewels were missing. This horse looked like he was jumping since no feet actually touched the ground. His neck was heavily arched and head was slightly bowed. His mane and tail were carved out of wood. His eyes were wood rather than glass. Mrs. Nordstrom said the reason he has a wood mane, tail and eyes was so they could hold up to the rigors of a traveling carousel that was being set up for fairs and then taken down, put on a truck and transported to the next location. All this information helped me appreciate this carousel horse's uniqueness. Mrs. Nordstrom said I didn't have to purchase the carousel horse if I didn't want it. She had a buyer that collected Herschell-Spillman carousel horses and very much wanted to purchase this one if I didn't want it. She told them I had first chance since I called first. At that moment I was still trying to get past the horse's horrible paint color. While I was still examining the horse, Mrs. Nordstrom offered Mother and me a cup of tea. How could we resist an offer from such a sweet older woman, and besides, it would give me more time to ponder my decision.

Mrs. Nordstrom took forever to return with two delicate teacups on saucers on a silver tray with sugar lumps and cream in silver containers. "How lovely," I said, and reached for a teacup. Mrs. Nordstrom asked us to sit while we enjoyed our tea. Mr. Nordstrom followed with two more teacups for him and his wife. While sitting and enjoying the freshly brewed Earl Grey tea and the company, I was reminded of the antique carousel horses flying about my head in the shop with the red door all those years ago. The conversation was about why they were selling so many treasures, downsizing to a one-story retirement home, and I started to tell my story of the Brooks antique shop and the flying horses. I continued telling them how impressed I was with the sight of those horses, all painted Chinese red and black, all those years ago. And at my age $2,500 might as well be a million. I explained that I never thought I could ever own an antique carousel horse.

Mrs. Nordstrom stopped drinking her tea. Her mouth dropped and she looked at me like I had said something wrong. I thought maybe I should not have shared my story or mentioned the dollar amount. One of those long silent moments passed with the Nordstroms staring at me and me back at them. Thankfully, Mrs. Nordstrom broke the silence. She said, "We bought this horse in Brooks from an antique dealer who had purchased an entire carousel and the horses were all red and black." She got up and walked over to the horse and pointed down the hole in his back where the brass pole came out. She said, "Look, you can still see the red paint!" Mr. Nordstrom explained that they repainted the horse red, white and blue in 1976 for the bi-centennial. That explained the hideous paint job, I thought!

The reality of the situation was almost too difficult for me to comprehend—could this be one of my flying red and black horses that had haunted me for decades? I carefully put down my cup of tea and went over to see the red paint for myself. Yes, it was a bright Chinese red inside the hole. I turned to Mrs. Nordstrom and gave her a hug and said, "Thank you." I surprised myself when I began to choke up so that it was hard to talk. I finally croaked out, "You have kept my horse for me all these years!" My mother could see how emotional I had become and wondered if I would be able to pull myself together. There was no way I was leaving without that horse!

The sale went smoothly until Mr. Nordstrom saw my cashier's check from my credit union. At that moment I wished I would have stayed with one of the big commercial banks since he had never heard of my credit union before. It was early Friday evening and the bank had already closed so there was no way to confirm the check was genuine. I explained that it was a local credit union for teachers. I told him that I taught at the local community college and was able to join it. I don't know what part of my explanation put him at ease, but he was fine with the cashier's check after that.

I asked Mr. Nordstrom how he planned to remove the horse from the brass pole since the pole went from the floor through the ceiling. There was no way I was putting a hole in my ceiling to mount the carousel horse. There had to be a better way. With some help from Mother and me holding the horse, Mr. Nordstrom pushed the brass pole to one side and it dropped from the ceiling. We carefully laid the horse on their sofa while it was removed from the pole. Mr. Nordstrom was pretty proud of the brass pole since these poles are very heavy brass and expensive. He said that he had wanted to use it to remount the carousel horse they were keeping since this is an old brass pole from a genuine carousel and the other is not. Mrs. Nordstrom interrupted her husband by saying, "I wasn't supposed to include the brass pole." Mr. Nordstrom said, "A deal is a deal." I could tell that there was some tension between them over the brass pole. Hoping to smooth things over, I explained my intention was to purchase some sort of stand and not use the pole permanently; however, I did want the brass pole for now until I could secure a proper stand for the horse.

Seeing the carousel horse lying on the sofa made me appreciate how big it was. What if it doesn't fit in my SUV? I loved my Ford Explorer. This was my second Explorer and one of the best things about it is that you can shop all day and always get all your purchases home. Hopefully this shopping trip would not be the exception. Before we left home I had thrown in some quilts to pad the horse if we purchased it. I went out with Mother to get the car ready. Now that we were alone, she asked where I intended to put the horse since its color was horrible. I said I planned to get it refinished. She asked how much that was going to cost. I am not sure if all mothers have the same gift, but my mother always says what I am thinking before I have the courage to say it out loud. I put the back seat down and spread out one of the quilts.

I helped Mr. Nordstrom load the carousel horse and it fit perfectly. Yes, my Explorer came through again. I covered up the horse while Mr. Nordstrom went back for the brass pole. I could see Mr. Nordstrom's hesitation in loading the brass pole. I assured him I would return it. My husband worked in Portland, not too far from their home; he could bring it to work one day and they can pick it up. Mr. Nordstrom looked at me like he didn't quite believe it would ever happen. Mother and I drove home talking about the Nordstroms, their house and the red and black flying horses. The carousel horse needed a name, so I named him Woody. I felt like a lifetime goal had just been achieved.

When we got home, my husband carefully unloaded Woody and brought him into the house and carefully laid him on the living room sofa. Next he brought in the long brass pole. Being a civil engineer he stated the obvious, "This pole will never work." I agreed and explained to him how they had the pole going up through their ceiling. John's reply was that this pole was so long it would go clear through the ceiling into the second floor of our house. Again I said, "I know and I have another idea." I quickly went online and found a free-standing carousel horse stand and ordered it. "The problem is solved," I said as I walked into the living room. "The stand should be here in a week." I explained that I promised to return the pole once I found an alternative.

A week later the stand came and it was just perfect! Woody was sitting on his new stand, with legs in mid-air like he was prancing. Woody looked perfect except with the colors orange/red, white and royal blue, it was a horrible color combination for a carousel horse. I thought that I would call Carol in the morning; surely she will have some ideas about refinishing Woody. I talked to Carol the following evening after work. She said she received my photo and could refinish him at her home. I hung up the phone. Perfect! Carol will give Woody a makeover.

Fast forward nearly a year and a half. Woody was coming home completely redone. He was a soft dapple grey with a darker grey mane and tail, my absolute all-time favorite horse color. His saddle was dark brown and he had white crystal jewels on his bridle and around his saddle. Carol found working on Woody to be therapeutic as she was going through a divorce. And Woody would soon celebrate his 100th birthday looking better than new.

Today Woody still sits on his stand "prancing" in my living room. Woody is the centerpiece of our Christmas celebration. We place three small, narrow decorated Christmas trees sitting around him, with a teddy bear in his saddle and ribbons flowing down from his brass pole. An electric train circles his base and the wrapped gifts go in the middle. Woody is a constant reminder to me that dreams do come true, but only if you hold on to them.

About the Author:

Rebecca Hillyer was born and raised in Salem, Oregon. She attended Oregon State University where she graduated in 1980 with a BS in Secondary Education—Social Science. Rebecca received her law

Behind Colorful Doors

degree from Willamette University College of Law in 1984. After spending 18 years in private practice as a trial attorney she came to Chemeketa Community College in her current position as General Counsel.

Additionally, Rebecca has taught adjunct at both Willamette Law School and Chemeketa and served as a pro-tem judge for the City of Keizer. Rebecca volunteers her time as a Teen Court Judge, Willamette Moot Court Judge and mentoring law students and young lawyers.

She is a member of the National Association of College and University Attorneys and serves on the board of the Marion County Bar Association as Treasurer. Rebecca also is a member of the Association of Threat Assessment Professionals and was a speaker at the 2014 National Conference.

Rebecca has been practicing law since 1984 and is admitted to practice both in Oregon and Washington State, as well as Federal District Court and The Supreme Court of the United States of America.

Rebecca's hobbies include showing dogs where her kennel boasts 20 Best in Shows and numerous "Top 10" nationally ranked Golden Retriever in both conformation and agility. In her spare time Rebecca loves gardening, relaxing at the Oregon Coast and her latest passion - painting with watercolors.

164

7

The Acorn Door
Robin Richardson and MAD MacNeill

Our door, the one we have now, and not the one that came with the house, is acorn in color and in nature since it is solid oak with a clear finish.

When we bought the house, years ago, the original door had peeling white paint but was so badly damaged by neglect and the energies of the boys who lived here when it was a halfway house for street kids, that it was beyond repair. Of course when you buy your first house, you quickly find that money is in short supply, so we made do with plywood gussets and more screws and it held together.

Our present door appeared about a year later. It was installed in a house of similar age, which was about to be demolished. It was black, and solid, and better yet, the same width as ours. But when we asked the contractor about it we were told it was already sold.

We had turned up at the demolition sale looking for oak flooring to put down in our house over the splintery side grain fir flooring, horribly refinished with grinder dips and scores by the previous owners. We cut a deal with the contractor because the house was coming down in the morning

167

and it was already almost noon of the day before. We worked by flashlights through the night pulling up the top-nailed oak strips with crowbars and hammers and by morning we had most of it up and in rough bundles.

And the door? Come morning, when the wrecking crew turned up, it was still there, untouched.

"Well, since the guy paid for it and didn't come back, if you want it, help yourself."

We did. We brought it back to the house along with all the flooring and carefully leaned it up against the front porch railing before we dumped all the flooring, still full of nails, on the front porch.

After a couple of weeks of pulling nails we had half of a five-gallon pail of used nails and a repeating crop of blisters, but we also had a good supply of neatly bundled nail-free oak strip flooring, and a door.

Our 1899 wreck of a house was not pretentious. It was built for a middle class customs official, on the standard Edwardian model, with a gracious staircase, but without any gingerbread or fancy stuff attached. The front porch had plain square pillars in clusters of three on the corners, and the railing balusters were, likewise, simply square.

But the front door was big—fully forty inches wide and seven foot three inches high. Seven foot three? I guess builders in 1899 were free to make a door whatever size they liked. The new (to us) door was also forty inches wide but only six foot nine inches high. It was also a different panel configuration with a smaller window and it was black. Our house was a vibrant yellow with white trim. Black did not fit into this color scheme. So with some trepidation, we gently scraped off a small section of paint to discover … oak. Wonderful, turn-of-the-century solid, indestructible oak with a deep golden brown hue, or "acorn." While we had no qualms about replacing the rotting cedar with oak from the same period, we wanted the replacement to be the same style.

Fortunately, I am the son of a carpenter, grandson of the owner of a building supply company, and great grandson of one of the contractors who helped build Brighton Pier in England. None of my forebears were still with us when we bought the house, but the talent for dealing with buildings was firmly ensconced in the genes.

My wife, Mary Anne, is a native of both Vancouver and its West End, and possesses a remarkable faith in my woodworking abilities. This is not blind faith as her family has a similar genetic history, including shipbuilders, house builders, upholsterers, and a grandmother who did all her own plumbing and electrical. When we first viewed the house with an eye to purchasing it and I had detailed all its shortcomings in exact and depressing detail, her exact words were, "But you can fix all that!" As it happened I could, though I often say, with some truth, we are now in the thirtieth year of the first five-year plan.

So I proceeded to deconstruct the door and reassemble various revised parts to match the original's panel and window sizes. It was a workman-like solution, and fit perfectly, if you discounted the out-of-skew doorframe which left an elongated triangle of light, and cold air at the top and bottom.

And it was now stripped of all its black paint, given a few protective coats of clear finish, and presented the world with a lovely acorn sheen.

In the years that followed, we gradually began to prosper to the point where we could tell our bankers more convincing lies about our finances and we were able to secure a second mortgage and begin the essential work of house restoration.

This involved raising the whole structure three feet, removing the old crumbling stone pillars and posts and replacing them with a modern earthquake-resistant continuous foundation and new walls, so that when the house was set back in place, it was a full two and a half feet higher and had an extra thousand square feet, with eight-foot ceilings. And all this happened while continuing to live in the house. Brilliant and cheap. At the time, it sounded really easy.

The day of the "lift" Mary Anne was in the house, since the house raisers assured us there was no danger. They failed to assure our Scottie dog, Caelte. I stood out on the sidewalk to watch. The process was so smooth that the house had risen more than six inches before I even noticed. Inside, it was a different story. As the six huge pneumatic jacks began to take the strain of lifting 80 tons of house, the whole structure made a sound which Mary Anne could only describe as "clicking." A clicking that made the hair on the back of her neck rise. Caelte found it even more upsetting and bolted for the front door. Mary Anne followed her and arrived to find that the jacks had begun to straighten the house out and the door was solidly jammed in the frame. Thinking quickly, she reversed direction and headed for the back door with Caelte close on her heels. It opened to reveal a yawning chasm where the porch had been removed by the house raisers because it was "not structurally integral." That is the technical term. Their description was more succinct and unprintable.

So dog and mistress fled back to the living room and tried one of the three windows that led to the front porch, and . . . victory! It raised perfectly. Caelte was quickly picked up and put out on the porch and Mary Anne clambered after her. The front porch is "structurally integral," but by this point it was also almost three feet higher than before, and the steps had been removed to allow access for one of the two huge beams that supported the now floating house. So I had to scrabble past all the house lifters' debris to grab the step ladder at the back of the house and bring it back to the front so the two escapees could be brought back to terra firma.

It took very little time to pry open the door and rehang it and we sat on the two immense beams for a month until finally the house came down to rest permanently, a full two and a half feet higher on the new foundation.

Now the process of going up was unnerving but incredibly smooth. So smooth, our old cat Mr. P., slept through the whole three-foot rise and only awoke went Caelte was dropped on the porch a few feet from him. The process of returning to earth was much more traumatic. The house raisers dropped one side at a time and they dropped it in about five seconds; it looked like a slow lurch to one side and then, after a brief pause, the other.

Unfortunately, the mason got the new chimney bases wrong and the main one was an inch higher than it should have been. Still, the house warped to accommodate it. Balloon frame houses like ours warp quite easily, plaster does not. And again I was outside looking in, while Mary Anne was inside with Caelte. So they had the once-in-a-lifetime experience of having a wall of plaster bulge out at them and begin to shatter. I know you can see this coming but of course the warping also jammed the front door shut again, and we had a repeat of the first exit, except for the running for the back door because the lack of porch was reinforced by my having screwed the door shut so no one stepped into space accidentally.

Once more, the new/old front door was refitted and there it remained in clear oak, in contrast to the rest of the house to which we added royal blue and sky blue to enhance the yellow and white.

There comes a time in everyone's life when the generation ahead moves on, and in our case, both my mother and Mary Anne's grandmother died within two years of each other, and in the fullness of legal time, which is much slower than real time, being based in a previous century, two small inheritances made their way to us.

A large inheritance, I think, must be an easier thing, because it brings a lot of freedom, though usually at the cost of a lot of responsibility. But a small one brings to mind the ability to do those things you may well have given thought to under the general category of "if we had the money to spare." And that is where we were. We treasured our relationships with both mother and grandmother and we wanted to use the money for something to remember them. And one of the most frequently considered items under the spare money list was restoring the stained glass window beside the front door. We knew what it looked like because Mary Anne had been raised in the neighborhood and remembered it, and she probably was more inclined to remember it because it depicted a schooner under full sail, such as what her great grandfather had built.

Our original owner was a customs official. At the turn of the last century that meant shipping customs, and most officials were recruited from the merchant marine, a natural posting for a ship's purser or captain. The stained glass window supports this theory. The inheritances made it possible to commission a stained glass artist, and we worked with him over the period of a year to achieve a quite wonderful re-creation of the original. Not only was he the kind of person who had developed several techniques of his own for making glass windows look like they were old, he also had an immense collection of old glass salvaged over a lifetime of work. On top of that, he charged so little that there was room in the budget for a second window.

Of course, our thoughts turned immediately to the window in the door. A stained glass window would mean the hallway would go from a room anyone standing at the door could survey, to a kind of private outer sanctum. But, what to put in it? I don't think the door had anything but plain glass in it from the beginning. I don't know this for sure, since the original glass was replaced at least once, probably during the reign of terror known as the halfway house era. But regardless, we were on our own.

The nautical theme, however, seemed appropriate, and when the words "compass rose" were first mentioned it seemed like a natural. A natural reinforced by the fact that my mother, though christened "Susan Rosa," was always known as "Rose." And our stained glass man came up with a perfect MacIntosh rose for the center, and a selection of "jewels— round faceted pieces in different colors, for the four points.

With a couple of consults for choosing specific colors of glass, we arrived at a final design and then we waited, and waited, and waited, all through the summer until one day we got a call that it was ready. It exceeded our expectations and the two windows came back with us. I carefully installed them behind clear panes of safety glass for protection. And there they remain.

Our once plain door is now a plain oak door, but with a wonderfully colored stained glass window that casts beautiful patterns of color on the hall walls whenever the sun shines through, and conversely, glows in intricate color at night if the hall lights are on.

And behind the now colorful door? Well, that's another story.

To B&B or Not to Be?

When we bought our house in 1984, neither of us had any intention of opening it as a Bed & Breakfast. Our prime motivation was financial security, since we were renting an apartment. Rent controls had been lifted on January 1 of that year, and our rent had promptly doubled. Yes, doubled. Looming on the horizon was Expo '86, Vancouver's engagement with the fun of a World's Fair. The experience of friends of mine who were renters in Montreal prior to the World's Fair there in 1967 was that rents were going up and up, and probably more up than that. The only defense was to move out of town, or find some way to purchase a property.

Now this was an era of high interest rates. They had peaked at something close to 20 percent per annum in the previous year, but not until they had brought the housing market in Vancouver crashing back to earth. Perhaps it was even a bit below earth, because houses listed for a half a million in the fall of 1983 weren't selling at a hundred and fifty thousand six months later. Interest rates had settled to what looked like an unbelievable bargain of 11¾ percent. I shudder when I think of that now, but at the time, the interest rate drop and the bottoming out of house prices looked like the only opportunity we were going to get, so we took it. Still, even by bringing in Mary Anne's brother Jay as a co-purchaser, there was a limit to what we could buy, so we bought the one house we could afford.

It was a wreck—an urban wreck, to be sure, on a postage stamp property, in the heart of Vancouver's West End.

Those who know Vancouver will understand. Those unfamiliar should know that Vancouver, British Columbia, Canada, is a small city of some six to seven hundred thousand, with the geographic peculiarity that its downtown is situated on a peninsula confined to the northwest of the city as a whole. Stanley Park occupies the most westerly part of the peninsula; the downtown business district is situated on the eastern portion. The West End occupies the section between them. It was the first suburb of the city and our house was built as a white collar residence in 1899.

The original owner was the only resident for a few years, and was followed by an accountant, and then a widow who took boarders for over 40 years and preserved the house from any kind of modernization. There followed a period of many landlords including a federal political candidate who used it as a campaign office and installed a hundred-line phone system with multiple telephone jacks in every room. Had we been less than scrupulously honest, we had the perfect set up for a boiler room or bookie operation. And then, finally, there were the two social workers who ran a halfway house for street youth. The youth seemed to specialize in taking their collective angst out on the walls and doors, and so when we finally acquired the house it was battered throughout.

It leaned decidedly to the southwest, one side being about three inches lower than the other, sitting on wooden posts set on exposed stone and mortar pillars with considerably less mortar in them than was safe. Some of the posts were still solid. Some of them were not and one of them I removed by pulling it out in handfuls of sodden sawdust before replacing it. We were now secure from rent increases. But meeting the mortgage and utilities pretty much sucked up our collective incomes every month.

Which brings us to the point everyone gets to fairly quickly after they buy a house—money. We first set on the idea of running a day care. After all, our daughter Niall was just two and our son Alec was in school, so it made sense that we could charge a couple of other people to look after their kids and put a little cash aside.

And this is where Fate intervened in the form of a citywide scandal involving alleged child abuse at a well-known day care centre. Suddenly, anyone starting a day care center was in the position of trying to prove they were not going to molest little Sue or Johnny. How do you do that when you haven't ever looked after any children but your own? The answer is, you can't. Interview after interview crumbled on the same issue and after a couple of weeks we were so demoralized we decided we needed another plan.

And Fate intervened again. This time in a positive way. The city had decided to host a World's Fair, but as the time drew nearer, realized that there was simply not enough accommodation for the expected number of visitors. The city's solution was to let anyone open a Bed and Breakfast for a set thirty-dollar fee. The great B&B experiment started.

The second floor of the house had only one bath, and a sink in one bathroom, and a toilet and sink in the tiny room beside it. There were four bedrooms:

the small back bedroom where Jay slept, our bedroom in the middle, and a large bedroom which we had designated as Jay's living room at the front of the house. Beside that was a small bedroom for Alec, and Niall was consigned to a crib in the pantry downstairs. That was it. Where were guests going to sleep?

The Second Rule of Running a B&B is: You Must Be Flexible and Think Creatively. I'll get to the first rule later.

Mary Anne and I bought a cheap futon couch to sleep on in the living room and moved our clothes into the pantry with Niall. Alec and Jay retained their small bedrooms and Jay gave up his living room. That gave us two bedrooms available for guests.

We placed our bets, put out the word we were open for business, and soon bookings began to trickle in and we were in a frenzy of preparation. Renovating the bathrooms, adding a toilet to the larger one with the tub, and covering the splintered floors with some salvaged wall-to-wall carpeting. I was in the middle of installing the carpeting in the front room when Mary Anne asked how long I would be.

"I'll be done when I'm done," I said irritably. "There are no guests until next week."

Short pause.

"Um, except for the ones I just booked in for this afternoon," was the reply.

I was down to the last corner when they arrived, and we managed to put their luggage on the installed part of the carpet while Mary Anne made them tea as I finished.

The trickle became a flow, and then a rush, and by the last months of the Fair we found ourselves fully booked in both rooms. We had made over three thousand dollars that year. It was enough to install an ensuite bathroom in the closet of the large front room and fix a myriad of other small and nagging problems.

Probably the biggest surprise was how much we enjoyed the company of a wide variety of strangers. And that is The First Rule of Running a B&B: You Must Love the Company of Strangers.

There is no getting around it. If you don't like people, you have no business being in the hospitality trade. This chapter is being written at the request of one of the people who stayed with us that summer, and we have not only acquaintances, but firm friends both in the city and abroad who came into our lives first as guests at Ashby House. That enjoyment continues. Over the years we have been hosts to people from almost everywhere in the world, and often in the most serendipitous of combinations.

One summer we had a guest from a kibbutz in Israel, a family from a farm in Alberta, and Lady Jane from England. The topic of conversation over breakfast consisted of farming, more specifically the trials of silage. Lady Jane joined in with gusto describing herself in impeccable English as a "farmer's wife, you know." The height of hilarity was when the Alberta farmer explained that the main problem was how dry his area was, which brought the response from the Israeli, "You think we aren't in a desert?"

When the Berlin wall came down, we had a visiting economist from West Germany explain to us that it would take about five years to integrate the former East Germany into the economy. Within a few weeks we had another economist, this one from East Germany who, when I repeated what the first had told us, simply laughed. "We will be lucky if it is complete within 50 years." His explanation was that there had been 50 years of communist rule in East Germany and it had taught the population how to survive, and they survived by cheating the system. "Now they will have to learn to think for themselves, and the old ones won't be able to, so they will have to die off before integration will be effective."

Probably the most bizarre was a guest from Switzerland who was a refugee from a tiny German-speaking area within Romania. They spoke a dialect of German that had been isolated for several centuries and was unintelligible to anyone from Germany. But we also had a much younger guest from Texas. It turned out his father had emigrated from the same area over 50 years previously but he spoke the dialect and had taught it to his son. So the two of them babbled away to each other nonstop, delighted at last to have someone who spoke the same dialect.

Each of our guests usually brings some special knowledge or perception with them and the breakfast table is the perfect setting for an exchange of ideas and opinions. The staggered nature of bookings adds to the mix since the guests around the table often change every day or so and this increases the variety of the experience.

In the last season we hosted guests from Norway, Niger, and Cuba, among many others, and learned from and enjoyed them all. Think about that. How many people get to talk to a native of any of those places in a relatively intimate setting without ever leaving the comfort of their own home!

What's in a Name?

There is a world fraught with peril in finding a name for your B&B. I say this only because our neighbors, at one point viewing our success in luring particular parts of the world to our door, and in their infinite scorn, decided they could enhance their income by proving they could run a B&B in a much more businesslike manner. They set up a thoroughly professional website of limitless detail, dismissing B&B's such as ours with the phrase "stuffy Victorian," and sublimely named their new offering as the "Pigs Fly Inn." I remain uncertain as to whether this was a not very sly intimation of the quality and character of the guests they expected, or to their flying pig weather vane. They did not prosper.

I, on the other hand, was highly tempted to name our B&B "Ashby-de-la-Zouch-by-the-Sea." The idea came as a historical reference. My great grandmother's house in England, being Roseleigh, was in the town of Ashby de la Zouch. This is a name familiar to any still alive who have read Sir Walter Scott's "Ivanhoe." If you haven't, it is still available at your local Amazon page for under ten dollars in paperback.

During both the First World War and the Second World War, Ashby de la Zouch was also the site of a major convalescent hospital for wounded servicemen, and being tucked comfortably in the exact center of England equidistant from the English Channel in the east and the Irish Sea to the west, was jokingly referred to by the soldiers as "Ashby-de-la-Zouch-by-the-Sea."

My view was that as we were in Vancouver's West End, equally situated between Coal Harbour to the north, and Sunset Beach to the south, we could lay claim to the name. It was Mary Anne who pointed out that "by the sea" would inevitably lead to the impression we were indeed next to a beach and not perched at the top of the hill a safe eight blocks away from either source of salt water.

I remained adamant in my choice and set off to the local hardware store with visions of the name in brass letters sprawling along the main beam of the porch roof. And then I discovered the price of brass letters. Our budget was not a large one. It extended past the use of cardboard and markers, but not to the infinite distance of 27 letters at over five dollars each. And this was 1986, you understand, and a dollar was worth a lot more, as indicated by the fact they were still made of paper and had not yet become coins.

I clung to my vision, however, and came home with solid brass letters which spelled economically, "ASHBY HOUSE," and so it remained until years later when I took the time to make a new sign in flowing relief script which reads, "Ashby House Bed & Breakfast."

The Third Rule of Running a B&B is: You Must Never Show Surprise! The routine at our house offers breakfast for guests from 8:30 a.m. until 10:00 a.m. each day. So it was around 9:00 a.m. with six of our eight guests, all from Europe, sitting at the dining table, and Mary Anne and I busy in the kitchen when there was a huge "crash" above our heads, loud and strong enough that it caused the pot rack over the island to sway ominously. Then silence. The guests in the Wilde Room that night were a young couple from the U.S. Northwest. They were the only ones not yet in the dining room.

I looked over from the stove to see everyone at the table looking into the kitchen. I confess I felt like that much maligned innkeeper, Basil Faulty, caught in the headlights. I am also not one of those people who takes surprises in stride. I usually freeze, but I managed to stifle the obvious verbal exclamation, and instead put the hot frying pan back on the stove, and stepped into the dining room.

The next thing I heard was the door of the Wilde Room, the room directly above the kitchen, slam shut and hurried footsteps coming down the front stairs. The front stairs are visible through the dining room door if you are sitting on the far side of the dining table. Before I could move through the dining room to intercept whoever was approaching, I was distracted by the intense look of concentration on the face of the French gentleman staring through the door to the stairs. It went through panoply of emotions quite plainly, starting with shock, moving through astonishment, and ending with a look of pure satisfaction.

She entered the dining room. A young woman in the full flush of youth and solely clad, or perhaps draped, in a housecoat designed by one of those haute couture houses that advertise in men's magazines of a certain type, to entice rather than cover. The Frenchman continued to stare and a quick glance around the table proved he was not alone. I turned my attention to the young lady, being very careful to look straight in her eyes and not let my focus drop to the more alluring views below. A mere raised eyebrow in the finest host tradition was enough to elicit the words, "The sink seems to have fallen off the wall!" "Ah," I said, in my best, seen-everything-in-the-world tone, "That would explain the crash."

She stood transfixed, much to the satisfaction of the entire table, who had all stopped feasting on breakfast and were instead feasting their eyes, and I added, "Perhaps I should come and see what can be done." And with that I ushered her out of the dining room and up the stairs to the Wilde Room. She paused at the door and let me enter ahead of her. The Wilde Room is our smallest room, and has an equally small ensuite bathroom with shower, sink and toilet. I only had to take two steps into the room to encounter a pair of naked legs extending out of the bathroom, which on the third step revealed an equally naked young man, with a bent plastic supply tube clutched in each hand. Water seeped out of the tubes and trickled down his arms to the floor, where the sink lay still in one piece but obviously now bereft of any plumbing.

I mentioned that I am not very good at the third rule: Never Show Surprise, but the situation really didn't surprise me; it was merely the logical consequence of having a sink "fall" off a wall and then trying to stop the water while seeking help. Most people try to do this while clothed but I try to be open-minded in these situations.

So I stepped over the naked man and popped off the cleverly disguised access panel and turned off the water valves. Then I stepped back, and being careful to keep my gaze confined, made my way back to the dining room. I congratulated myself on the way down the stairs for not laughing, but as soon as I reached the dining room, the highly amused looks of enquiry from the entire table seemed to require some explanation. "It seems the sink fell off the wall," I said, and fled to the kitchen. Europeans are not naive, and a wave of laughter followed my exit. The couple never appeared at breakfast for the rest of their stay.

The strangest guest who ever appeared at our door, and just as an aside, this was not the one who appeared for breakfast in a full and luxuriant jester's costume, complete with little silver jingly bells on his hat, was the Minotaur.

It began with the usual email requesting the Whistler Room for three nights. The request explained that the husband had stayed with us before, and although they now lived in town, he wanted to stay over for his 30th birthday weekend. All was arranged, and we looked forward to seeing someone, for the name given was the wife's, for a second time.

At the appointed time, there was a ringing of the front doorbell, (we still have the original mechanical Victorian doorbell) and Mary Anne answered it. Standing on the porch was a young woman she had never seen before who confirmed she had a booking and asked about parking. We have three off-street parking spaces nearby, since parking in our neighborhood is highly restricted to residents only. Mary Anne showed her where to park and the woman went to fetch the car which was close, but parked illegally, and Mary Anne returned to the house. The second ring of the doorbell announced that the guests had parked and arrived. When Mary Anne opened the door, there stood the woman, and slightly to one side and behind her stood . . . a Minotaur. Well, to be accurate, a man wearing a full Minotaur head mask complete with nose ring. For those of you who slept through the classical mythology class, a Minotaur is a half man/half bull of Ancient Greek origins.

"I forgot to mention that Minotaur was coming to stay," the woman said. True to form, Mary Anne simply said, "Well, welcome. Shall I show you to your room?" And took them up to the room, where she asked if they would like some tea. Tea is served in the dining room, so as she came back down the stairs she had to ponder how the Minotaur was going to manage this.

In due course they came down the stairs. I had returned from whatever errand I was on, having missed all the excitement but in time to be informed by Mary Anne what had happened. As they came down the stairs I recognized the man now appearing sensibly without the mask as someone who had stayed with us about a year ago.

We were disappointed to learn that the mask was just part of the costume, and he had foregone putting on the whole thing, because, in his words, "It gets very hot, and it smells a bit." Still, there are very few B&B's that can reckon even half a Minotaur among their guests.

So You Want to Run a Bed and Breakfast?

Some years ago we were guests at the wedding of the daughter of some friends. It was a large reception with several hundred in attendance and seating was assigned. We were surprised to find ourselves sitting at a table for eight with six other people we had never met. Our hostess soon appeared and explained to us that these other three couples were all thinking of retiring and opening a Bed and Breakfast, so she was sure our years of experience would be of interest to them.

Understatement! They pounced on us with a barrage of questions as soon as the situation was announced. We started by asking if they were starting up a B&B, or purchasing one that was already up and running. One couple told us they were looking at buying one on Vancouver Island. The price, we were told, was about one and a half million.

"Do you have one and a half million?" I asked. They acknowledged that, yes, they did. "Then why on earth wouldn't you buy a condo in Hawaii and put your feet up and enjoy the rest of your life?" We then got into the details of the work involved, the return on equity, the importance of location, and all the nefarious details of success or failure. Suffice to say not one of the couples ventured into the business. And the moral to all this is simply a repetition of The First Rule.

We have and continue to enjoy the guests that stay with us. And more importantly, we have become much more knowledgeable and relaxed hosts over the years.

We have really never approached the running of our B&B as a business, with capital expenditures carefully calculated against expected income. We have simply adapted our natural sociability to entertaining and being entertained by the company of others, and though we charge most of them for the privilege (there are some who have moved to the complimentary category by virtue of long association), that is simply a necessity that allows us to continue with this wonderful window on the world.

About the Authors:

Robin Richardson and Mary Anne MacNeill bought the house that became Ashby House Bed and Breakfast in 1984. They had, before then, run an amateur theatre company in the city, producing 20 plays over a four-year period. In retrospect, they assert that they are simply producing the longest running improvisational performance with a permanent set and an ever-changing cast of characters. Performances continue daily.

Their first published novel, "The Fourth House," was released in 2003 and is now out of print. The revised version will surface as an e-book in early 2017.

The full story of the B&B is now being written and will appear whenever the guests give them enough time to finish it.

8

The Pale Green Door
Dr. Leroy Goertzen

Finally!! Spring Break was here! I finished my last paper for the week and placed it on the prof's desk the morning it was due. Check! And there was that Greek exam. I pulled an all-nighter drilling myself with vocabulary and points of grammar and syntax. But I think I aced it—and good thing because I needed to make up for bombing the previous one. Check! Now, with the last class behind me and the car packed, I could at last distance myself from the daily grind of everything that looked, sounded, smelled and felt like school. Oh—and WooHoo! I wasn't going to have to walk the one and a half miles to my part-time job down the hill in the Old Market, one of those I-wouldn't-t-work-here-unless-I-needed-the-money kind of jobs. The owner, a shrewd little beady-eyed man with crazy-thick glasses and a very scary stare, employed some rather seedy people. I must admit, however, working with some of the local riffraff was a positive, eye-opening experience for this small town farm kid. I needed that job far more than it needed me. I should be thankful for the experience. The minimum-wage pay was extra!

I've enjoyed quite a few Spring Breaks through the course of my academic pursuits and now, looking back, I marvel curiously at the nearly euphoric sense of excitement and release I felt anticipating this time off. But the change of pace and the time away from the rigors of the academy, if only for a week, make that a week with two weekends, was a welcome respite. I could taste the freedom from deadlines and the intense schedule that accompanied them. I could use eight hours of sleep. Hey, maybe I could even sleep in—now there's an idea whose time has come. No late nighters—no early risers! Not this week. I'm crossing my fingers.

I was headed home. Yes, home! No South-Florida beaches, Arizona deserts or crowded Polynesian islands. Home! I never understood the allure of traveling to some popular spring-break resort only to have to jostle with a crowd of students with nothing better to do than hang out and party. To be around more students was just a bad reminder that you were in college, and would soon have to go back to classes again. Nope, that wasn't for me. Besides, my conservative, traditional-thinking parents would never have permitted it. Such a foray into leisure, self-pandering and lack of a regime and boundaries was beyond their capacity to even imagine. My goodness! What value could possibly come from that? And so, happily and necessarily, my destination was home and the familiar sights, sounds and smells of my upbringing. Though it doesn't begin with "s," I would be remiss not to mention the tastes of my mom's cooking. She was sure to prepare a few of my favorite dishes while I was home, at least that was the script playing in the back of my mind. Actually, my mouth was watering for homemade noodles sautéed in my mom's onion-laced creamy ham gravy. Kielka and schmont fat is what it was fondly called in my home. I'm convinced it tastes better when called by its traditional name. Whatever the case, it didn't make the college cafeteria menu and I was really hungry for it.

It occurred to me as I left the city limits of Omaha behind that I might even get in on Smorgasbord, the fund-raiser sponsored by the community high school music department. This annual event included supper and the spring band concert. It had become a very big event for a very small town. Henderson nearly doubled in size on this day. In and of itself, this was a meal worth going home for! Non-Mennonites from miles around descended on the town in droves to enjoy verenika, kielka and schmont fat, schaubla, kluptz, worscht, kumpzt borscht, pluma mos, rugga brot, partzlike, apple priescha, schnetya, plautz, kohl salat and zwiebach. These dishes were part of a menu that featured many of the traditional German dishes that had been brought to America from the Old Country—authentic recipes prepared in the old ways. Most of us hailing from Henderson and other German Mennonite communities, were brought up on this food-off-the-land. But to have the entire menu spread out over the length of the gym, fastidiously attended by familiar faces, many of whom were relatives, was a sight for sore college eyes and a delight beyond description for institutionalized taste buds. I could smell the verenika in my car traveling 75 mph down the interstate. Just thinking about it weighed on my right foot, even as I saw the 60-mph speed sign to my right signaling that I was entering the city limits of Lincoln.

To be entirely forthcoming, do I need to mention that going home had other benefits? By now I may have had quite a bag of clothes needing to be washed. No, I don't believe I recall mentioning that, but there is some likelihood that my suitcase was stuffed with dirty clothes. Quarters were hard to come by in college. Washers in the dorm were always occupied or broken down. They were possessed! Clothes dryers ate my socks! The basement laundry room was dark and scary! My mom enjoyed sharing in my college experience! Ahem.

Now, spring break in Nebraska needs definition or explanation. No—description. You could be traveling in a late winter or early spring snowstorm, the wet kind where a late cold front out of Canada meets an even stronger warm front forcing its way up from the Gulf. The heavy snow accumulates in a hurry and sticks to the road, resulting in road closures, power outages, cancelled meetings and activities, and best of all, school snow days! An unofficial, unscheduled winter break! Or, you could be headed for a week of farm-work, volunteer of course! Springtime on the farm launched a flurry of activity as the rich, dark soil thawed in response to the sun's increasingly warm rays. The frost had done its work, mellowing the fallow ground as last year's stubble almost magically decomposed. By now, farmers were anxious to get into the fields, particularly if it had been a short fall. Late snows and early rains, as welcome as the added moisture, just increased the worry and stress as planting season was bearing down on the almanac, and there was so much tillage yet to be done. Everyone who is part of the agricultural community understands the quandary; it either rains too much or too little; the winters are too cold or not cold enough; the summers aren't quite warm enough and lack the heat units to produce full, mature kernels, or the summers are too hot too soon and mess with pollination. Lyrics of a tune from the country band Alabama say it well, "I don't know how our crops survived the drought and too much rain. It must have been a miracle. How else could you explain?" That's exactly how I remember it. The weather was seldom ever right. In case you didn't have anything else to talk about, you could always grumble about the weather. Negative, gloomy attitudes notwithstanding, what often made the difference, other than the miracles, was the timely, determined, persistent work of the farmer. No one understands seasons better than they do and the opportune nature of work therein. Farmers know well the wisdom of Solomon: "There is a season for everything, a time to sow and a time to reap." When it's time to sow, get on with the sowing. God forbid that the weather might get in the way! That was a prayer.

Fortunately, today my drive on I-80, now heading west out of Lincoln, would be escorted by dry conditions with temperatures in the high 30's and a slight easterly breeze. Having driven this stretch of the road on more than a few occasions, my gold-toned, two-door 1971 Malibu Chevelle was on autopilot. That was a good thing because my mind was racing miles ahead, focused on a visit I was paying my grandfather. My mom had hinted in a recent letter that he hadn't been doing well and that I might want to see him the next time I came home. Most sons who have reached some manner of responsible, attentive adulthood understand well that such hints from one's mother are not really hints at all. Neither are they suggestions. Mothers seldom suggest. But they don't stoop to the level of pleading. I refer to them as "motherisms"—pithy sayings that mean so much more than what meets the ear. These sayings are highly nuanced for they come immersed in the context shaped by years of having been together and having heard her voice and seen her mannerisms. It is the art of telling you to do something without telling you to do it knowing that your conscience, really her conscience at work in you, will tutor you to do the right thing—her thing. And so I was going to stop by and see how he was doing, and give him a chance to catch up with my life as well, although I couldn't imagine that taking him long. Though I loved and respected my grandfather dearly, I wasn't really looking forward to the visit because, quite frankly, he seemed conversationally challenged at times. At least that is how it seemed to me. The presence of pregnant pauses was uncomfortably awkward. And I didn't always know what to do with short-sentence responses. Like an unprepared prosecuting attorney, I ran out of questions fairly quickly and hoped the court would soon be adjourned.

My mom's dad was now in his mid-80's. He lived on his own in the house he had had built long enough ago so that it was the only house I associated with him. The two seemed rather inseparable. My grandparents lived in town, now long retired having passed on the family farm to the only son of their nine children who chose to follow his father's vocation. Living in town seemed like a big deal to me

at that time, though now, having spent most of my
life as a suburbanite in large cities, I don't quite
understand the mystique it held over me. It seemed
huge, a vast network of streets running north and
south, east and west as far as the eye could see! In
reality, it is tiny. I can jog around the entire town in
less than 30 minutes. And I hardly jog.

The town was Henderson, a thriving but
rather plateaued rural village of 750 people, all of
whom easily fit into half a section including the
downtown, the parks, golf course, swimming pool,
school, churches, grain industries and all housing.
Main Street ran a straight two blocks north and south
with no stoplights or stop signs. You could make a U-
turn at either end. Dragging main, something of
course I never did, could take nearly five minutes at
five miles per hour. That gave ample time to see the
sights such as the hardware store, the IGA grocery
store, the local bank and post office, the printing
press for the local newspaper, a café or two, and an
assortment of other small businesses. Of course, as a
rural community, the town serviced a much larger
area populated by farmers. As a case in point, the
large Mennonite church had several hundred more
attendees than the entire population of the town. And
there were two other well-attended Mennonite
churches within the village limits.

My grandfather lived on the corner of one of
the primary east-west streets on the perimeter of the
larger town square. The large Mennonite church
which my family and many relatives attended was
directly across the street. That always seemed rather
appropriate to me considering the spiritual demeanor

197

of my grandfather. It seemed natural to connect my grandfather's location to the church. Without a doubt, he was a churchman. As I entered the town from the spur that led from the interstate, I drove by the large brick church and its ample parking lot on the south end of the property. I was enraptured by a flood of memories. One in particular was more than a bit unsettling. We were playing softball during a summer Daily Vacation Bible School recess. I swung hard and hit the ball solidly. Oops! Not good! I pulled a hard foul ball into left field—way left—right through one of the stained-glass windows of the south chancel. There was a quiet gasp as we watched the ball fly, calculating its trajectory. Then we heard that all too familiar ball-meeting-glass "crack." What followed was terrifyingly profane: The blessed and beautiful Virgin Mary and Babe fell 20 feet to the sidewalk below and broke into a thousand shards. That was an unfortunate, rather unholy moment for all of us as we began contemplating what proper remorse and penance might look, or feel like, once the pastor put his gaze upon the missing Madonna.

I pulled my car to a stop in front of my grandfather's home. Because he lived directly across the street from the church, his side of the street, and it was rather wide street for such a small town, had been striped for parallel parking in order to accommodate Sunday morning worshippers, particularly the large numbers of families traveling from the countryside. Every Sunday my father parked the car on the church side of the street directly opposite my grandfather's home. We only parked on his side when we visited. That made it clear that we were there to see him. One must do these things properly.

I got out of the car and leisurely made my way up the short familiar sidewalk that cut a straight path from the street through the grass right to the front door. I passed by a couple of old American elm trees that were being ravaged by the infamous Dutch elm disease that spread through the Midwest in the 60's and 70's. These fast-growing, hardy trees, planted during the dust bowl of the 30's to provide vegetation had succumbed almost all at once to this deadly disease. Like most of these magnificent elm trees in town, they would soon need to be removed. I recognized all the well-known cracks in the concrete; one uses them for playing hopscotch when chalk is contraband. Really, it makes for a much more interesting game, certainly more argumentative! I climbed up the few steps to the small, raised concrete porch that served as nothing more than an elevated entry to the home. I stood there in front of the pale green door attempting to rehearse again in my mind what I had hoped to talk about beyond the trivial, "How are you feeling?" and "What did you do today?" My thoughts rebelled. As I began to reach for the familiar handle to the screen door, it dawned on me that, other than my own, I had not entered any home more frequently than this one, not by far.

The front of the house included a large picture window, a common feature of homes built here in the 50's and 60's. It gave the front room where everyone gathered a view. Of course, the view works both ways, so standing at the door I could see my grandfather sitting somewhat bent forward in his chair at the far end of the family room. He was reading. His unbecoming glasses were lodged halfway down his nose. I almost expected him to be reading the Bible which typically rested neatly next to the chair on an end table, as it had been for as long as I could remember. It was a King James Version with sullied, tagged page ends where one's hands and fingers rub the edges, and over time, leave a brownish tinge on the thin India paper. The leather was worn, having been rubbed off by extensive use. He had newer ones which family members had enthusiastically seen fit to give him, but like a pair of well-worn jeans, he preferred the one that had seen him through the thick and thin of life. I was familiar with that Bible. I had read it and heard it read by my grandfather since I was old enough to remember.

He was reading the Henderson News, or as we fondly quipped, the Local Liar. In small communities, particularly those where citizens are genealogically interrelated as Henderson was, the margin between what is presented as news and gossip is narrow. They are easily commingled since it is assumed that everything is everyone's business. All residents are on a need to know basis, and all think they need to know, though not equally so of course, and that too is a source of gossip—err—news. Editorial freedom provides the perspective that may make plain the difference between news and gossip. One can never be too sure. Letters to the editor offer correctives when these differences seem to have been obscured a bit. But as the worn out aphorism states well: It is what it is. Some might contend that there is a moral obligation, one grounded in support of community, to stay current on local affairs, which is local-speak for staying abreast of the gossip. Of course, this is all rather redundant since a daily visit to the local coffee shop on main street offered the same information in real time, updated daily at mid-morning, noon, mid-afternoon, and evening as the locals took a break from work and the retirees escaped household chores and boredom.

Front doors in Henderson are seldom locked, and if so, only at night. One could literally just walk right in, which typically I would have done since other aunts, uncles, and cousins would already be there. But Grandpa was alone and I was alone, so I intended to knock so as not to alarm him, though I doubted that that was actually possible. I couldn't recall ever seeing him raise an eyebrow. My mother swears otherwise. I guess she should know. As I raised my closed fist and leaned into the door I experienced that all-too-familiar déjà vu moment. I suddenly remembered having been in a similar position dozens of times in the past, leaning against that very door, forearm covering my eyes. I could almost hear it and found myself saying in my mind, "One one-thousand, two one-thousand, three one-thousand . . . TEN ONE-THOUSAND—Wolf in Town!" I have absolutely no idea how this rather pointless and preposterous game came to be. I just remember playing it a hundred times—ONLY after dark. One wanted the fear factor of the terrifying wolf to be heightened exponentially as part of the game. Just the thought of hiding from the wolf so as not to feel his jagged teeth and have him fill his ravenous belly was scary enough, as it played out in the dark shadows of the bushes and trees that outlined the house under the light of the moon. Moonless nights were hideous! I remember participating apprehensively in the game as a child with my older siblings and cousins. As I recall, they found it rather enjoyable, devilishly so, to find ways to increase our primal fear of the wolf. Nightmares were sure to follow.

With the counting aside and having arrived safely "home," escaping the village wolf, I quietly opened the door and stepped into the small entryway. Contours of a home suited for life on the farm were apparent. The entryway was tiled, hosting a large carpet for wiping one's shoes before entering the carpeted front room. To the side there was a recessed area to hang one's coats and place one's boots. I was overcome abruptly by that warm, heartfelt sense of familiarity with a place I had been so often before, though not recently. Stepping from the cold into the entryway of my grandfather's house is an experience that lacks lucid description. The transition from the dry, cold, nostril-freezing air to the warm, tight, pungent odor of that house was exhilarating. How do you describe the smells of a home where someone you love and cherish has lived for 40 years? It's a menagerie of smells, quite real and yet quite imaginary because they are evoked by our memories and suggested by our feelings, but as real to us as the noses on our faces. I could still smell them: Baked ham, pan-fried potatoes, homemade baked beans, pluma mos, fresh-baked zwiebach, all commingled with the smell of old furniture in the living room, the same soap and cleaners venting from the bathroom, and the same cologne and perfumes emanating from Grandpa's bedroom. There's no formula for such a thing. It can't be reproduced; it's one of a kind. It's priceless and became lost forever at my grandparents' decease and the sale of the home except in the furthest reaches of my memory. But that wasn't at this moment.

My olfactory system was inflamed, creating a flashback into my childhood, memories resurrected from times and places no longer in existence, ancient odors making contact with my senses once again, exploding into mental pictures and feelings that drew me back into reliving those precious moments. Opening that pale green door and stepping inside took me back to earlier days. I found myself peering into the living room enlivened by all that was familiar to my spirit—a place to call home with people I knew as family. What a feeling! The room oozed with warmth, love, security, peace, joy, happiness, contentment, well-being, faithfulness and an array of other attributes too numerous to name. In a way, it's rather strange. These qualities were never imposed or even discussed but they permeated the atmosphere of that room and the people who gathered there, leaving their scent on all of us in different ways. In my heart, I sensed a deep emotional, even spiritual, bond with that place, baptized and sanctified by its memory, still living on its fumes.

I could hear their voices, multiple conversations taking place simultaneously in the crowded living room. Couches were filling and folding chairs were being dragged in from around the house as needed; the piano bench was already occupied. People kept coming in, passing me by as they entered the house without knocking, allowing the cold air to rush in immediately behind them like some uninvited guest. They promptly and vigorously took off their wraps, hung them up and looked for a place to sit. I could hear the familiar greeting, "Komm aul enn!" coming from several warm and cozy onlookers. A variety of smart comments spoken in low German were bantered about as only those who know each other well can dare or afford to express.

Seating was, as we would jest, Mennonite style: The men sat together next to my grandfather at one end of the room, and the women gathered at the other the end closest to the kitchen, bathroom and stairs to the basement, a rather convenient and pragmatic arrangement. Children were, well… just everywhere and teens either participated in the adult conversation or found somewhere to hang out. Believe it or not, my best friend (and first cousin) and I claimed the small bathroom as our private domain. Older teens that could drive might drag the town square for a while, revving their engines here and there to keep the carbon from building up, or so it was explained.

These ad hoc meetings were a weekly affair. My grandfather's proximity to the church made it convenient for his children to stop in following services on Sunday night before they went home to prepare for the work week. We all went to church on Sunday night; there was programming for everyone. It doesn't really matter what it was and so it isn't worth describing. It was just the right place to be and the right thing to do. When the church opened its doors, you ought to be there. You were expected to be there. Relatives would know if you weren't! You might be asked in a happenstance-kind of manner at coffee on

Monday morning what you might have been doing the night before. Enough said.

After church, my mom's clan got together at the head patriarch's house to debrief. Now, they wouldn't have called it that. But there was a lot to catch up on, and I'm not talking about the evening church service. There really wasn't that much to say about that. No, a lot had happened on their farms the previous week and there was lot about to happen that was grist for the mill. The farm program needed further calculation and criticizing; the weather needed more hand-wringing, brow-tightening concern; the markets needed assessing as they deliberated about when they ought to sell the corn they had not yet planted. Who ever said Mennonites don't gamble!? During the summer, concern for the crops needed to be expressed and their progress evaluated, typically one farmer against the other. Precipitation needed to be reported and compared. Somebody always got more rain. Though politics was not front and center in most conversations, it was clear that the country needed correcting. And because we were pacifists, the war in Vietnam was, well, it was just awful! There were reports of draftees burning draft cards and running off to Canada. What was this all coming to? And that was just the start. Property taxes were going higher because the school had proposed another bond measure, and no one seemed to have the gall to say no to kids getting a better education. Now, there was some debate as to whether adding a second gym really improved education. For my dad, learning and sports were at different ends of the life and education spectrum. One was valuable, and the other, well.... Furthermore, defining "better" was pretty deep water for anyone to wade into. You did so at your own risk. The room was filled with country folk who had eighth-grade educations who all seemed better educated than most high school grads I knew. I never could fully comprehend just what that might mean!

Hearsay reigned supreme. Someone always had an inside track to what was really going on because they knew someone who knew someone who was somehow involved at the center of the matter. Experts quickly emerged in the group. But it took an expert to understand the farm program. Now there has always been some question as to whether or not it was ever intended to be understood; sometimes it's best leaving some things a bit ambiguous so that there's plenty of room for interpretation. Furthermore, it gives farmers something to talk about. Anyway, the small talk gave clear evidence of men and women who were undoubtedly comfortable with sharing their minds about most everything. But it was mostly small talk related to the doings of the previous week and what might be ahead. The affable environment just didn't facilitate deep conversation. As the saying goes, quiet waters run deep, but these were not quiet waters.

As I slipped deeper into my memory, it occurred to me that I had come through this door hundreds of times, virtually every Sunday night for 20 years, and many more times in between. No wonder it all felt so familiar. But no entrance was more familiar than the one on Christmas Day. Every Christmas morning, my cousin Dennis and I raced gustily to my Grandpa and Grandma's house following the church service. Yep, I grew up going to church on Christmas morning. We had all been there the night before, entranced by the Christmas pageant. But it was the easiest of services to sit through because of the anticipation of celebrating Christmas at Grandpa's house with all the cousins and aunts and uncles. It was a short race, usually more like an obstacle course as we jolted between cars and trampled over piles of snow heaped up against the curbs. With the closing "Amen" and an orderly, dignified dismissal to the Narthex, we bolted from the church, with permission from our parents of course, down the steps across the half-frozen sidewalk, over the pile of dirty snow, across the slushy street—without looking—and into my grandpa's yard. We would meet at the front door, nose dripping and exhaling plumes of white vapor, coughing like a car with a flooded carburetor from the rapid intake of cold air. There was no need to knock, ring the doorbell or get all civil, because the door was unlocked and we knew what to do and where to go.

Dennis and I hurriedly and shoddily hung up our overcoats, brushed and wiped the snow from our shoes and continued the race into the kitchen and down the stairs to the basement. We were following our noses urged on by rumblings in our stomachs. Most Mennonite homes had second kitchens in the basement; you could never have too much room for preparing food, either for the next meal or for the canning room. The women were congregating there organizing themselves quickly and efficiently as one might expect, considering how many Christmas dinners they had prepared in that same kitchen. Short spurts of low German were interspersed with responses in English as multiple generations found their place in whipping together the traditional Christmas dinner. "Who's cutting the ham?" asked the elder sibling. Another responded shortly, "Gary likes to slice the ham!" He was volunteered by his wife, one of the younger siblings. Everyone knew that Gary liked nibbling on the trimmings! Hors-d'oeuvres. Of course that word wouldn't have been used by German Mennonites. Ach! It was French. My mom started frying the potatoes. She had boiled and sliced them the day before and kept them covered with cold water in the fridge overnight. They were fried nice and brown in a large cast-iron skillet seasoned in home-rendered lard, and then salted and peppered. Esther questioned, "Has anyone checked the baked beans? They haven't been stirred since this morning when I put them in the oven!" One of the in-laws, spoon in hand, grabbed an apron and reached for a hot pad; they got right on it. "And let's have the girls start putting food out on the tables." The kitchen rustled and bustled with quick decisive movement accompanied by chatter and laughter as pans were clanging, doors were banging, and potatoes were sizzling. "How's the ham? As good as last year?" "Jo! Daut schinkje fleesch schmakjeit scheen; et es ne kjleene mot soltijch." As I visualized this in my mind, it was like ballet—poetry in motion. It is often quipped that "too many cooks spoil the broth," but this doesn't apply here. There can't be too many cooks in a Mennonite kitchen because "many hands make light work." Everyone's given a job to do and everyone does their job—well—I might add. Knowing your way around the kitchen is a virtue; one aspires to embrace it.

Christmas dinner was enjoyed in shifts. Though Grandpa had a large oak table that could be extended to what seemed like a country mile, it still couldn't accommodate everyone. And so the men and boys ate first followed by the women and girls. The food was all out on the table in relatively common serving bowls and plates. After it had been properly blessed, you would simply grab whatever dish was in front of you and pass it on. Well, that wasn't actually how it went because we never mastered Emily Post-approved table etiquette. Daut es fer dee Enjlische. Amidst the commotion of filling one's plate, grabbing a bite all the while keeping up the conversation, serving bowls were inevitably stranded until they were hollered for by some starving soul at the other end of the table. And so the process would begin again—and again. You learned quickly to fend for yourself and to ask for what you wanted. Otherwise, you just might waste away from hunger.

As my mind drifted, the chattering and clamoring at the table faded. Still standing just inside the pale green door, peering into the living room, I could see couches and chairs were filling once again as the men had made their way up from the basement following dinner. Children of all ages were finding their spots on the carpeted floor, anxiously, indeed, impatiently waiting for the program to begin. There I was, sitting next to my dad, mouthing the words to the Christmas poem my mother had suggested that I recite by memory. The women, finally finished with cleaning up after the Christmas dinner, were coming up the stairs to join the rest of us who were now anxiously awaiting the start of the afternoon festivities.

But look! The program had begun! I could see and hear my mom and two of her sisters singing a trio accompanied by the piano on Christmas day—the popular "Star of the East." Sometime during the Christmas program, when all the younger kids had been coaxed and cajoled into doing their parts, someone would inevitably but pleadingly volunteer the aunts to sing. It seemed to come as a complete surprise, but everyone, pretenses notwithstanding, knew it wasn't. The sheet music would appear mysteriously from the piano bench, though that is exactly where it had been left the year before. My mom and her siblings would dilly-dally around contending they were out of practice, the piano was out of tune, one or the other had a cold or some other reasonable-sounding objection, but the pleading and the cheers only grew louder. "Come on!" "We want to hear 'Star of the East'!" Finally, at everyone's incessant urgings, they would get up from their chairs and make their way to the piano. I can still see them deliberating about the song, cackling about who would sing the melody, the alto and the second soprano. It had all the appearances of being an ad hoc first performance. But no, no, no, no, it was a Christmas tradition, including the whole cavalcade of cacophony that preceded it. And so, finally, after the full measure of required badgering had taken place, the accompanist began playing the introduction, the aunts would begin to sing, and then, STOP. Most of us knew they would stop; they always did. They always needed a second, and sometimes a THIRD START. But they needed to stop. We were actually hoping they would stop. Now, it needs to be said that most Mennonites in our community were fairly musically inclined and had a rather low tolerance for pitchy out-of-sync music. Even the young-ins knew when it was time to start over. Well, they would look at each other questioningly, talk quietly amongst themselves in Plattdeutsch, shake their heads confidently and agreeably, and then begin again. And ohhhh they would sing! "Star of the East—Oh Bethlehem Star. Guiding us on to Heaven afar…." And we all just loved the serendipitous chorus: "O star that leads to God above! Whose rays are peace and joy and love! Watch o'er us still till life hath ceased, Beam on, bright star, sweet Bethlehem Star!" Occasionally, they would suggest that others might replace them-—"Let the younger generation have a chance." That was never taken seriously because it just didn't seem right. It had become their song, their part of the Christmas tradition. They gave a peculiar meaning to Christmas we all longed to be part of. Some things begin and end with the same people, and it ought to be left that way for posterity to remember. Legends are made that way.

Still standing there in the entry way, just inside the pale green door, I could hear a hush fall over the group. The conclusion of the song brought applause, modest applause because listeners should not provide an opportunity for performers to think more highly of themselves than they ought. I doubted that that would ever be a problem in this setting, but pride goeth before the fall, and one could never be too careful about falling, or sinning, for that matter. The hush quickly dissipated the applause because, typically, the reading of the Christmas Story followed. And before the group might get too carried away, Grandpa had quietly picked up the Bible. Children, flush and proud from just having sung a song, recited a poem, or played a tune with their instruments, were now prompted with earnest compulsion to sit quietly at their parents' feet and listen to the family patriarch read the beloved account of the nativity—the story that brought us all together on this day in the first place. There were gifts, bags of candy, and fun galore, but we all knew, young and old, that the story was somehow central to everything. It was a sacred moment amidst the hubbub of celebration.

As children were getting settled on the floor next to their parents, a situation necessitated by the lack of room—a strange parallel to the story we were about to hear—grandpa would simply state which of the nativity narratives he was about to read. "Today, I've decided to read about the story of Jesus' birth from the book of Matthew." I could sense some additional excitement in the room! Only occasionally did he read the Matthew account that features the coming of the Wise Men from the East. I loved that account, as most young boys did. Think about it! A long journey through the desert by camelback, tracking a star, murderous intrigue, treasure, an improbable escape—it was all fodder for our vivid imaginations. What character might any one of us cousins want to take up? But one dare not ask too much about that because the reverent tone of the reading coming from the white-haired elderly man sitting at the front of the room, holding the Bible ever so confidently, made clear that the story was no

Hardy Boys mystery novel. It was real. Jesus, the Savior of the Word, had truly been born in Bethlehem. It could have been yesterday. Wise men traveled for months following, of all things, a star in the night sky. How does that work? Arrayed in Babylonian garb, they kneeled before the baby Jesus offering gifts suited for a King, not a baby. How did they know? An angel warned Joseph of King Herod's treacherous and murderous intent, and helped him escape with Mary and the baby Jesus. But still, young children really died in Bethlehem because of the rabid fear and suspicious jealousy of a wicked ruler. The baby Jesus must have been someone very special but very dangerous for a king to want to kill him. The story was mentally vivid and emotionally intense. Pacifists though we were, I always felt a tinge of rage at the injustice of it all.

      I wouldn't describe Grandpa as a great reader, but the story unfolded slowly, carefully, with pause, so that we might take it all in. As I grew older I anticipated that he might offer explanation or perhaps application. But no, the preponderance of the story itself was allowed to leave its God-ordained impression. My mother would come to read the story the same way as she carried on the tradition in her family. But the story was always followed by prayer. As a child I thought Grandpa's prayers were long in the same way that I thought this room where we congregated was huge. Of course neither was the case. But Grandpa's prayers were nothing to trifle with, or giggle or fidget through. When he prayed, it was as though heaven came down to listen in on what this elderly man had to say. I always sensed a strange but familiar aura come over the room disrupted only

213

by an occasional whine or snivel from a little one followed expeditiously by a quick "Shhhhhh." It was a sacred moment, not to be disturbed or disrupted. Truly, we were at the manger in the presence of the angelic band. Silence and listening were in order. The family, led by its patriarch, was connecting with the Divine on this most sublime occasion. For just a moment on a hectic Christmas afternoon, the baby Jesus—the promised Messiah and very Son of God— would be remembered and cherished with the same wonder and adoration as that offered by the Wise Men and the shepherds so long ago. Grandpa's intercession made clear that we were all part of the Story, and the Story ought to be a part of us.

We are all part of the Story, and the Story ought to be a part of us. I guess that is why I was standing in the entryway of my grandfather's house, just inside the pale green door. As providence would have it, this Story of stories traversed the continuum of time and space and made its way down through the generations to my grandfather. He lived the Story and invited his family to become participants in it with him. We all long to be part of a story greater than ourselves, one that brings a deeper sense of belonging and meaning. And even more when our personal story is being written into THE STORY. Passing through that door connected me once again with the Story—my extended family's unique experience and journey into that grand Story of eternity.

My concern about sustaining conversation with my grandfather suddenly dissipated into the familiar smells and sounds of that living and breathing home that had borne the Story so well. Opening the door was like turning a page of a well-worn book, like the well-worn book my grandfather read on Christmas day, and every day. Come to think of it, that is the story our families found so endearing, irresistible, and in the end, redeeming.

Suddenly, gaining a new appreciation and awareness of my whereabouts, I heard a familiar voice calling out from the far end of the room, "Wäa es et? Komm aul enn!" I took that as my invitation to step away from the pale green door, turn the page, and begin writing the next chapter to the story.

About the Author:

Leroy Goertzen is a farm boy from a small Mennonite community on the plains of Nebraska. Farming didn't take so he went to college, earning a B.A. from Grace University, a Th.M. from Grace Theological Seminary, and a D.Min. from Talbot School of Theology.

He is no longer fit for the farm but enjoys visiting. Instead, God prepared him to serve as a pastor, and in more recent years, as a professor training students at Corban University seeking to enter vocational ministry.

More importantly, Leroy is married to Karen, who fell in love at first sight in August of 1975. They have three adult children and seven grandchildren.

9

The Black Door
Bonnie Hull

Our flat was on the second floor of an Edwardian row house in London. Roger and I moved the table in front of the bay window so we could sit and watch life go by on Woodbury Crescent. London seemed big and gray and cold that fall day when we arrived and found a flat to rent.

Mrs. Ishin took a very long time bringing us the keys, and our son Zach and I sat outside the front door in the rain. From down the Crescent came a lady with a thermos of tea, some "biscuits" (which we learned meant cookies) and some "sweeties" for Zach. We waited, crouched like the foreigners we were, refugees, in the corner of the front garden. How were we to make a life in this place, we wondered?

But she did eventually come, Mrs. Ishin, herself from Cyprus long ago and now the owner of many London rental flats, the empress of north London rentals, maybe. The key was produced to the ornate black door with a leaded glass window, the door was opened, and we headed up the stairs to find a home. In time it did become our home. From the bedroom we could look into the back garden but that garden "belonged" to the downstairs renters—Sophie and her parents Odile and Nestor, who were French.

217

On the street Sophie once asked me if I had been to Disneyland, if I had a color TV, and if we had a Cadillac. "No," I said. Then Sophie said, "Are you sure you're American?"

One day I looked out to see Sophie arranging flower petals on the windshield of a parked car, and later an impatient man brushed them off and drove quickly away, missing the small message from a foreigner.

Zach's teacher in the second level infant's class at Coldfall Primary School was Mrs. Corboy, from New Zealand. "Tsk tsk, Zachary" she often said when he forgot capitalization or misspelled a word. But her room was full of warmth and lively children and animals and fish, and Zachary played Joseph in the Christmas pageant at school, and "Mary" was a tall girl from Pakistan.

We learned to order "a wheaty loaf" at the bakery, what "plimsolls" were for school, and Zach quickly discovered where one could go to buy "sweeties" in the late afternoon.

By the spring we had friends and they included Jeff and Miquette and their daughter Alice. Miquette taught art history in the university program Roger (also an art historian) was administering, and worked at her beloved Tate Museum guiding groups. She was born in Scotland to a Scots father and a French mother, but London had become her home. Jeff ran for Parliament as a liberal and invited us for a Robbie Burns poetry reading contest where we drank scotch, ate haggis and recited poems. Jeff was the last man standing.

In the spring when we hiked through the muddy Stour Valley in search of Constable sights/sites with a group of college students, Miquette showed up in her "wellies," the only logically dressed person on the coach. She had a big laugh and loved to talk about any and all art and the ideas that made art happen. As a friend she was a "gem" and our friendship extended beyond our year in London.

Five years later we passed through London on our way to a family wedding in Ireland. By then Miquette and Jeff had a "new" house in the Kentish Town neighborhood, and a new baby boy named Duncan. It was a small but very lovely house with a simple green front door, complete with a brass knocker. The sitting room had a fireplace and William Morris wallpaper; the back garden was an oasis; the kitchen was compact and cheerful. Jeff took us to the National Liberal Club on the Thames where we sat in deep old leather chairs and had a drink and talked about art instead of politics.

Roger and Miquette wrote back and forth a lot over the years. They compared teaching and manuscripts and art historical ideas. From Petworth House she wrote, "I was invited to give a lecture on Turner to a group of art tutors who work in this area. I seized the opportunity eagerly because the paintings here have been rehung as they were in Turner's day and there is a display of his water colours. I have just been for a walk in the glorious grounds. Love to you both."

In one letter she included this note under the weather category: "This winter I have really been noticing the little spots of light, intensely beautiful because of their rarity, for example, the light shining on the chimney stack of the Old Assembly House pub in the morning, which turns just those bricks at the top of the building a warm orange." I loved this image, and wrote a poem shamelessly stealing her imagery:

Tidying Up

Miquette and I
have been emailing,
she in London,
me here in the far west.
The Tate is
making her retire this spring.
No more solitary morning walks
through the galleries.

It isn't that
she can't think of projects.
We discuss our crowded closets,
our unwritten manuscripts,
the old books and clothes to be discarded.

The problem is that
all the things she plans to do
seem like tidying up for her death,
even though
she sees the little spots
of rare morning light
glint off the Old Assembly House pub
turning just those bricks
at the top of the building
a warm orange.

I sent along the poem and she responded that I was no Mallarmé. True enough.

In 2008 we emailed back and forth about the death of a mutual friend, Miquette remembering the time she and Adele once met...

"...a very sprightly old lady in her early 90's who knew Claude Monet! Isn't that staggering? It made me question all my notions of history since I have classified the Impressionists into a neat packet in my mind marked "history", e.g. a long time ago. This lady followed in the footsteps of her father as the chef of a restaurant L'Hostellerie des Vieux Plats in the little market town of Gonneville-la-Mallet where impoverished artists painted a wooden panel in the dining room for a free meal. Monet painted two of these and much later commanded the father (in 1924 when the daughter was about 5) to send him some of his excellent Calvados and hare pâté, saying, 'You'll make plenty of money for your daughter's dowry selling these panels so you can afford to give me some free food and drink.' Calculating old so and so, wasn't he? Unfortunately when the father died most of the contents of the restaurant were sold due to a family feud and that included the two Monets, one of which is now in an American gallery."

Good stories, encouragement regarding creative projects, and family news continued to fly back and forth until the very sad news that Jeff had a harsh cancer, that the chemo was hard and that Alice and Duncan, now grown, came home frequently to help. Some time went by; we hadn't heard. Late in 2010 Roger wrote to Miquette hoping that Jeff was still alive and if not, that Miquette had found a peaceful place. We never heard another word. We were busy, life here rolled on.

One evening near New Year's this year we began talking over dinner of Jeff and Miquette, of our young selves, of the wonderful letters and stories, of Alice and Duncan, of why we had never heard a word after a friendship and a correspondence of thirty years. In the way of the modern world I "Googled" Jeff and Miquette Roberts.

Sitting in our candlelit dining room, starting our own new year, we learned that early in 2010 Jeff lay dying in the Kentish Town house. When the phone call from the doctor came, Miquette raced downstairs to get the phone and fell the length of the stairs. Miquette lived on for 10 days, but Jeff died the day after the accident, without learning of Miquette's death. And so for us, long after the event, far away, the black door swung closed.

About the Author:

Bonnie Hull is a working artist, and has co-curated exhibitions at the Hallie Ford Museum of Art and the Bush Barn Gallery in Salem, Oregon, as well as exhibiting widely. At the heart of Hull's art practice is drawing. Also a quilt-maker, Hull has had three exhibits of her quilts in the fall of 2015. Hull now operates a cooperative gallery, Compass Gallery at the Willamette Heritage Center. She has written a blog since 2007 at bonniehull.net., and is a published poet.

10

The Slate Door
Dr. Katie Hunsucker-Brown

Looking behind that splattered slate overhead door one would be uncertain of what hour it was. Doc certainly lost track. The initial 10 hours were a normal busy summer day at the vet clinic located on the plains of South Dakota. Summer was a busy time. There are puppies and kittens to spay, neuter and vaccinate. Brood mares are cycling and ultrasounds need to be done, uteri infused with antibiotics, and don't forget to artificially inseminate the mare at the perfect moment only Mother Nature knows. Foals and horses require special attention because they are fragile. Lameness in horses is a never-ending problem. Horses might have a touch of pneumonia, or have a laceration to repair. Bulls are steadily coming through for breeding soundness exams before being turned out to pasture with the cows. Goats, sheep and anything else that has four legs could also walk through the door at any given moment.

The number of trucks and trailers in the parking lot was an indicator of the chaos ensuing behind the large slate door which seemed to be open more than it was closed during this time of year, resembling a bit of a revolving door. The open door allows onlookers the perfect view. At this moment

Doc had already worked well over 10 hours and seemed rather pleased that it might be a "short" day. Last week she averaged 15-hour work days while not on call, but this week she is the doctor responsible for after-hour emergencies. She hoped too soon. As the door closed behind her with the chance of three hours of freedom before returning to the clinic for another night of mare watch, the dreaded cell phone notified her of a missed call. The cement walls of the clinic block all cell reception. This was both good and bad. Doc listened to her voicemail and her spirits sank. Jen, a horse client, just found a severely cut-up horse. Doc called her back and confirmed that it would be best for Priscilla the horse to come in that evening rather than waiting till tomorrow. Jen lived over a half hour away but promised to hurry. There was no use for Doc to go home for 10 minutes so she spent the time answering emails and gathering supplies for the laceration repair. Everyone else had high-tailed it out of the clinic, so there was no help around.

Jen arrived quickly with Priscilla. The wounds were vast, deep and debilitating for Priscilla and adequate repair was essential. Doc knew she had her work cut out for her. One laceration spanned seven inches across the right shoulder. In the grand scheme of things, that was not a huge concern. The mass amount of muscle always promoted quick and efficient healing with minimal scarring. However, the two cuts over the left hind leg were concerning. One was on the back aspect of the leg, near a joint and very close to the tendons. The other laceration, higher up and in front of the leg, was approaching the bone. Doc got right to work. The horse was sedated; the wounds were clipped, scrubbed and flushed clean. Local anesthetic was placed around the edges of every laceration. Doc sutured the easy one first—the shoulder, despite it being at least three times longer than the other injuries. It came together nicely. With lots of time, frustration, stress, stubbornness and determination the other two came together, eventually. Due to the nature of the leg, the tension across the cuts was great and it was difficult to get the edges apposed. The swelling in the leg complicated the situation. Sutures kept breaking or pulling through the skin and knots would not hold due to the tissue tension. While Doc worked, she visited with Jen trying to distract her from being worried about this new horse she just bought. The conversation transitioned to Jen's precious two boys, recent hailstorms that destroyed her husband's soybean and corn crops, crazy helmet-less motorcyclists in "SoDak," and her relatives in the area. In rural America, it seems everyone has more cousins within a mile radius than cows in the local fields.

The last two cuts were sewn together on the leg. Doc wrapped the leg hoping to minimize movement and prevent the sutures from pulling through or breaking. Deep down, Doc was uncertain of Priscilla's prognosis. She gave the horse the best antibiotics she had in her arsenal, loaded the mare up on pain meds, and reiterated the instructions to Jen. Strict stall rest was mandated and she wanted to see the horse on Friday to ensure that tendons were not infected or injured. At that time, Priscilla would need a second dose of antibiotics and a bandage change.

Three hours had flown by. Frustrated at how much time had passed, Doc reminded herself how severe the wounds really were. Doc was tired and hungry and hoped to go home for a quick break before returning to the clinic for the night but before she could close the door, the phone rang. She moaned "Ugh, another emergency!" She answered the call and on the other end was a frantic, hysterical lady: "My granddaughter's dog was attacked and guts are hanging out! I can't get hold of my vet. CAN YOU HELP ME?!" Doc took a deep breath and said, "Yes, I am actually at the clinic. Get here as fast as you can!"

Panic struck Doc. This was not good. This was REALLY not good. It was written on her face as she moved behind the door. Adrenaline kicked in. Surgery needed to be set up and endotracheal tubes needed to be pulled. Part of Doc didn't want to even get things set up. The prognosis for these cases was always poor. The dog would probably die, like the other one she saw last week. This surgery required an assistant. Someone needed to help get a trachea tube placed, run anesthesia, flush the wounds, and fetch necessary supplies while the vet attempted to remain sterile during surgery. Rural vets occasionally have to do surgery solo but that's not ideal. Doc typically had to call her boss and clinic owner, Dr. Dave, for critical cases but he was busy that evening with his family of six. Luckily, Ralph, Doc's younger sister (nobody knows to this day why Ralph received this nickname from Doc in their junior high days, but she is proud of it) was in town from Oregon and was available to help. Ralph was an elementary music teacher and Doc was fully aware that this situation would be slightly intense and out of everyone's comfort zone. Yet this was the only option. Doc called Ralph and told her to grab her night items and make haste for the clinic! They had surgery to do. Truthfully, Ralph thought it was all a joke but she figured she'd best head for the clinic.

Doc readily prepared for surgery before the owner, "Frantic Granny," called again. She wasn't sure exactly where the clinic was, as truthfully it really is in the "middle of NOWHERE!" Providentially Doc was wearing a red smock, went outside and served as a beacon to bring Frantic Granny in from the road.

It was easy to see panic on everyone's face, as a crying Granny jumped out of the car and was met by Doc, who couldn't smile and was holding back tears. Breakfast was hours ago, dinner (the noonday meal in rural America) came and went without any recognition, and supper was ignored for a full plate of suturing Priscilla. The grumbling complaints of Doc's stomach were accompanied by nausea and shakiness. Vet school taught Doc the art of ignoring hunger but that is another story.

Daisy, the dog, was life-flighted in Doc's arms to the exam table. A quick assessment was made. In a brief moment Doc determined the dog was a small land shark that wanted to devour her. No vitals could be taken without suffering a non-mortal wound from the snapping jowls. Amidst the excitement Doc concluded "guts" were coming out. The "guts" were thankfully comprised mainly of fatty tissue and no intestines were noted. This was all good news, really good news, but the prognosis was still poor. With hearts pounding and palms sweating, time was of the essence with Daisy's life on the line. Doc had the owner set the thrashing dog on the scale to obtain a semi-accurate weight to calculate anesthetic medication doses, which were swiftly administered with the tiniest needle. Thankfully that little poke went fairly well and no one lost an appendage. While working, Doc explained the gravity of the situation, risks associated with the procedure and the protocols to follow. The owner was bluntly informed of the poor prognosis, as the dog would likely die. This didn't reassure the already hysterical lady. Doc was of the opinion that truthful information is better than a false hope, especially in a crisis.

One of deep faith, Doc put one hand on the dog, one hand on the sobbing owner, bowed her head and asked God for wisdom and provision as the dog quickly fell asleep. Granny was told "good-bye," and Doc rushed the sleeping dog to the prep area to be prepared for surgery. Ralph had not yet arrived, but Doc proceeded to prep the patient anyway. Once an animal was anesthetized, there was no time to wait! Intubation proved impossible, but Daisy was breathing on her own so intubation was postponed until Ralph arrived. Doc started clipping and cleaning around the wound. Clipper blades are vicious to guts and a far cry from sterile, complicating the task. Adrenaline was rushing through Doc's veins as she monitored the whirring clippers next to the guts, and the rise and fall of Daisy's chest verifying she was still alive.

Ralph finally arrived in a rather leisurely mood. She had been enjoying a relaxing evening at the neighbor's house experiencing the true South Dakota hospitality of "make yourself at home." Doc clearly emphasized this was an EMERGENCY, this dog's life was on the line, and the stakes were high. Together they first needed to pass the trachea tube. Ralph did not think it was fun, or easy, to hold the tongue and pull the mouth open exposing the arytenoids, the gate to the trachea. After some sweat and frustration the tube was finally passed. The dog was immediately placed on its back and the clipping and cleaning process resumed. No matter how hard she tried, hair was still around the puncture wound. This was far from ideal as the hair contaminated the intestines, held dirt and nasty debris that could potentially enter the abdomen during surgery, and the location of the hair was where the skin and muscle needed to be closed. Any surgeon would prefer not to have hair in the incision site as this increases the risk of infection.

After Doc removed all the hair that she could, she started scrubbing the site where she would enter the abdomen alternating between a chlorhexidine scrub and alcohol. Experts say the process needs to be repeated three times. However, Doc had learned in her short career that three times was not enough. South Dakota animals must be dirtier. Sometimes it takes 20 cycles.

While Doc was in the process of scrubbing, she was barking orders at Ralph. Daisy needed to be hooked up to the anesthesia machine. The machine was a monster of barrels, canisters, tubes, and dials. Miraculously, Ralph was able to connect the tubes, turn on the canisters of oxygen and adjust the dials for the appropriate flow of oxygen. The pup was still sleeping under injectable anesthesia so the gas anesthesia was not yet needed.

Ralph then attached the heart monitor to Daisy. This small machine had colored cords and clips tangled everywhere. Each colored clip had a specific location for attachment for an adequate reading. Doc had used this monitor regularly and she told Ralph exactly where to put each clip. Finally, the pulse ox clip was placed on Daisy's tiny tongue to measure blood oxygen levels. Ralph was instructed to wet each clip with alcohol for better contact, avoiding alcohol directly on the dog's tongue. Yes, the dog was asleep and probably wouldn't taste it but Doc's motto was, "If you don't want it done to you, don't do it to an animal."

The tiny machine was actually a human pediatric monitor but used on anything from cats to cows, horses and dogs at this particular rural clinic. The machine was an all-star of versatility. Unfortunately, the machine had been kicked and dropped a few too many times when calves or horses woke up with no warning. That meant the machine could be fickle in operation. Ralph plugged the machine into the wall, and pushed the power button. That was a moment of truth. Doc didn't have time to coerce the machine, Ralph didn't know the tricks, and surgery was more important. The machine started chirping—music to Doc's ears. Something about the annoying chirp, beeping, and screeching was so soothing to any veterinarian.

Doc quickly scrubbed up her arms and hands as Ralph monitored the dog. Doc had already sterilely opened her surgery pack, suture, and instruments. She donned her sterile gown and gloves and made it explicitly clear to Ralph that herself, Daisy's belly, and the surgery pack were not to be touched or she would experience the wrath of Doc. The surgery pack was organized for easy access. The sterile drape was located and trimmed for Daisy. An egg-sized hole was cut in the middle and the drape was strategically placed so the puncture hole and guts were all that could be seen. Ralph was tasked with obtaining the sterile fluids from the microwave to keep the intestines flushed and wet using a sterile syringe and needle.

Doc wasted no time cutting into the dog. Three layers were cut through and the abdominal contents were found in just moments. Upon thorough examination, no guts seemed to be punctured or torn but they certainly needed to be thoroughly flushed with sterile saline. A common saying for any veterinarian is: "The solution to pollution is dilution!" Clean, dry gauze was packed around the exposed guts limiting contamination of the abdomen, minimizing the introduction of dirt and bacteria into the abdomen where it would be trapped forever leading to peritonitis which would be a fast death.

Up to this point, Daisy cooperated splendidly. Then the regular soothing chirp of the heart monitor began to pick up pace and herald the premature awakening of Daisy from anesthesia. Doc yelled at Ralph to push the black button on the metal canister and turn the dial to "2" so that Daisy would immediately receive inhalant anesthesia via her trachea tube. After a few moments of angst Ralph figured it out. This was a seemingly impossible task for any person who helped Doc, with the exception of E, who was eight years old, but that is another story.

It was time to flush the abdomen until squeaky clean—a challenge—as there was visible hair and dirt on the guts. Ralph was instructed to put the needle on the syringe and insert the needle into the bag of sterile saline and pull up 60 milliliters (mL). Assuming this would be an easy task, Doc was irritably impatient. Ralph grew up on a ranch and put countless needles on countless syringes when vaccinating cattle. Yes, this syringe was substantially larger but the concept was the same. Anxiety or exhaustion was causing Ralph to not function like a competent adult. Time was ticking and Doc was fearful the clock would run out and the scoreboard would be Doc-zero and Death-one. Ralph finally drew the 60 mLs up and put the cap back on the needle. Doc instructed her to remove the cap and spray the guts with the fluid being careful not to touch the sterile field. Shaking uncontrollably, Ralph tried to remove the cap of the needle and ended up dropping it on top of the guts. Not good! That cap was not sterile and despite the guts being already contaminated they didn't need MORE contamination. Doc may or may not have said a bad word. Thankfully, Ralph knew better than to grab the cap. That would have caused Doc to say more than one bad word. Doc grabbed forceps, snatched the cap, threw both items over her shoulder and they clanked to the floor. They were contaminated and could not touch anything clean so the floor was as good a place as any for them to rest. Ralph started flushing the guts. Dirt was rolling off and Doc massaged the guts trying to release more of the inorganic matter. A total of four, 60-mL syringes were used to wash away the unwanted material. A thorough flush of sterile saline should wash away any nasty bacteria, invisible to the eye, left by the "perpetrator" dog's mouth. Finally, Doc couldn't find any more nastiness and instructed Ralph to flush with one more syringe for good measure.

Daisy was breathing at a normal rate and the worse part seemed to be over. The act of manipulating intestines and flushing is rather painful for any creature, causing blood pressure to increase and requiring a greater quantity of anesthetic. Ralph set aside the syringe and sterile fluid and was instructed to decrease the concentration of anesthetic. Doc let out a long sigh and donned a clean pair of sterile gloves. Her previous pair of gloves was contaminated from interacting with the guts sprinkled with dirt and debris.

One "small" task was left—sewing the dog up. There was no room for error. One failed knot, one wrong bite, one improper placing would spell disaster later. Dogs returning for failed sutures and having guts hanging out is NOT COOL. This had not yet happened to Doc, but her career had been relatively short as she had only one year of practice under her belt. The three tissue layers were sewn together with three different suture patterns. This process was routine for most every surgical procedure so Doc could speed along trying to remain mindful of any compromised stitches. If there was any question of integrity or placement, Doc would start over. Time was ticking and the battle of time versus quality pulled in every direction. Trying to remain focused, Doc pushed forward. The skin came together perfectly and, in the grand scheme of things, that was most important because that was what the owners saw and cared about. Doc was pleased. Gas anesthetic was turned off. Oxygen levels were maintained for five additional minutes while Doc cleaned up and removed all the blood from Daisy's underside and she was given an injection of antibiotics.

Daisy continued to breathe steadily and she was moved to a cage with heated blankets and water bottles. Hypothermic animals do not process anesthetic meds well and can experience severe complications. After the dog was situated in the cage, Doc ignored the mess in the surgery room and hustled to the horse room.

There was a brood mare in a stall that needed her routine six-hour ultrasound to determine if she had ovulated a follicle which would demand immediate artificial insemination. This range mare and beautiful foal off the plains of South Dakota were familiar with the routine. Doc was able to lead Horse #69 into the stocks, turn on the ultrasound machine, sedate the mare and give a muscle relaxant. Doc donned the glamorous full arm rectal sleeve and put her left arm up the mare's rectum as far as her shoulder to vacate all the feces. She then adjusted the settings on the ultrasound machine and inserted the probe back into the mare's rectum with her left arm. Amidst the black and gray of the screen, Doc quickly made out the outline of the ovaries and recognized the two large familiar black circles that represent follicles on the left and right ovaries. As she retracted the probe she assessed for fluid and relayed the information to Ralph to be recorded in the breeding book. The mare and her colt were returned to their stall all within 11 minutes. The mare had not ovulated so Doc and Ralph could proceed to bed. Had #69 ovulated they would have artificially inseminated her and bedtime would be delayed by at least an hour. There were as many as 30 other mares on the property that receive similar care everyday, but thankfully, they were not all on frozen semen and didn't require six-hour ultrasounds.

Doc took a deep breath and instructed Ralph to head to bed. Ralph reminded Doc she had not eaten since 7 a.m. and should eat the supper sent by the generous neighbors. So often the need for sleep overruled the need to eat for this doctor so she had lost over 15 pounds since starting the job one short year ago. Doc realized how hungry she was and inhaled the grilled chicken and pasta salad in no time flat as she checked on Daisy one last time. She threw on some semi-clean scrub pants and a smock before crawling onto a cot in the middle of the clinic. An alarm was set for 12:30 a.m. to check on Daisy and another alarm was set for 4 a.m. to check #69, who would likely ovulate within the next 10 hours. It was already 11p.m.

Lights were out, but a cacophony of barking, known as Bridgette, was arising from the adjacent kennel room. Ten minutes passed, but the dog refused to shut up. With fiery anger Doc arose, put Bridgette in her portable kennel and hauled her 50-

pound butt outside to the isolation kennel. At last, the peace of night had settled on the clinic. Doc crawled back into bed and promptly fell asleep for what seemed like only moments.

Bliss was interrupted by the obnoxious blare of her 12:30 a.m. alarm to check Daisy. Daisy was found coherently peering through her cage. The tension in Doc's shoulders dissipated a degree and she crawled back into bed to await the 4 a.m. alarm. The midnight stroll to check on Daisy brought the clinic to life and soon the other boarding dogs in the kennel area were vividly awake. After 10 minutes of an escalating headache, everything quieted down allowing Doc to drift off to sleep. One clamor was traded for another as the phone rang.

Doc stumbled out of bed to grab the phone. It was "Jolly June," the local bartender who just arrived home from work. Patches the dog had explosive diarrhea and was vomiting. Patches was morbidly obese, diabetic, and had an issue with cortisol. In patients with diabetes, vomiting and diarrhea episodes increase the risk of electrolyte imbalances, which may spiral out of control. Doc was worried Patches could be in diabetic ketoacidosis (DKA), meaning he would die a terrible and miserable death if not promptly treated. Doc instructed her to come in immediately, as June lived 45 minutes away.

At this point, Doc was wide awake, anticipating the oncoming excitement. Patches was their "only child," creating an attachment as deep as the ocean. While waiting, the blood machines were turned on, fluid and intravenous catheter supplies were readied, and kennel space cleaned and cleared as Patches would likely be staying at the clinic. From the phone conversation, June caused Doc to wonder if Patches was trying to die. Truthfully, due to the garbage food he was fed, Patches probably should have died a long time ago. Doc hoped she didn't have to euthanize Patches in the middle of the night, but she prepared the supplies for euthanasia anyway. The events from the rest of the day and a half had wearied her heart. Euthanasia is one of the hardest tasks for a veterinarian, not because of required technical skill, but rather the emotional burden of comforting a grieving client and the pain of watching a family member die in their arms.

June arrived and Patches walked himself into the clinic—an encouraging sight! There was always hope for dogs that could walk on arrival. Doc quickly pulled some blood as she discussed the recent events of June's household. June revealed she had not administered insulin to Patches over the previous two weeks because life was busy for her and her husband. To resolve their guilt, they decided to give Patches an extra-large dose that night. A foolish idea. The rapid blood test was run to test for glucose levels in the blood and it read low. This low level could be explained by the extra insulin administered earlier. Doc took another deep breath and was relieved Patches' problem was an easy fix. Doc also discovered sesame seeds on Patches' butt, which suggested a diet rich in hamburgers, not a benefit for a diabetic dog (or any dog).

To treat Patches, Doc administered dextrose, distributed bland chicken and rice food, and an antibiotic. June was informed that Patches would stay at the clinic for further monitoring and it appeared all would be fine. June, the jolly bar lady, wasn't tired and wanted to chat and make small talk and share all of Patches' daily habits and doings. Inside, Doc was screaming, "Just do what you are supposed to do and I wouldn't be up at 2 a.m. having this discussion!" But she refrained. She made the excuse she needed to go check a mare, which was kind of true and June finally left. Ralph rolled her eyes, realizing that the chief complaint of "my dog is dying" was a little far-fetched. Nothing could be done about it now.

To maximize possible sleep time, Doc decided to check #69 early, hoping to sleep until 7 a.m. Doc and Ralph performed the 11-minute mare ritual. The mare was refusing to ovulate, which meant more sleep and in her present state of delirium, Doc was not convinced she could pull off the task of artificial insemination without a glitch. With Daisy and Patches both doing well, an exhausted Ralph and Doc crawled back onto their cots where sleep found them quickly.

Like a living nightmare, the phone rang again, just minutes before the 6 a.m. hour. Doc staggered out of bed groaning, holding her throbbing head as she felt it was going to explode. "Smart Stan" was on the other end of the line and told Doc he was in the clinic parking lot with a colicing horse that had been colicing for three days. The pain med and trailer rides Smart Stan self-prescribed didn't cure the horse. He apparently was on his way to work and it was convenient to stop by. Doc told him she was in the clinic and would be right out.

She flipped on the light with despair and told Ralph, "We have a colicing horse. Up and at-em." Ralph groaned, "Are you kidding me?" Doc replied, "I wish." In a tizzy, they threw on yesterday's clothes, and stumbled out to the horse room after checking on Patches and Daisy. Doc opened the slate overhead door to let in cool fresh air. This familiar door was bound to be open the rest of the day, allowing the world a perfect view of the chaos unfolding behind it. Ralph kept complaining that the air seemed so thick, likely from the steam created by the tension in Doc's body. A gray mare was led into the horse stocks where Doc had spent much of her time in the last 12 hours. Doc grabbed her stethoscope and handed Ralph the thermometer. From growing up on a ranch, Ralph knew to place the thermometer up the butt to obtain a reading. Doc started performing her physical to gather vital signs. She listened to the heart rate. It was 48 beats per minute, which was unremarkable. Respiratory rate was 28 breaths per minute which was a normal rate. Oral mucus membranes were not purple. Purple membranes suggest a twisted bowel, a grave prognosis. Bowel sounds were decreased in all four quadrants. The cumulative findings of the vital signs and physical led Doc to believe an impaction was the likely cause of colic, but additional testing was needed: a hematocrit and rectal palpation.

While tests were performed, Smart Stan was sitting on a stool, running his mouth and trying to be funny. Sleep-deprived Doc had no sense of humor. Doc sharply told Mr. Stan to be nice and warned she might burst into tears and leave the clinic with the horse still in the stocks until Dr. Dave came to the clinic as the previous 12 hours were rather cruel.

Blood was drawn and placed in tiny plastic tubes (capillary tubes). The tubes went into the centrifuge to be spun at a high velocity. The resulting separation of the blood was used to determine hydration status.

While the hematocrit was running, she performed a rectal exam on the horse. Once again, the large yellow sleeve made an appearance on Doc's arm and inserted into the back end of the horse. No "road apples" (poop) were present within the rectum, signifying the horse was not passing poop and was possibly impacted. With Doc's arm still within the rectum, she ran her hand gingerly over the horse's innards. In the lower left abdomen her hand was alerted to some distended and hardened guts, confirming the diagnosis of an impaction. An impaction was a hardened, nearly obstructive mass of poop. Doc withdrew her arm and prepared the horse sedative and nonsteroidal anti-inflammatory (NSAID) which she administered intravenously. At this point Stan had left and continued on to work.

A bucket of mineral oil was prepared as well as a bucket of warm water. The nasogastric tube, fluid pump and lube were gathered. For the procedure to begin, the nasogastric tube was passed through the horse's nose, avoiding the trachea, and pushed through the esophagus to the stomach. Doc warned Ralph that the passing of the tube could cause a bloody nose for the horse and the end result would be comparable to a war zone. The tube passed with minimal effort. Doc instructed Ralph to pump in seven pumps of water through the tube to ensure proper placement in the stomach and not the lungs. Anatomically, tube placement in the lungs is impossible in cattle, but in horses the placement in the lungs is likely and fatal.

The first few pumps occurred without a hitch. Doc let the fluid flow into the stomach and tried to create a syphon off the stomach. On the first attempt, there was no stomach reflux or coughing, both signs of proper placement. This was repeated an additional three times and the positive signs all stayed consistent. Doc wanted to ensure the tube was within the stomach because mineral oil in the lungs is fatal, and if there is any reflux, additional oil could cause a ruptured stomach or aspiration pneumonia. Doc instructed Ralph to pump in half the mineral oil. After Ralph stopped pumping, Doc lifted the tube and pump out of the bucket over her head to ensure fluid was still freely flowing into the stomach. If mineral oil was not freely flowing, the stomach could rupture and kill the horse. Oil was flowing, so Ralph pumped in the rest of the oil. Doc blew in the end of the tube to ensure all the oil was passed to the stomach. Everything went smoothly and the horse was cooperative. The passing of a nasogastric tube was always a bit stressful for patient and provider. Everyone breathed easier when the tube was pulled and no one was injured or killed.

Next, Doc instructed Ralph to fill the oil bucket with warm water to give the horse an enema. It was best to approach the impaction issue from both ends. Doc donned another signature yellow glove on her arm, applied some lube, and carefully inserted the same tube she put up the horse's nose into the mare's rectum. Any type of rectal tear in a horse is BAD news. Doc instructed Ralph to pour half a quart of ivory dish soap into the bucket and start pumping. With Ralph's vigorous pumping, all the fluid was swiftly deposited. Doc was careful to stand off to the side in fear of the horse straining and dousing her with poopy water—the last thing she needed.

As Doc and Ralph cleaned things up, Doc contemplated what to do next. It was 7:15 a.m. now and Ralph was at her wits' end. Doc told her she could go home, hoping to soon follow. A second before Ralph passed behind the horse to leave the room, the horse coughed and the previously deposited fluid squirted out of the mare's butt with great speed and trajectory, traveling 15 feet before hitting the wall on the opposite side of the alley. Doc and Ralph looked at each other laughing uncontrollably. They bent over and laughed even harder, reminded all would be okay. Such a funny sight! After they gathered their composure, Ralph left and headed for the house. Doc remembered the hematocrit needed to be evaluated. Upon reading the levels, she determined the horse was dehydrated and needed intravenous (IV) fluids. An IV catheter needed to be placed and IV fluids should be started. The additional hydration would hopefully aid the horse by hydrating the impaction to allow for passage.

Eight o'clock was coming quickly, the normal start for scheduled appointments for the day. Doc craved a change of scenery as the stresses of the night haunted her from the walls of the clinic, but fluid therapy was needed. Deciding she was going to be a responsible adult today, she grabbed the supplies and got to work. Vet techs would be arriving in about 10 minutes and could lend a hand. Doc clipped and scrubbed the horse's neck over the jugular vein. A 14-gauge catheter that was five inches long was passed with ease into the jugular vein. The catheter was capped and fastened with suture and glued to the skin with tissue glue and then flushed. The gray horse was backed out of the stocks, only for Doc to remember the stall where she needed to put this horse was occupied. For that matter, every stall was occupied as there were so many mares being housed for breading purposes.

Lynette, one of the clinic's loyal employees, arrived at that perfect moment. She had just finished her breakfast of Mountain Dew and doughnuts. She always arrived early to get a start on chores before chaos unfolded at 8 a.m. Lynette was perplexed as she observed Doc's haggard appearance. Doc told her to take the mare and colt in the fluids stall to the round pen so fluids could be hung for the grey mare. Moving slowly was never part of Lynette's style. She moved the mare and ran to storage for two, five-liter bags of fluids to hang for the horse. Doc was already fastening the fluid lines to the mare. Lynette let down the fluid pulley and positioned the bags while Doc hooked up the bags to the fluid line. Lynette and Doc situated the bags and lines quickly, and the fluids seemed to be running with no problem just minutes before 8 a.m.

Doc performed another sweep of the clinic with Lynette to check on Patches and Daisy. Both dogs appeared to be recovering well and Lynette was told their feeding, medication, and care instructions. Doc had a busy day on the books and needed someone to be attentive to the patients. Before the day spiraled out of control, Doc thought she should touch base with Granny and June to give an update.

When Doc got off the phone she turned to find Dr. Dave looking at her with a curious look. He said, "What is that all about? Rough night?" referring to the horse in the stall hooked to fluids. Doc raised her eyebrow and said, "Rough night? You have no idea. That horse is the least of my worries!" She spewed out the events of the last 12 hours into two minutes flat and Dr. Dave just laughed and said, "Sounds like a doozy." And as a typical male, with no real sympathy, he turned and walked out the door. Doc was too tired to care. By now it was 8:30. Doc's morning surgery patients had not yet arrived, so she elected to hightail it home for some fresh air, a change of scenery, a much needed shower, and some breakfast.

Home was lovely, but the sweet relief of freedom and sunshine was tainted by the woes of the previous night and the busy day to come. After a shower, change of clothes, and a few moments of silence, it was clinic time once more. Ralph was sleeping on the couch, out cold. With darkened circles under her eyes and weariness only few comprehend, Doc crawled back in the truck with her cereal bowl in hand and headed for the clinic, eating as she drove the straight, empty roads.

Action resumed with gusto upon arrival at the clinic. Doc neutered a dog and performed a dental on a geriatric dog with a severe heart condition, which complicated anesthesia. Thankfully both procedures were successful and both dogs were soon up wagging their tails. Doc helped with the reproduction mares by plating and reading uterine cultures, doing ultrasounds on several uteri, and fielding phone calls to order semen in for the next day. Dinner passed again without any notice.

Horse teeth floats were up next. To properly float horse teeth, a large diamond bit on the end of a drill is applied to the edges of the teeth to eliminate sharp points and promote better feed efficiency and control for cowboys when they ride. The Wayne family were regular clients, seasoned horse handlers, and quick to offer help, making the task at hand enjoyable and efficient. Virgil, their two-year-old son, thought Doc was super cute and attractive. He brightened her day by wanting to be up in her arms every moment she was free from working on a horse. Doc was reminded that those moments of connecting with clients and their families are worth the difficult times.

Unlike the previous night and early morning saga, today's tasks seemed to flow smoothly and ahead of schedule. A client called needing 85 head of cow to be pregnancy checked that afternoon. Some people do not plan well and call at the last minute needing work done which drove Doc crazy. Often those in the farming and ranching industry have a hard time planning ahead and scheduling things because animals don't have a schedule. Due to the efficient manner of the day, there was time to get those cows through a chute and "armed," a slang term for pregnancy checking. After the laborious previous few hours and the lack of time outside, Doc convinced Dr. Dave to let her go. Anything related to cows made Doc giddy and in her book, "pregging cows" was happy time! Doc finalized bills, instructed the techs on what needed to be done and packed the necessary supplies and equipment. Pregging cows for the Toss ranch was a low maintenance job as the brothers didn't need vaccines, cow dewormers or ear tags. All Doc needed was her arm, an OB suit, overboots, steel-toed boots, and rectal sleeves. Easy enough!

Ralph had arrived earlier in the day after her nap and was back to work helping Doc. The sisters jumped in the truck and headed south despite the late hour for pregging. Eighty-five head of cow work paled in comparison to the work of the previous 24 hours. As the truck rumbled southward, the rain started to fall. Cattle work was usually halted by rain as the wet environment increases the risk of large abscesses from vaccination. Since there were no vaccines to be given, Doc pressed on, convinced the rain and some happy time would wash away many of the stresses and trials of the previous 24 hours.

The producers, Scott and Charlie, were ready for them when they arrived at the farm. Doc quickly put on her OB suit including waterproof pants, and a waterproof top with elastic in the arms to support the rectal sleeves that span from the fingers to shoulder. Doc pulled on her steel-toed boots which she covered with rubber boots. She grabbed her bottle of lube, some extra gloves, and an orange oil-based marker, anxious to work. Ralph slipped on a pair of boots, grabbed the notebook from the truck dash and listened to instructions while they made their way to the chute. Ralph was to keep a tally of the animals that passed through the chute, pull the sale barn identification stickers, and pour anti-fly liquid on each cow. Scott ran the chute as Doc pregged the cows. Pregging cows was a rather dirty job, yet a very common job for vets in rural America. Every cow that passed through the chute received an arm up their butt to feel for a calf. Doc needed to determine if the cows were pregnant. If the cow was pregnant, she determined if the calf would be born soon or several months from now.

Most of the cows were either not pregnant, which vets call "open," or very close to calving. These two ends of the spectrum made Doc's job easy. The rain continued to fall and the mud was congealing. The cows were rather "loose" meaning their poop was runny like diarrhea. The recent diet of fresh grass created a loose poop, normal for cows. Not long into the job Doc was covered in poop, but she didn't mind. The mess was expected when putting an arm in the butt of the animal. Poop had to be evacuated before one can fully feel for the signs of a positive pregnancy. Also, when the animal was squeezed in the chute to be contained, a cow may strain and fight causing poop to shoot out. As anticipated, cows dislike an arm up their butt so strain causing poop to fly. Doc was usually behind the cow and wore this flying poop. An occasional cow needed a dose of antibiotics due to respiratory infection, which slowed the flow, but otherwise cows were filing through rapidly.

Doc put her arm in another cow. This cow didn't have a baby in her so Doc yelled out the word "OPEN." Before she could remove her arm and step out from the line of fire, the cow strained, and poop shot out over her arm and directly into her face and open mouth. Runny poop trailed down her neck and into her shirt. A waterproof OB top couldn't stop the assault; only a hazmat suit would suffice. Ralph started laughing uncontrollably and ran to the vet truck for the stashed wet wipes and paper towels. Scott scrunched up his nose, and refused to offer any assistance as he was trying to not gag. He shut off the chute and walked away for a bit while Ralph cleaned up Doc's face and removed the poop from her mouth the best she could. As they both laughed, Ralph told Doc the poopy mess was payback for the torture Doc put her through the previous 24 hours. The whole event was like a pie-in-the-face contest at the local county fair. Just replace the poop with some fluffy cream; the only difference would be that Doc really tried to refrain from licking her lips as the smell and taste were drastically different.

After a vigorous wet wipe facial, poop was still streaked down Doc's face but now she could see and poop was out of her mouth. Work resumed to normal in three minutes flat. All the cattle passed through the chute in less than an hour. In the end, everyone was muddy and soggy from the rain. But Doc certainly won the award for the dirtiest person! She stripped off her top layer of pants, shirt and boots. Scott and Charlie insisted she go in the house to clean up before she faced civilization. Doc happily agreed. It took a good 15 minutes to get her face, neck, and arms clean. The poop that went down her shirt would have to be dealt with later. It was a minor issue after the events of the previous 24 hours.

Looking and smelling like a cow really didn't bother Doc.

The cheery sun was quickly descending in the western sky as the two sisters returned to the clinic to close out the day. Another long day, or maybe one could say two long days, were mostly in the books. The large slate overhead door that seemed like a revolving door was still raised, meaning there was more to be done before Doc could rest her head on a pillow for some much needed sleep. However, the end was in sight and the worst seemed to be over. Daisy was barking with plenty of attitude in her cage and eating like a normal dog. Patches' blood sugar levels were approaching normal; his poop resembled a normal log and he had his normal carefree attitude back. The ol' gray mare had been discharged by Dr. Dave when Smart Stan came to check on her, since she had passed several large piles of poop throughout the day due to the aid of the mineral oil. Doc was relieved to see all her patients bright-eyed and bushy-tailed. The memo book miraculously had no notes waiting, meaning Doc could taste home. Finally! These two days would never be able to be repeated, but Doc was aware of the reality that there would be many more long days with revolving doors, sleepless nights, and humorous stories (even if in retrospect) in her career. The adventure behind the slate door had only just begun.

About the Author:

Katie Hunsucker-Brown, Doctor of Veterinary Medicine, grew up in Montana on a ranch, attended college in Oregon, earned her vet degree from Colorado State University and found her way to South Dakota where she works as a veterinarian on the plains. She also spent two months in Rwanda providing veterinary care for the livestock of widows and orphans affected by the genocide. Cattle are her favorite animal and every day is an adventure.

Katie lives on a small farm with her husband, Paul, who works as a Physician Assistant at a rural, low income clinic. Together they love comparing medical cases and stories. In their free time they enjoy running, playing games, exploring South Dakota via kayak, and spending time with their church family.

11

The Lime Green Door
Jovanka Mrdja

My doors are rustic and I can see wood grain all over them. They burned in the sun and the lime green color is almost gone, except in the deeper layers of lines and cracks created as the tree was growing. As I opened them, a field full of wheat and poppies awaits me.

Growing up in communist Horgoš, a border village between Yugoslavia and Hungary in the late 1950s, I remember flying over those fields when I was small, as some pilots would take us for a ride while they sprayed the fields. Wheat fields were like a big gold carpet that would wave from the sudden blasts of a plane or the wind.

A few years ago, I made a special journey returning to the area, probably trying to bring back the happy days of no worries and less political turmoil than my home county is experiencing now.

My Communist Childhood

My first memories go back to a villa. It wasn't ours; it was given to us. My parents paid for the lodging by working at the big company. Later I learned that the villa used to belong to a German family that had been expelled from our country.

255

Apparently, they collaborated with occupying forces during World War II and returned to Germany without ever being paid for the house they lost. We never knew for sure if they really participated or even sympathized with German forces during the war, but many were forced to leave indiscriminately just because of their names and ethnicity. Often I think, what if Germany hadn't let them back in? What happened to them? Would they ever return to our village and claim their house? I will never know that, but to this day I still wonder.

My parents were agronomists, experts in soil management and field-crop production. As a young and university-educated class of intellectuals in the war-ravaged country of Yugoslavia, they were sent there to live in the bread basket of our country. They started their careers and young family there. They truly had no choice where to live. It was a decision made at the upper level but I am grateful and happy that we had such a different and rich upbringing in the remote part of the country. We lacked nothing— elementary school, cinema, theatre; there was even a music school, kindergarten and lots of other institutions to make our childhood perfect.

Three of us were born between 1956 and 1960. The villa where we lived was impressive with a high entrance and spiraling stairs like in the movie, "Gone With the Wind." I was barely two, but I do remember the white doors. They were massive, high, and had shiny golden knobs. I thought of those doors as something so sophisticated and refined; the golden knobs were such an elegant touch, almost royal.

Our village had vast and open streets; there was a lot of dust but I loved the fine smell of ozone after the rain. We ran with geese and played with them. They chased us and we were afraid of them but we still went and teased them. Nobody ever looked after us. We were the kings of the streets no matter what that scary, big male goose thought. We taught each other how to ride bikes.

"We are lucky. We live in a free country," my mother said. "Over there," she said pointing north to Hungary, less than a mile away, "is not so free." Over there was harsh communism. She told us stories about the first days in the village of Horgoš. She said hundreds and thousands of Hungarians were crossing the border daily, coming from the north, escaping communism. My country opened the border door and let them come in. There were no closed doors for them. We helped them come and stay in our country and move farther to Canada, Austria and to America. To me, these stories were fascinating. I imagined thousands of Hungarians coming with small suitcases made out of cardboard, hiding at night, and crossing slowly in fear, but determined to go. I felt sorry that they had to leave all they had, their homes, belongings and family members. I couldn't imagine having to make that kind of decision and how hard that must have been.

Later when I started school, I discovered that we also lived under communism but a different kind, or so everyone said–a communism with a face, with a soul, and that cared for the people and workers. We believed we were special. Our communism was humane; we didn't suffer under the regime and totalitarian government.

The day any child started school, each pledged an oath to become a healthy young pioneer who will study well, be strong and alert, and support our leader Tito and our beloved country. Everyone received a red triangular scarf that became part of our uniform, along with a blue-toned hat and white shirt. We girls often put bows in our long hair to look more feminine and even more innocent. We were a picture of perfect, obedient and brainwashed children. And, indeed we were, except that we didn't know it. Our parents knew it, but I guess they would leave it to us to judge, decide and figure out the real picture of our perfect society later in life.

Our schools were good with teachers proud of our (and their) achievements. We competed with other schools in the country. We had exchange visits and got to see almost every corner of our country. We traveled by trains or sometimes a short day journey by bus. Sometimes we spent two weeks at places known for their facilities for children. Most of them were actually built for that sole purpose.

I recall a high step and dusty doors of the trains with a yellow, almost opaque glass, and the unique smell of train tracks. Black and white photos of our most beautiful holiday places—lakes, mountains and cities— along with inscriptions in all major European languages, were posted near the windows and clearly stated, "Do not lean over the window" along with "Water is not drinkable."

Many things seemed perfect. The school organized our holidays. Our parents also contributed a little money to our vacations which were mostly paid by the government. A few chaperones would annually take us to the Adriatic Sea where we spent time swimming, playing, reading and enjoying freedom. The color of the Adriatic would make me compare and dislike every single sea I'd see later in life during my travels. There is no such great, limpid, azure color anywhere else in the world.

The first few days at the coast we always burned. First we were red, then we would peel and gradually became tanned. We even competed there over who was going to be darker and for how long. Later, when we started going alone to the coast, we swam nude. Our country was known as the second best place for nude tourism in Europe, after France.

Our schools organized camps where we would spend at least two weeks with chaperones, teachers and some parents. Books were read, and we had a sort of curriculum during the days. Summer was not to be wasted; previously accumulated knowledge was to be retained in the long period of free time.

The school boys were often looking and targeting the foreign girls so they could be some sort of hero among themselves. Some even married later, if love survived between the summers. For the girls to watch that was a humorous affair but the boys were serious. It was a matter of pride and success to have a foreign girlfriend. German and Swedish blond ones were particularly good catches, since there were fewer among us.

Places we stayed at the coast would vary but I remember we started in the south and slowly moved north. My favorites were the islands. They were less crowded and harder to reach. Only the ones who made the effort to come and stay would appreciate remote places more.

The mornings started with a run to the beach to find the best place which normally was a partially shady spot under a tree. A towel was placed on the spot and that meant that only we could stay there. Endless hours of sun were interrupted with sudden decisions to swim for hours. As we grew older, no parents could control how much we stayed in the water. Our prune-like fingertips was the only indicator of how much we enjoyed the blue, salty waters of the sea. We competed playing with balls and splashing foreigners who were timid and less noisy. What were they thinking of us, I wonder.

My very first holiday without my parents was at Lake Ohrid in Macedonia. I loved the camaraderie among us and the lake was fine for swimming. We learned Macedonian songs and explored some monasteries from early Christian times.

The following summer we went in the complete opposite direction to the mountains of Slovenia, to the place called Kranjska Gora, where winter sports were popular and the best skiers lived and practiced. I remember the walks in green, lush meadows with summer wildflowers in many colors. Those days are so vivid in my memory that I still think of them as places of perfect tranquility, and imagine paradise to be like this.

As we traveled, we sang some popular tunes and slept on the luggage racks giving more room to the ones below. It was like sleeping on an uncomfortable grill but it was fun and different. After all, we were going to learn how to swim, how to march, and read. Every morning we were given some orders—which books to read and what to do. Our days could not be wasted; we must be strong youths, who would defend our humane communism and our esteemed leader, Tito. We must be perfect and straight, upright and with placement. No army can march if the feet are not perfectly formed for long walks. Our medical care paid for specially made shoes in case you had some issues walking or standing perfectly upright. I remember those shoes. They were made out of the best goat leather. They were so soft, yet specially designed to support the perfect arch of a foot.

Truly, there was nothing wrong with our society. All doors were open. We traveled, we left our country, and we returned. Many communist countries didn't allow passports for their citizens in fear of them never coming back.

If one wanted to study abroad, one got a scholarship. You wanted to visit Italy, or the Far East or Iraq, or Sweden, Germany, France? No problem, the doors were open; they were swinging in all directions. Some opened, some closed, but we thought they would never be closed for us. We had a perfect formula: Our strong leader will protect us; our strong army will defend us; our politics of the nonalignment movement initiated by Tito will keep us independent. All the leading and powerful countries respected us and respected Tito, and we believed this would last forever.

Our parents took us on an annual journey and these were the best times of our lives. My father said, "We will explore our own country first," so we went. Over the mountains, crossing bridges, going to the coast. We went to the lakes of Macedonia, villages in Serbia and the mountains of Slovenia. I didn't see at times how lucky we were. I didn't realize that my own counterparts in the world didn't have the same privileges.

After some serious explorations of our own country, we took off and visited our neighbors. We went to Prague, Vienna and Budapest in 1969. That was just a year after Soviet troops arrived in what is now the Czech Republic. I remember being frightened after seeing a real tank in the center of Prague. It was sitting quietly near major square as if saying, "Watch it, because we are watching you!"

We had a car, a small Fiat first, then a Škoda (Czech-made, quite a reliable sedan) and then a French Renault model. Most importantly, we were mobile. We traveled through open doors; we easily crossed the borders. We didn't need a visa for practically any country in the world. We thought we were a class above. Our communism was perfect. We only wanted to see the perfect side of it and we did.

Our school days were full of stories about our country's struggle during World War II and partisan fights with local and foreign enemies. Our daily radio and television news always started with the speech from President Tito. We were used to it. He traveled extensively to exotic places and we traveled with him via our television or radio. We were so proud of how many world leaders respected him and came to visit our beautiful country.

We traveled to Belgrade occasionally to visit my grandmother who lived in a nearby village. As a youngster, I was always asked the question, "Have you ever been to Belgrade?" "Have you ever seen Tito in person?" That was probably the most prestigious thing to happen to anyone of us! I remember being proud of that question, thinking I MUST be special if I even have a possibility of seeing Tito. We did travel to Belgrade often to visit grandma but we never saw Tito.

My friends would have been impressed for sure as later we moved closer to my grandma, and when I started a new elementary and secondary school in Belgrade I did meet Tito many, many times. But at that time it was not as important for me as when I was a young child in a remote part of my country.

When we moved to Belgrade, I met and greeted so many world leaders, such as Richard Nixon of America, Haile Selassie of Ethiopia, Reza Pahlavi of Iran, Indira Gandhi of India, and many others. They were coming to visit our country to see President Tito. Our school was conveniently located at the main entry point of Belgrade. We were often summoned to leave our classes and get out to the streets to warmly welcome visitors. Cheering the visitors was our duty and we would miss many classes because of it but our happiness seemed endless.

Normally after such an interrupted day, we would not return to classes.

One of the places we played after school was a big park with a fortress that was built in Roman times. Basketball was a game all boys played and the basketball courts were practically everywhere and for free. That park was a magnet for all of us. You could hear the balls bouncing all day, any day, all the time. At night, those places turned into disco clubs and that was quite fashionable at the time. Music records were brought from abroad and if they came from England, the epicenter of modern music at that time, even better. You were the star just because you brought the record!

What is fascinating is that we truly had a good life. Books were very important and we read world literature—French, English, and our own; we truly were world citizens. We read Russian books as part of our curriculum: "Anna Karenina," "War and Peace," Pushkin poems, Mayakovsky revolutionary poetry, and Esenin love stories. Our publishing companies printed forbidden books, and many were smuggled from what is now the Czech Republic, as well as from the former USSR. Solzhenitsyn became a household hero. Václav Havel, who would become the first president of the new free Czech Republic, had his plays printed and performed in our theatres.

How can I explain to anyone that we were happy? Equality was important and we never wanted to be different. We wore uniforms in schools to appear the same. Of course, some of us were luckier than others, but truly, we tried to blend in and to be the same. We learned to cherish our "Brotherhood and Unity," which was the slogan cast in stone and would never be challenged!

It was unimaginable for many that our country might EVER be involved in any war. War was something that didn't happen in Europe anymore, and in particular in our peaceful and stable country.

Was That A Utopia?

I have no answer, except to think it was impossible and expensive to have such a perfect country for a long time. After all, socialism was not new to Europe. Its best examples still exist in the Scandinavian countries. I reckon it is a mentality—a Balkan mentality, whatever that may be, positive or negative.

Yugoslavia was created at the end of World War I. It was natural for many Slavs to finally live in one country that would be ruled by one government, certainly not foreign. The idea finally materialized at the end of the war, and it was embraced by intellectuals and educated people, who were the first to contemplate and believe in it. Before World War I, various parts of the country were simply parts of different empires such as the Austro-Hungarian or Turkish empires. At the Paris conference in 1919 at Versailles, Yugoslavia was created like many other new countries, with new borders and two autonomous parts as one new, bigger, and hopefully better place to live.

The economy of the country was based on agriculture, textiles, tourism and small industry. For about 20 years the country prospered financially yet struggled with political changes. An autocratic king, who tried to bring peace to the region and in the process created political enemies, would cost him his life. All this would lead the country to the division based on nationalism as society clearly did not recognize the different nationalities and some, like Croats, believed that the new Slav country was not equal. Macedonians were discouraged to use their original surnames. Instead they would change them to sound more Serbian. The problems were swept under the carpet and the discontent was brewing.

As World War II broke out, Yugoslavia was divided and destroyed in a matter of a week. During that terrible and dark period many people were killed, some by the enemies but many in battles based on nationalism that was never resolved, and at times, encouraged by the opposing sides.

After the war, the one and only unifying power that fought against the enemy formed the new government. The elections were monitored and firmly controlled by the communists led by Tito, who was the charismatic leader during the war, and represented the power that controlled the region. At one point at the end of World War II, it was important to have a buffer zone in the Balkans (Yugoslavia was covering almost the whole region) and the West helped us. The simple fear of the spread of communism orchestrated from Russia helped the West to embrace our model of communism. We had factories that were managed by workers, not by some remote, aloof, and rich owners who did not care and banned workers' unions. The West appreciated the peace in the region. We had medical care that was paid by contributions from our salaries. We had jobs and they were almost always considered to be for life. Factories built, owned and paid for the accommodations that they provided for their workers. Dental care was free, too.

But if people wanted their own companies, that was possible also. Small companies that could have a maximum of 17 employees, and were considered a kind of capitalist model, were allowed. Our country opened the door to something new, possibly communism with a happy face, with people in mind.

Factories reopened from the ones that survived the war. Many new foreign companies such as Fiat, Renault, and Citroën opened car factories. The new country also created a class of workers who left villages and came to the cities; industry was a prime goal for economic development. Many institutes opened with scientists who applied their knowledge that they got from our or other reputable universities. Small appliance factories opened, as well as big steel smelters, and coal and other mines. We started building hotels along lakes, mountains, and the Adriatic coast. Our country had an open door to all new and progressive ideas, as soon as they were in the developing world.

Slowly TV started broadcasting our own programs. Before the early 1960s we were importing TV programs from Italy, England and France.

In other words, nothing was missing. We were informed and we followed the world. Television was and still is the biggest door through which we were provided information about life, changes, politics and disasters. There was very little, if any, censure on news or information.

We didn't have all the luxuries that the West had but we lacked little. After all, we could find someone who could buy the latest record in London and play it at our parties at home. Parents normally went to visit relatives in the countryside on weekends since many had cottages; we had our small apartment for our parties. The world music scene was not so bad (in our minds we significantly contributed to it) and international trends were followed. Many years later after I moved out of my country, I recognized some tunes. Our musicians clearly copied some well-known themes.

There were times when our small country invited world-renowned artists and performers. I remember our FEST, which was a movie festival. Robert de Niro, Italian film actress Claudia Cardinale, Richard Burton and Elizabeth Taylor were personal friends of our President. Sofia Loren was just one of many stars pictured with Tito. He loved movies and for him to have international stars as personal friends was seen as a prestigious honor.

I remember going to a Ray Charles concert. I was young but I knew who he was. Our music teacher in high school was so enthusiastic; he always encouraged us to go and see artists in person. Tickets were not hard to get. It was not even pricey. I was barely 15 but I did go to jazz festivals. Tina Turner came and performed at one big sports stadium. We all went—my whole class. Santana came, too. I wish I could remember all of them!

The world of music, movies and theatre was there with us. We lived it; we were part of it. We had that open door, too. Museums mushroomed all over the country. World exhibitions were coming regularly from big European centers to our country. For us, we saw no limit.

I started traveling on my own. In retrospect, I admire my parents for never saying no. We had passports since we were 18 years old and we could go on our own—west, east, anywhere, if we could afford it.

I worked many jobs to make sure I would have enough for a month or even two months of travel. I would arrange what I wanted to see and we would go by train or car: Greece, Italy, France, Czechoslovakia, England, Germany–even East Germany was on my agenda and I explored it fully. We would travel every summer. August was a busy month and we always went to the Adriatic. The narrow roads were a big challenge but that was what we wanted to experience. It was unimaginable that all that would cease. In our minds, everything could only become better in the future.

When I graduated from the university, I faced my first problem. There was no work to be found and I became restless and disappointed. Jobs that I could find were not adequate, not for any length of time, and my independence was not possible. I lived with my parents for some time. I looked around and realized I must leave, and I did.

I went to England where I could work for a period of one year as a tour guide. When I reached the deadline, I returned to my country and found work with a foreign tour company, but at least I had work. I simply continued to travel as a tour guide. The language curriculum in our schools was demanding, requiring at least one or more of the most important world languages. As a result, I knew many fluently.

The best part of my job was that I could show the world my perfect little country tucked between the mighty West and the controlled East. It had it all—natural wonders and monuments worthy of being declared World Heritage Sites.

Happy days continued but not for long. Tito died in May 1980 and rumors started. What is going to happen to our country? Did we have a charismatic leader who could hold on to the paradise he created? Can we be united and keep what we have? Should we be prudent and smart and recognize how good we have it?

It does surprise me to see how a hot-headed few could start the unimaginable. It started with the economy. People were seeing less and less money in their pockets. The blame game began on that basis. The national debt was suddenly so high and someone had to pay it. But who should pay? The organized Slovenians, who had factories that produced the best quality products, or the Croats, who had the immaculate coastline and were the envy of the world? Many foreigners visited annually and left hefty amounts of hard currency. Or should Serbia, which produced the food, pay the debt? The other provinces were simply tagging along contributing various goods. We would be a country that would not import anything but oil which is not found in the Balkans. We had it all, or so we thought.

All of the sudden we could read something we never believed could be published. Nationalistic, bombastic news prevailed in daily newspapers. The blame game continued. "Boycott Slovenian products! Do not go to the Croatian coast!" and "Do not buy Serbian bread!!" I ignored all of it but others complied. I saw people I thought were my friends from school and assumed they would think the same as I did. You think you are smarter than people who are not as educated, but to my amazement, I saw those people leading the madness. Hot-headed hatred became the norm.

Then a few new politicians appeared. Where did they go to school? Where were they educated? They must have lived at the same time in that good, old Yugoslavia. Why then did they speak a different language and have different goals? They all had provincial, parochial quarreling minds. How come I was not aware of THOSE people? Who opened the door to this?

In disbelief, suddenly I saw what I feared. The war! Those who could see it were prudent. But how many would take suitcases and leave everything behind?

Could you leave all you have and go somewhere where it is supposedly just as good or better? After all, where is it better? You have a job for life, medical and dental care, four-week holidays, and maternal leave of one year, or three years if you have three or more children. All that covered for free! Do you leave and hope for the best? What if it is not better? Do you slide into a job you don't like? You have higher education. Maybe you are used to decent money with which you can support your family. What if all that disappears and you are not able to have any of it?

The doors were still open but not for long. England introduced the visa requirement for us. Germany followed, then France, Belgium, and almost all the European countries, one right after another. Meanwhile, while Eastern Block countries after the fall of the Berlin Wall were getting more freedom, we were getting restrictions. Now I can't travel? I now need a visa? In my mind, it could never happen but it was happening. Slowly but surely the doors slammed closed on us.

I was in Belgium, illegally, waiting for help, working, and hoping I didn't get caught. Months passed, a year passed, and my problem was not solved. Another year passed and I was organizing some possible escape plans. Luckily for me, I had some money saved and my company bailed me out twice when I got arrested at the border crossing. I was not put me in jail, though, since the only thing I did wrong was to go from one country to another.

As help from the Belgian government arrived and I was transferred to my new country of Canada, what was ahead of me was another period of learning by doing menial jobs and getting accustomed to many new ways. Even though everyday life was easier, I still had to pay the bills, and everything was new to me. I coped, but in the interim, about five years of my life was not as productive as those of my counterparts in

Europe. For many of my countrymen, this was the exact opposite of what happened to them. They slid daily into poverty year after year, and it is not over yet.

Reflections

Now, many more years later, when I go to Belgrade and see what happened to my country, I become numb. So many things have changed.

There are schools that are corrupt; teachers are paid under the table to give students good marks; and universities produce an army of unemployable young who are lost. Factories are closing, as it is cheaper to import goods from India or China, and few can fill up their pockets with a profit made by pricing the products higher than they are worth. That is not only the case in Serbia; it seems to be a worldwide trend. Outsourcing seems to be the way to go. At some point I see our workers being the ones who work for very little and we are the country where big, foreign companies are coming for cheap and poorly paid workers. We turned into a third world country.

How could that happen and why? How come all the doors closed and my country is now chopped apart and parts of it are in constant conflict with each other? Is it part of an international conspiracy? Is it because we had to pay the debt that was amassed by that "beloved" President Tito? Why do we now have so many more doors between us? Who built and then closed them?

I want to find out. Returning on a regular basis doesn't give me the answers. I am more and more surprised and puzzled. Losing my country marked me, made me somewhat bitter, nostalgic and wounded. Yes, I am one of the losers; the ones marked as "Yugo-nostalgic," unrealistic dreamers of a utopian society.

Was my early life just a dream created by those in power? Was it possible to have such a society? Why are we now divided and bitter toward each other? The blame game goes on and I look at the politicians who manage different parts of my country now. Who are they? Did they live in different times? Who educated them? How can an ideal society disappear so quickly as if it never existed?

We now have separate flags, national anthems, and different internal and international politics. Was the past all a big dream of an unrealistic leader? For me it was not. I lived it and loved it!

The train that used to take me overnight to the Adriatic coast is now impossible to board. It exists but constantly knocking on the door of the border guard for yet another border crossing, to yet another country, is just too long and too much to bear.

I often think that my generation is to blame. We didn't vote; we ignored the signs of trouble and we were tucked into a cushy present with our personal goals. Mind you, we studied, worked, and were ambitious, but we didn't see the danger. It was covered in the form of rhetoric and promises by incapable politicians at the end of an era. When new politicians appeared, we believed them or we wished to see a brighter future. It was not to be. The country got divided, destroyed and bombed to death. The worst of all is that we did it to each other. It was like tit-for-tat. The old wounds that we believed were healed during the long, prosperous time after World War II, reappeared. The hatred I never believed was possible at that level, ruled. Madness, insane bloodthirstiness, and revenge for the past wars were dragged out and presented to the ones who listened, and even to the ones who didn't want to listen. The reality was that some couldn't see it or wish to see that that kind of politics leads nowhere.

My country lost too much. Historic monuments were systematically destroyed or damaged. One in particular hurt me so much, I sobbed. The famous Bridge of Mostar collapsed in November 1993. The elegant bridge withstood so many regimes and wars, but not this war between us. I was 10 years old when when I saw it for the first time. Memories of my toes sinking into soft asphalt near the bridge on a hot summer day are so vivid. My father told us the story of the famous builder Hayreddin, and the Sultan's order to build the bridge, and the rumor that the mortar used to build the bridge was made from eggs. It all seems so unreal, and that famous arch that appeared so light, yet built of stone, is gone. That arch was a symbol of our unity, or so I thought. Built by occupying forces of Turks, passing to local Bosnian knights, surviving the Austro-Hungarian annexation and exploitation, and arriving intact at the twentieth century was quite a miracle, and now it is gone.

Watching on TV as the bridge crumbled, I realized it was too late. Insanity prevailed and took the best with it. At that point, my soul was sure I would never see any of my old monuments again. Lucky for me, I was wrong. I would return to Sarajevo and Mostar in 2004. Everything seemed fine but mistrust was everywhere. If you opened your mouth and spoke, your ethnicity was immediately exposed. Is that really, truly, so important in life?

In my family we never talked about who we are. It was simply known that we are Yugoslavs and now I am "Yugo-nostalgic." Many blame us for dreaming about an unrealistic lie or life. Both are right. What happened to me is what is happening to many nearby in Europe now, just a quarter of a century later.

Wars—unimaginable, destructive, meaningless—are raging again. As I was helped 25 years ago, I want to help refugees now. I see, at the very small village where I was born and lived several happy years, they erected the barb wire. My little village is mentioned almost daily in the newspapers. I read that in Horgoš, on the border between Serbia and Hungary, Hungary doesn't want more refugees from Syria, Afghanistan, Iraq and Pakistan or anywhere else. Enough is enough. The doors must be closed they say.

I wonder, what if we had closed the door to them just 60 years ago? What would have happened to the people of Hungary or to many who were clearly coming from communist regimes? The West could have said that the Hungarians were obviously communists and maybe were infiltrating our society and trying to spread communism even farther into the West. But they didn't. Don't get me wrong. I am not blaming Hungarians for their behavior. It just happens that I was born in that little village, and because of that I was curious about the decision to erect the barb wire. Yet now I see doors closing all over Europe, the USA, and my adopted country of Canada.

Why are we destroying hope by being paranoid over some refugees? We are better off; we should help. Maybe they can contribute and assimilate into our society. Maybe they have degrees we are not aware of. We shouldn't judge. Maybe they had a perfect education, nice holidays, went to universities and were full of hope at one time in their lives. Maybe they hope to return to that monument they remember from earlier holidays.

Maybe we should be more humane and see through the open door as I saw on the other side of my lime green door. We'd see a better world if we could just change, for a moment, and open that door of hope as I had done as a young child. Essentially, I believe in the goodness of people. Politics is what makes us divided, but truly, we all want to live, to have a better future, to work, to progress. The essence of any human existence is to improve and to create a better life than the generation before. We hope for that but the curse, karma, or whatever we name it, is now our reality and daily struggle.

About the Author:

Jovanka was born in a small village near the Hungarian border, growing up in the village of Mol and the city of Belgrade where she finished elementary and secondary school, and got a university degree in art and history. Jovanka lives in Vancouver, Canada and is a tour guide by profession, employed by an American company, working mainly in Eastern and Central Europe, with an occasional detour to her good old Balkans, ex-Yugoslavia.

12

The Green and Gray Door
Laura Alyson Manger

If there is one thing every kid looks forward to, it's summer vacation. Was it not having school work that I looked forward to? The sports or arts camp I'd attend? Playing with the kids down the street and not coming in the house until we were called in for dinner? Not one of those things was even on the radar. I had freedom to play…all day, the whole day. Riding bikes around the neighborhood, playing with my Barbie dolls, swinging on the swing set to see if we could get the poles to rise up just ever so slightly out of the ground, playing in the sandbox that my great-grandfather built for us, or competing in kickball against my dad and brother in the yard.

But this summer was different. There was a whole new adventure waiting for me beyond the acre that I called my playground for 10 years.

As Sophia Petrillo, the character in "The Golden Girls," would put it, "Picture this…Brooklyn, 1947." Well, picture this: New Jersey, 1986. My parents, Bill and Nancy, were teachers, so they too had two and half months of freedom from the daily grind of the high school classroom. Along with my younger brother by four years, Bobby, our family made a huge purchase—a brand new, 1984 GMC

Vandura 2500 van. Little did we know in 1984 that "the van" would take us places we could only imagine.

Of course it had two front doors—one for the driver and one for the passenger to enter what looked like a cockpit. For a ten-year-old, it had so many gadgets and gizmos it may as well have been inside an airplane. Our family's previous cars, bought in the 1970s, were never this high-tech.

What really caught my attention was the sliding door. It had green and gray stripes of varying widths on the outside. With the silver handle, you could pull up and slide back the big-as-a-barn door to take three steps up to the "room" that was laid out. The interior was as cozy as one would imagine with light green, soft fabric on the walls, and seats upholstered in light and dark green. How exciting it was when we noticed the arm rests! Can you believe that each seat had its own set? Bobby and I not only had our own seat, but we could rest our arms or lay a pillow down to fall asleep without touching. Gone were the days of both of us saying, "He's touching me," or "She's poking me." Though not the sole reason for buying the van, it was an added benefit that Bill and Nancy enjoyed!

All four captain chairs would swivel and could be facing each other around a removable table with built-in cup holders. Obviously, this was a feature we only used when we were parked safely and not driving down the interstate or country road! What we call the "third row seat" today was a couch that would fold down into a queen-size bed. The floor was a Kelly green carpet and the windows had blinds AND curtains! What a luxurious vehicle for our family of four and now we were thinking that our van really could become a home.

And one summer it did.

I cannot believe how Mom did it in the non-internet age, but the trip took months of planning. The Rand McNally Road Atlas was always open, as we planned where we wanted to go and what we wanted to see. Before Google, there was mail and the telephone. Yes, Mom would call or write to the local Chamber of Commerce office in the area we wanted to visit. In return, they would write back and send brochures on the local attractions. She also visited the local motels in the area to pick up their nationwide directory. Can you imagine calling the motels directly to get rates and to find out if rooms were available? It seems so archaic today, and time-consuming. Who has time for that? We did, but then again, we had no idea of the "time-saving" technology that eventually would be coming down the pike.

Every week, our mailbox would be filled with treasures from far off places. Spreading out the brochures and maps on the dining room table, we dreamed of the places we'd only read about in our textbooks at school. Places like Mt. Rushmore, Yellowstone National Park, and the Great Salt Lake peaked our interest as we perused the brochures.

The route was planned. We were just about ready for our three-week trip across the United States, taking the "northern" route out and the "central" route back home. Joining us on this epic journey were my grandparents, Bob and Helen, and my 88-year-old great-grandmother, Laura. They, too, had purchased a van a few short months after my parents. It was the exact same make and model but the only difference was that their van had blue and gray stripes on the outside and a navy interior. Since my grandparents lived only six miles away, our families did everything together. Looking back, how funny it must have been to see the "twins" in each of our driveways when we would be at each other's homes.

Bob was a factory worker nearing retirement, but had plenty of vacation to take while Helen was a recently retired bookkeeper from Sears & Roebuck. Family was important to them and so they were not going to miss out on this adventure.

In an era prior to cell phones, we borrowed CB radios so we could communicate between the two vans without having to stop. We created handles for each of us: We were "Green Hornet" and my grandparents were "Blue Bird." Could we have been more creative with the names? Sure, but CB pros we were not. We kept it simple and based it on the color of our vehicles! It worked for us.

Like any good planners, our family had a back-up plan. Just in case the CBs weren't going to work...paper signs. Yes, we gathered our craft supplies making construction paper signs with statements or questions. "Bathroom Break," "Hungry," and "Gas" were our terms for communicating. During the trip, Bobby and I were charged with posting the signs on the back window. We anxiously awaited a reply from my grandparents' van following closely behind us.

Since suitcases would be too bulky to maneuver in the tight space and the question arose as to where we would put them when all of us were sleeping, Mom had the ingenious idea of using crates. We each had a different color crate and our clothes would be folded and placed inside. The crates fit perfectly under the third seat which kept our home on wheels neat and organized.

Route planned? Check.

Vans packed? Check.

Ready to embark on our three-week trip? Most certainly!

On our first day, we left our comfy central Jersey home, passing through the rolling green Hunterdon hills and around the small lakes and ponds that dotted the landscape. We approached the dense evergreen woods and the steep peaks of the Pocono Mountains to make our way to Interstate 80. The clickety-clack of the tires rolling over the cement highway would lull me to sleep and I actually slept most of the way through Pennsylvania. (No worries, I have since made numerous trips across the Commonwealth to see all of its splendor!) Waking up in Ohio, the day wore on and we made it through Youngstown and Cleveland. Going from the Appalachian Mountains of central and eastern Pennsylvania to the flat plains of Ohio leaves quite an impression on a ten-year old. How different, yet beautiful in its own way, the landscape is.

Our first overnight stop would be the KOA Campground just north of Toledo. Our list of to-dos to set up camp would become a familiar ritual in the days and weeks to come. Camp was established with our 10 x 10-foot, screened-in canopy tent dubbed our "dining room." Dinner was cooked on the propane stove and all of us gathered at the picnic table. We took walks and played on the sandy beach of the campground's lake. We were not alone along the shore. Many other camping families spent the evening lakeside. Some even ventured into the cool, dark water of the KOA lake. Not us. Bobby and I were content with building sandcastles with our plastic buckets and shovels. As the sun set and night was quickly approaching, we strolled back to our campsite for our first night of sleeping in our vans.

Up and at 'em early the next day we rolled down the highway traveling through the crop-filled fields of Indiana and Illinois, making stops for bathroom breaks and lunch at the rest areas along the interstate. The land was flat and went on for miles, just like the long stretches of interstate we were cruising down at 55 miles per hour.

Before long, we were spying the only thing that separated us from Iowa: The Mississippi River. The rivers aren't as big in the East, so to see the Mighty Mississippi firsthand was quite the sight to see. In my 10 years on this earth thus far, I had never seen a river so big. The mile-long bridge taking us over the muddy waters flowing south took us through the city of Davenport.

Stopping in the little town of West Branch, Iowa, the home of former President Herbert Hoover and our cousins, we "camped" at their house, a visit we wish could have been longer, but the road west was calling us back. Making a turn north on Interstate

29, we entered South Dakota to make a rest stop at the welcome center near Vermillion. Greeted by a concrete pillar teepee (and a plaque noting its significance), a representation of the dwellings the Sioux lived in, we took in the sights and native culture while stretching our legs after a long journey. From the bluff, high above the water's banks, we had a view of the Missouri River, the other mighty river of the Midwest as it was making its way downstream towards Omaha, Nebraska.

Heading west once again, but this time on Interstate 90, we began to enter terrain unfamiliar to our East Coast eyes. We have entered the Badlands. Why in the world would we want to stop, let alone spend the night, at a place with such a name as this? When we were planning our trip, we found out the Badlands were named by the Lakota Indians because of the extreme differences in temperature, the scarcity of water, and the rugged terrain. Times have changed and modern conveniences have made life in the Badlands more bearable. But one thing was for sure– the colored rocks and their unique formations that line horizon were gorgeous. The reds, pinks, and tans that were embedded, looked like someone had taken a large paintbrush to the rocks.

Arriving at the campground that would be our home for the evening, little did we know that this would be one of the most adventurous nights of our trip. The wind had picked up significantly overnight and the whistling through the canyons echoed through the camp. The wind was so fast and furious that the vans were rocking back and forth as if they were row boats on the ocean, ebbing and flowing with the swells of the waves. My family was nervously awake most of the night, but I was blissfully unaware as I lay on the mattress on the floor behind the captain chairs. No one could believe that I slept through the whole thing, nor could I fathom their description of the frightful night they experienced! Too bad the one who slept the best was seven years too young to take over the driving the next day!

We ventured out into the Badlands National Park, winding our way through the colorful buttes and valleys, stopping at vistas along the road to snap 35mm memories of a land that seemed to be out of a sci-fi movie that took place in some desolate wasteland. The random and oddly shaped peaks, points, and flat ledges that make up the Badlands, truly revealed the reason the Lakota Indians called it that name.

Just a short jaunt away we made our way to a cabin in the hills…the Black Hills, that is. There was a camp tucked away in the valley near Keystone, South Dakota. There, you could tent camp, relax in your RV, or rent a cute little log cabin. From the brochures sent our way months before, we knew the cabins would be the perfect respite after days of traveling. This also gave us a "home base" since we would take a few days to explore the southwestern part of the state.

The one-room cabin was no bigger than 12 x 12. There were two bunk beds and a single bed so there wasn't much room for anything else within the four walls of the cozy cabin. There was a water spigot outside our door which was where we had to pump the water up from the ground. It was a subtle reminder to appreciate how quickly and easily we can get our water at home! Just a short walk down the road was the community bath house. We spent the evenings on the front porch, sitting in the beach chairs we brought with us from home, and ate our meals at the picnic table. It was quiet and peaceful in the shadows of the Black Hills.

While in Keystone, we found a little general store near our cabin. We were able to stock up on our necessities that were diminishing as we added miles and memories to our trip. It was a quaint little shop with everything from food to tools to clothes. I bet their motto was, "If we don't have it, you don't need it." It was here I learned that there were more versions of the English language than I realized. I can vividly recall the moment at the check-out counter when the cashier asked if we wanted our groceries in a sack. All I knew about a sack was that it was a large burlap bag–and certainly not a bag for our grocery store food to be placed in! The cashier must have noticed the overly puzzled look on my face and was able to "translate" her word of sack to my brown paper bag. Thirty years later, the moment still sticks with me.

Our spirits were not dampened by the rain that fell as we toured Mount Rushmore. From the visitor's center we could see the larger-than-life heads of the great American leaders carved into the granite. They were all larger-than-life personalities when they led our country, but here they physically were. For 14 years, several hundred men carved four faces into the side of the mountain until 60-foot heads of George

Washington, Thomas Jefferson, Theodore Roosevelt, and Abraham Lincoln were revealed.

From one stone carving to the next, we traveled about 20 miles south to the Crazy Horse Memorial. It was quite the undertaking and it is still not complete to this day, which is no surprise since the finished monument is supposed to be over 600 feet tall and over 500 feet wide. But from what can be seen thus far within the tan and reddish-colored stone that make up the mountain, Crazy Horse is an amazing stone monument protruding from the pegmatite granite mountainside. History and Native American culture abound as it is a memorial to all the Native American tribes. It was a solemn visit that caused me to reflect upon our earliest inhabitants of our country.

How two men had the vision to create these works of art on the sides of mountains (and in South Dakota of all places) still amazes me. Looking on from a distance into a carved mountain, you feel so small in comparison to the gigantic piece of art that is looking back at you.

Back on the road, we reached Wyoming and continued on our westward-bound trek, arriving at the Grand Tetons. The majestic snow-capped mountains of the West rise so high above the horizon that you cannot imagine there is any way to travel over or around them. Back in our camping routine, camp was set up and we settled in for the night. Warm July days were enjoyable, but the Wyoming prairie greeted our morning with freezing temperatures. Who would have thought we should have packed our winter coats, hats, and gloves for a mid-summer adventure? Finding as many warm layers as we could, we did what we could to try and warm up...jumping, hopping, and rubbing our hands up and down our arms...hoping the friction would create some heat! Looking back on it, we must have looked like we were doing some native dance around the frost-laden picnic table! However, the shivers we experienced couldn't compare to the beauty of the aspen trees and the majestic mountains that lay before us.

Cold as it was, I could have stayed there forever, but Yellowstone was our next stop and reservations at a camp site in the park kept us moving right along. The winding country road brought us to the South Entrance of the national park and we soon found our home among the fir trees and not too far from the lake. Spending a couple days here would give us time to tour the park where we saw the big burly buffalo and a family of deer in the distance as well as a geyser up close. The smell of sulfur wafted through the air as if someone placed a pile of rotten eggs on the pathway to the viewing area. As we sat on one of the many wooden benches, we waited patiently for the next viewing of Old Faithful. The anticipation for what would happen was almost too much. How loud would it be? Would I get wet? What if it loses its faithfulness and doesn't shoot water into the air? Well, it is called Old Faithful for a reason and showed up on time, leaving our hearing intact and our clothes dry as a bone.

We were warned that the wildlife can get up close and personal; we were mindful that we shared the park with the bears. Though we can laugh about it now, it wasn't too funny when, in the middle of the night, nature called Mom. Debating whether to wait until sunup or be brave and make her way to the "outhouse with indoor plumbing" (which was only a campsite away), Mom chose the latter. All went well until she wanted to make her way back to our van when a noise was causing concern. "Is it a bear?" Do I stay in the bathroom?" "Do I scream for help?" were questions I'm sure Mom asked herself over and over. Again, bravery reigned and armed with just a flashlight, she made her way back to the van and passed the tent where the roar-of-a-bear-snoring from the man inside filled the cool night air.

Leaving the heart-pounding adventures of Yellowstone behind, we drove on the back country roads through the forests of Montana and Idaho. Bobby and I, who spent many hours on the interstate highways of the Great Plains playing the "License Plate Game" or the "Alphabet Game" (inevitably giving up or just skipping over the Q and X words), really had a difficult time on the Rocky Mountain byways. Few cars and even fewer signs were seen along the way. As a result, we passed the time looking out the window at all the greenery, listening to music on our Walkmans, or coloring in one of the many books we brought with us for such a moment. The monotony would be over soon since we entered Idaho Falls, Idaho and were back on an interstate highway.

The times when we were rolling down the road, making good time, were usually interrupted by the call of nature. With the appropriate sign in hand, Bobby headed to the back of the van to send the signal to my grandparents that a bathroom break was needed. Every two hours we'd have to find the next rest area to use the facilities. Hoping they were clean and that each stall would be stocked with toilet paper, we ventured in, along with all the other road warriors. These were good breaks for us to stretch our legs, walk around, and enjoy some fresh air before we headed back into the tight quarters of the Green Hornet or Blue Bird.

Continuing on our way south, Interstate 15 brought us into the state of the Great Salt Lake. Our western-most destination of this trip would be Salt Lake City, Utah, and a couple days of rest and sightseeing were on tap. As a reward of sorts for our nights in the vans or cabins, we opted for a couple nights in a motel. A real bed, air conditioning, and actually being able to brush one's teeth in front of a sink with running water were luxuries we came to appreciate even more!

Once we showered the "camping" off of us, we enjoyed the sights of the city. The sunny days and warm temperatures reminded us that it really was summer, so we spent much of the next two days walking outside. The towering stone buildings, like the Salt Lake Temple, cast shadows on the streets below. But then, we would walk through many of the beautiful city parks that were full of vibrant flower gardens. The reds, oranges, and yellows in contrast with the bright greenery created happy vignettes in the concrete jungle of the capital city.

Even though our family was not of the Mormon faith, one cannot be in the city and not tour the Mormon Tabernacle. How awesome it was to see the Mormon choir sing! The melodious sounds wafted through the air as if the heavenly angels were actually singing in the house of worship.

Our final tour of the area included the Great Salt Lake, spending time on the shore and wading in the sodium-dense lake that seemed to have a lavender hue. In the middle of the desert, it smelled like the ocean, as if we were along the Jersey Shore. How did something this large and this salty find its way to the middle of nowhere? With parents as teachers, every moment was an opportunity to learn. My Mom recalled reading about the rivers that fed into the area that brought many minerals from the mountains. Because the lake does not have an exit, such as another river leading out, the minerals stay in the lake. That is what makes it so salty and gives us the ability to float in the lake. Of course, Bobby and I had to try this out and we spent hours in the water just floating along.

Our time in the state capital was coming to a close and it was time for us to head back east. Driving through Wyoming, once again, we entered the city of Cheyenne in the early evening. The sun was setting as we settled into our campsite and had a restful night's sleep under the stars. Moving along the interstate, we traveled through Nebraska and Iowa. We didn't have any scheduled stops along the way, except one night in Lincoln, Nebraska. The miles of cornfields and the big black flies were the only memories along this stretch of Interstate 80. The flies were constant companions on our journey and they seemed to buzz incessantly around us. This meant that our rest stops were quick and our windows were kept tightly shut on these two days of traveling. One does not know the true annoyance of a fly until it is contained within in the narrow confines of a conversion van. At least waving the fly swatter created a fun new car game when the "License Plate," "Alphabet," and "I Spy" games once again became monotonous.

We reunited with our West Branch, Iowa, cousins for a night and then the next morning, the mighty Mississippi greeted us as we left Dubuque, Iowa, and entered the Dairy State. The river didn't look much different from the time we saw it for the first time in Davenport, but its vastness was still impressionable on this ten-year old.

Our destination was Green Bay, Wisconsin and time with family and more "refined" accommodations. We had been camping since Utah so it was nice to lay our heads down in nice comfortable beds. What a treat to play with our cousins, swinging the hours away in the sunshine or playing ball in the front yard.

But our time with them was not as long as we wished it could have been, because the road was calling us back. The northern-most part of our journey was through the Upper Peninsula of Michigan. Our vans ventured from the western side of Lake Michigan to the eastern shore of the same. We spent the day along the shore. The adults walked along the beach or sat in the low beach chairs, allowing the cool lake water to wash over their warm summer skin. Bobby and I had fun as we spent hours bodysurfing in the crashing waves of the lake. We were quite sore and maybe had a few black and blue marks on our legs, but it was a welcome change of pace and scenery from the countless hours sitting in our home on wheels.

Our family stretched out of its comfort zone when we took a dune buggy ride up and down and all around the sand dunes of western Michigan. The topless buggy raced across the sand and the wind blew hard against our faces. We held on for dear life to the seat in front of us because we were afraid that a quick ascent on one of the dunes would throw us from the buggy. Even though we were scared out of our minds, we were laughing hysterically at the adventure we were on. We would never have thought in a million years that we'd be that thrill-seeking to do an activity like a dune buggy ride. That's about as "extreme sporting" our family gets!

With our trip winding down, we just had two more days on the road…or so we thought. We left Michigan and headed for Ohio were we would spend the night near Youngstown. However, the wind changed and a severe thunderstorm was barreling across the plains. With the memory of the windy night in the Badlands still fresh in our minds, the thought of spending the night in the van during a thunderstorm was not on anyone's list of things to experience. The sky grew darker as night was settling in and the average eight-hour day of traveling turned into sixteen. Constantly looking through the back window, we could see the snake lightning streaking across the navy sky and the loud booms of thunder could be heard over the roar of the engine.

Trying to stay ahead of the storm, we drove through the Keystone State, arriving safely at home just after midnight. We were exhausted but the adrenaline rush of trying to beat the storm kept us awake and ready for a meal around the kitchen table…our own kitchen table next to an electric stove and around the corner from indoor plumbing.

As we were eating our late night meal of peanut butter toast or scrambled eggs (remember, we were just on the road for three weeks and the food supply had dwindled down), we reminisced about our trip while the thunderstorm was raging outside the back door. We were never more grateful to be safe inside our home.

Whether we were at a national landmark, a rest stop, or restocking our food supply at the local grocery store, the world appeared to me on the other side of that sliding van door. It opened up my eyes to the land and culture of a country so beautiful.

The door with the green and gray stripes opened up my love of travel, my desire to learn about new cultures, and my eventual self-proclamation as a "foodie." I've learned never to be afraid of what is on the other side of the door…you just never know if it will be the trip of a lifetime you won't soon forget. Adventure awaits . . . just by sliding open the door.

About the Author:

Laura Alyson Manger was born and raised in New Jersey before heading off to Eastern University in St. Davids, Pennsylvania. She loves to travel and enjoys combining her interests in history, food, and photography during her trips. So far, she's been to 45 of the 50 states, and looks forward to seeing the last five. Besides working at her alma mater, she is a freelance photographer who, in her free time, enjoys cooking, music, and researching her family genealogy. Check out her photography on Facebook at "Photography by Laura." She currently resides in a suburb of Philadelphia.

13

The Boise Green Door
Patty Walker Riley

The old car door is heavy and difficult to open now due to years of rust built up on the hinges. Laying my box of paper dolls on the running board, I grip the back door handle with both hands and pull hard. The Boise Green door swings open slowly. I grab up my box of dolls, scramble in and pull the door closed behind me. Sometimes I like to play by myself and this is my favorite place. My pesky little brothers, Eddie and David, like to play here, too. They sit behind the wheel and pretend to drive, while making all kinds of crazy roaring noises. They won't bug me today, though, because Mom said we have to take turns. Today is my day. I like my new home in Silverton, Oregon, but some days I just sit here quietly and daydream...mostly about being back home in Nebraska. I miss Bloomington and my good friends. I miss my Grandpa Walker and the fireflies, and my little dog Prince.

When I get really lonesome I like to pretend I'm back home. I close my eyes, squeeze back the tears, and remember when...

My Nebraska

"Patty, here's one," called my sister, Helen. I ran to where she crouched near a mulberry bush but it was gone. My brother Billy yelled, "Quick, over here, I see some in the weeds." I rushed over but they were gone, too. Not really though—they were there—but their lights were off. They're really hard to spot in the dark. Chasing fireflies was fun but it wasn't easy if their landing lights were off.

Catching fireflies on summer evenings was my favorite thing to do. On a hot, humid day in Nebraska, we could expect a rip-roaring thunderstorm and plenty of fireflies to catch. I poked tiny holes in the lid of an old mason jar Mom gave me so they could breathe and stuffed a leaf into the bottom of the jar so they could eat. They could live like that for several days, blinking off and on.

I could tell when a storm was brewing. I could feel it and smell it. But storms didn't scare me; they're exciting! I enjoyed hearing thunder way off in the distance and watching as dark clouds piled up along the skyline, pushing their way across the prairie and over the bluffs. Lightning flashes burst from the sky and the thunder rolled louder. I used to think it was God rolling potatoes across the floor of Heaven. Storm clouds hovered low over the river valley then tumbled and rumbled on towards Bloomington. Dad called us in before the storm hit full force. A too-close flash of lightning and a sudden, ear-splitting clap of thunder encouraged us to give up chasing fireflies and head for the house in a hurry. I scampered to the porch and flopped into a rocking chair to watch another brief but brilliant light show. I loved thunder and lightning storms almost as much as I did fireflies. When I went to bed that night, I had six in my mason jar. They looked like twinkling stars in the Nebraska night sky.

Bloomington is my home town. It's small, the people are special, and everyone knows everybody and what they are doing. Bloomington sits on a mesa overlooking the Republican River Valley and the bluffs of Kansas beyond. From our house, we could see fields of corn in the valley below and clear across to the other side where a narrow river, lined with cottonwood trees, glides along beside steep sandstone bluffs. "My Nebraska" is our state song and I learned every word.

My Roots

My ancestors all settled in Nebraska within 30 miles of each other. They came from Scotland, Norway, England and Germany. I am proud of my heritage and loved hearing stories about my grandparents and great-grandparents from faraway countries. I loved my Grandpa Walker; he was fun and really nice. People called him "Honest Bob," and he had a good sense of humor and Mom said he was a gentleman. Grandpa was a road superintendent but he did such a good job they made him Sheriff. The old river rock jail where he worked as sheriff stands in the county square in Bloomington. I walked by it everyday on my way to school. I miss Grandpa and the fireflies more than anything else.

My parents, Adah Lorimer and Charley Walker, met at a hoedown in Bloomington. Tall, pretty Mom loved to dance and big, handsome Dad literally swept her off her feet. They married in 1915 and reared nine children: Josephine, Frances, Charles, Ardess, Helen, Bill, Patty, Eddie and David. We were all born at home in Bloomington except for David. He was born in a hospital in Oregon but he thought he was born in Nebraska, too.

My name is Patty. I am the seventh of the nine Walker children and the youngest girl. I have four brothers and four sisters. I have hazel eyes just like my Mom, black hair, bangs and freckles galore. I like to chase fireflies, play dolls, and read books, and I think boys are a nuisance.

Bloomington Days

I was born in the Harboe place, a little house on the prairie, near Bloomington. The farm was perched on a bluff overlooking a deep ravine. Our nearest neighbor was the Bienoff family. They lived a mile away, as the crow flies, and spoke only German. We had a well, barn, several sheds, a couple of scrubby trees and an outhouse with two seats and a Montgomery Ward catalogue.

Dad raised corn, cattle, and hogs while Mom raised kids. The summers were hot and dry and the winters worse. Snow days were fun but not for Mom. When she hung clothes outside to dry, they froze stiff like boards. The house was warm so wet clothes hung everywhere. As a result, we had colds, coughs and croup. Mom told me when I was a baby I had pneumonia and almost died. The doctor came but he figured I was a goner and left. But Mom and Dad didn't give up.

Living on the prairie was hard for Mom, and Dad didn't like it either. It wasn't long before he decided to move us closer to Bloomington. Dad planned to start a truck line; they called it a dray line. When we left the farm, he kept a dray wagon and two horses. Then he and Mom drove to Omaha where he bought his first automobile, a 1925 Ford pickup. Before long he bought a used freight truck and started hauling cattle from Bloomington to Omaha. As business increased, he bought a second truck and began transporting merchandise, groceries, and cattle from Bloomington to Omaha and all points in between. "Walker's Transfer" was up and running and business was good.

Dad was happy with his job and Mom was happy to live closer to town. She met new friends, joined the Ladies' Aid Society and even hired a nursemaid now and then to help with us kids. Dad bought her a new sewing machine, in case she needed something else to do. Mom was overjoyed when Dad bought her the new electric sewing machine. She was a good seamstress and made most our clothes, except for the boys. They wore bib overalls all the time. With four older sisters, I always worn hand-me-downs. I was tickled when Mom altered a dress for me or used old material to make me a new dress.

Dad loved animals, especially dogs. He was a hunter and we always had one or two. Besides dogs and a barn cat, we had two horses, two cows, several pigs, a flock of chickens, rabbits and wild turkeys but not all at the same time. We had a big white turkey but he disappeared at Thanksgiving time. Dad liked birds, too. One time we had 14 canaries. Some were yellow, some were singers and all were messy. I liked the singers best but not cleaning their dirty cages.

Dad had a dog named Lady. She was a champion Chesapeake Bay, with brown curly hair. Dad had many chances to sell her because she was such a good hunting dog but he always said no. Lady loved water and would jump in anywhere at anytime. Our other dog was named Prince and he belonged to all of us kids. He was white with several odd-shaped black patches. I wondered why we didn't name him Patches. I could tell Prince loved me most of all and I loved him back. He was with me all the time and even slept in our bedroom. Prince was always poking his nose on my leg to get my attention and when I sat on the porch watching storms, he'd put his chin on my knees and look at me with his pretty brown eyes. When I scratched a special place on his back, his left leg thumped the ground. He had a long tail and when he wagged it, his whole body wiggled. Everyday when I came home from school, Prince was on the porch waiting for me.

Mom was always waiting, too, but in the kitchen. Even before I got to the door, I could smell supper cooking on the big black cast iron stove. Maybe it was rabbit stew or chicken and dumplings. I didn't care as long as we had dumplings. I knew there would be a surprise tucked away in the warming oven, made especially for us, hopefully chocolate pudding or cake. Mom was a good cook and my special times were with her in the kitchen. After supper was over and the dishes put away, she let me sit in front of the oven door and soak in its warmth as I read *Raggedy Ann and Andy*.

Then Dad rented Doc Sumner's place and we moved right into town. It was a stucco house with cement steps. From our house it was only a block down the street to the county square where the old courthouse stood before burning down years before. It was another block to downtown and two more blocks to school.

Bloomington had six dirt streets. Main street ran down the middle of town where all the businesses were located, mostly within one block. Not much happened in Bloomington except on the Fourth of July when everyone in town turned up at the county square for a big celebration and picnic. They shot off the cannon and square danced in the streets. Fiddles and banjoes played all sorts of music.

Everyone had an alley—narrow dirt lanes like wagon trails, that ran from street-to-street behind the houses. They provided easy access to backyards and barns. We used them as shortcuts but they were really for deliveries or parking for horses, or cars if you had one. One morning Mom let Ardie walk me over to see Grandpa and Grandma Walker. Their house was on a hillside and had a dugout basement. We were both happy and excited because Ardie loved them almost as much as I did. We were walking down the alley, through the fields to Grandma's house, and all I could think about was the nursery rhyme, "Little Red Riding Hood," hoping there would be no wolves hiding behind the fence posts. Grandma made the best cookies ever while Grandpa held me on his lap and told me stories. Grandpa also gave good advice. I remember him saying, "If you jump in a frying pan, plan to sit on blisters." I wondered why anyone would do that.

One summer day, Ardie took Eddie and me to Grandpa Walker's house. I needed to see Grandpa because I had something important to tell him. He was waiting at the door and grabbed me up into his arms. He was as happy to see me as I was to see him. Grandpa pulled up his favorite chair and held me on his lap while I told him about the big storm we had the day before. The wind blew and swirled around the house, tossing things about in the yard, and it got so dark. Ardie told him that Mom knew what to do even when Dad was away. She hollered really loudly, "Everybody, into the cellar. Right Now!" I whispered to Grandpa that Mom mostly talked really low and quietly so when she talked loudly, we all knew she meant business. I told him how I called for our little dog Prince to "Come" and he did, then we all headed for the storm cellar in a hurry, piling down the steps and into a dark, musty, icky room. It was really a root cellar where Mom stored jars of jam and fruit, potatoes, and other vegetables. Ardie explained how Mom and Chuck cracked the cellar door open to look around and we saw a funnel cloud drooping down from a churning black sky. We watched it snake around, then up and away it went. They shut the door and we waited until we were sure the storm had passed. I was glad to be out of there. It was like being locked in a dark, damp closet but it smelled worse. I always felt good after being with my grandparents. I'm glad they had a storm cellar, too.

I was four years old when we moved up the street to a big house on the prairie. It was only two houses away on the corner so I got to carry my dolls to our new home. It was called "The Walker House," built in 1873. Dad bought it from his sister Hattie for $3,100.

It was the biggest and prettiest house in town with lots of gingerbread on the outside. It had six bedrooms and three porches: a front porch for company, a screened-in side porch, and a cement back porch with a pump, where Mom did her washing. We had electric lights, running water, and two stairways. There was an in-house toilet and an outhouse, too, just in case. We had a barn, sheds, and small corral for the animals, plus a windmill with a cistern below. It was a dream-come-true for Dad and Mom and me, too. Now I could have playmates over. We had two mulberry trees in the front yard, a cellar door to slide down, and rain barrels full of water. Rain water made my black hair soft and shiny. On the top of the house was a lightning rod.

Living next door to us was a family with four boys. They hung around our house because they had their eyes on my sisters. My sisters weren't interested so the boys played with our brothers instead. Together they built scooters and go-carts out of orange crates and used wheels from old roller skates or little red wagons. They were built for racing but ended up mostly needing repair. The boys made rubber guns from sticks and inner tubes, stilts from 2 x 2s, used tin cans for walking or "kicking the can," and anything else they could dream up. When Dad gave the boys old tires, they talked us into curling up inside and rolled us down the hill. They laughed but I didn't; Billy liked it. The bigger kids didn't fit inside.

I'm glad they didn't try putting Eddie in one because Mom would have had a fit.

I was four years old the first time I visited school. I wore a beautiful yellow dress with matching underpants that Mom made for me. Ardie was proud to take me and I was felt honored when the teacher, Miss Shaeffer, invited me to the front of the room and introduced me to her class. She told everyone my name and said, "Patty, what a pretty dress you have on." I replied, "Thank you," and lifted my dress over my head, I added, "I have matching panties, too." That was the only time Ardie took me to school.

Billy and I had great times exploring the gullies that ran through the open fields behind our place. Some folks called them coulees. They were dry ditches except when flood waters from prairie storms gushed through to the valley below. It probably wasn't a safe place to play but we never ever saw any flooding or snakes. As we investigated, often barefoot, Billy collected rocks and bugs and I gathered wildflowers. If lucky, I went home with a bouquet for Mom. My favorite flower was purple and small like a wild rose but grew low to the ground on runners that spread out like a carpet. I made flower bracelets, crowns for my hair, and once, a necklace for my dog Prince.

We used the screened-in side porch a lot. It was closest to the yard and driveway. It was a good place to sleep on hot summer nights and we could talk as long as we wanted to. Sometimes we just lay there quietly, listening to the crickets chirp and the steady buzz of locusts in the trees. Our back porch faced south and was a good place to sit on sunny spring mornings. Though dressed warmly, I grabbed a blanket to sit on and cozied up against the outside wall, soaking in the sun while reading *Heidi*, one of my favorite books. My first grade teacher's name was Miss Van Steinberg. She knew I liked to read so she let me take books home on the weekend. Books took me to places where I'd never been before. I liked that because I had never been anywhere beyond Franklin County.

Winters in Nebraska were bitterly cold. One morning Dad hitched his horses to the wagon and drove two miles to the frozen river where he met with a few other men to cut and store ice. It was extremely hard work but Dad was as strong as an ox. As they cut out squares of ice on the river, he grabbed them with huge claw-like ice tongs and loaded them onto the wagon and drove to a hay-lined cave on the riverbank. There the chunks of ice were unloaded and stored until needed. Because of their hard work, we had ice for our ice box all summer long. Our ice box was a wooden cabinet with space above for a big hunk of ice and space below for food. We used ice picks to chip the ice into pieces when we wanted to make homemade ice cream. This was the best use of ice that I could see.

Late one freezing winter night, Prince and Lady, my dad's dog, started barking and barking, nonstop. Dad knew something was wrong. The barn was on fire! Men rushed in from all over town to help. One group formed a bucket brigade, passing heavy pails of water from one person to the next to pour onto the fire while others hurried into the burning barn to help Dad. They threw gunny sacks over the heads of frantic cows and horses and led them to safety. We lost one cow and the barn was destroyed. Hot embers glowed for days and it stunk something awful. Helen slept through it all. It was a good thing because she would have panicked. Later on, my brother Chuck admitted starting the fire. He was worried about the animals because it was below freezing that night. He wanted to warm the place up. He did.

Christmas was special and something we looked forward to all year. Dad always got us a tree. Once, during the Depression, we used a really big tumbleweed. Mom sat it on a round oak table and trimmed it with ornaments we made and strings of popcorn. It was different but fun to decorate.

On Christmas Eve, Dad and the older girls stayed up late, wrapping gifts and talking, while Mom prepared the turkey. Upstairs, the rest of us snuggled down in our beds, while visions of presents danced in our heads. It was so cold upstairs that we used hot flatirons or heated rocks wrapped in old towels to warm our feet. It felt good and helped us settle down, but not for long. Christmas came early at our house. When one of us woke up, we all did. Excited and ready to go, we could hear Mom bustling around in the kitchen below.

When Mom gave the word, we piled down the stairs, gulped our oatmeal, and headed for the dining room where we lined up in front of pocket doors that opened to the parlor where the Christmas tree was. I was second and eager to go. When Dad slid the doors open, my eyes popped in amazement—the floor was covered with brightly wrapped presents. We all gave each other gifts and it didn't matter what. Some were handmade and others bought with pennies saved throughout the year. Candy bars made of chocolate were my favorite but we didn't care; every present was treasured. Dad made doll furniture from orange crates and Mom upholstered them with pretty fabric. That was the best gift of all.

Our school was a three-story big brick building. There was a classroom and teacher for each grade and I knew everybody in school. Alice Royal was my fourth grade teacher and I loved her. She was always kind and helpful. At the back of our classroom was a row of revolving doors. When we pushed the doors open to hang up our coats, we faced a wall of shelves where we put our books and lunch pails. Everyday we had tasks to do to help the teacher. I got to straighten up the bookshelves and go to the basement to get water for the plants that we were growing. Mrs. Royal knew I loved to read and let me borrow books when I finished my other assignments.

One freezing winter morning, while on our way to school, we stopped for a sip of water at the downtown water fountain. I got too close because my tongue touched the fountain and froze there. It hurt bad and I couldn't get it loose. Billy and Helen tried to help me but it didn't work. I was bent over the fountain crying so maybe it was my warm tears that defrosted my tongue and set me free. It was awfully sore and it bled all the way to school. I thought of Grandpa's story about the frying pan and the blisters. That was the last time I ever drank out of that fountain.

My best friends were Clara Koehmel, Allene Hoagland, Daisy Strangman and Betty Moffett. All of their dads were farmers except for Betty's dad who was the local banker. They lived near the cemetery in a big house and she had really nice toys and dolls. It was always fun to go there to play. Daisy was seven years old and had more freckles than I did. One day she died of diphtheria. It was so sad; I thought only old people died. When we went to her house, there was a black wreath on the door. That meant someone was dead. Daisy was in a small white casket in the living room. I didn't want to be there and I didn't want her to be there either.

Hard Times

Mom loved flowers. She circled our house with sweet pea, sweet william and hollyhock. There was the fragrant smell of lilacs in the spring, sunflowers in the summer, and always a garden. She enjoyed being outside working in her garden and tended it carefully. In the fall, Mom gathered up her vegetables, canned some and stored the rest in the root cellar, along with crocks of sauerkraut and pickles. The Great Depression, severe winters, hot summers and the drought bought it all to an end.

Grandpa Walker told me that things were good when I was born. Horses were out and cars were in, along with all sorts of new inventions. People wanted the new things but they didn't have money to pay for it so they charged it. People that had money bought into the stock market. I didn't know what that was except it crashed in 1929 and they lost everything. Businesses didn't have any money either so they closed down and millions of people lost their jobs.

Before long, no one had money to buy anything. He said it was called The Great Depression; I didn't see anything great about it.

But that wasn't all. Then came the drought. In the Great Plains where we lived, the climate had changed. After years of good weather and rainfall, a long spell of dry weather created a drought. It was severe and lasted for years, causing the ground to crack and the topsoil to dry up and turn to powder. Strong windstorms blew in from the Rocky Mountains, swept up the powdery dirt and carried it clear to the east coast, spreading it from North Dakota to Texas. The Great Plains became a giant Dust Bowl.

One morning Ardie found Mom standing in her garden crying. All of her plants were dead. The work she had put into her garden was lost. I felt so sorry for Mom because she was proud of her garden. Now she was worried about a food shortage. Everything, even the sagebrush, dried up and blew away. They rolled all over town and piled up against the fences. We called them tumbleweeds. I saw several that were almost as tall as Dad and he was over six feet.

The year 1933 was terrible, mostly because Grandma Walker died and Grandpa was very sad and lonesome. I spent as much time with him as I could. I was seven years old when a series of windstorms hit the Great Plains and stripped the best topsoil right off the ground, creating thick, heavy clouds of dust that blackened the sky and moved across the land. Some people called them "Black Rollers." We called them "Black Blizzards." They rolled in like fog and at times we couldn't see three feet in front of us. It was frightening.

Sometimes the black blizzard would happen at night; people didn't see it coming and some got lost and died. One evening, Dad saved Ardie's life. She was at the opera house when a dust storm hit. Dad was worried so he tied a wet handkerchief over his face and went to get her. We didn't want Dad to go out in that black dust but he had to. He was gone a long time and we were really upset and anxious. Finally, they stumbled up to the porch and into the house. Dad said the storm was bad and it was so dark that they got lost. While trying to find their way home, he accidentally bumped into a fence. By feeling it, he knew the type of fence it was and where they were. He and Ardie followed that fence all the way to safety. Otherwise they would never had made it home.

We were in school one morning when the principal rushed in and told us a bad storm was coming and we were to go home immediately. Kids who lived on farms were told to stay in school until their dads came for them. We grabbed our lunch pails and ran for the door. My sisters were outside waiting for me. Chuck had Billy and we all took off for home. Girls wore dresses to school and Mom made the one I was wearing; it was special, with a black velvet bow at the neckline. I liked how my dress flounced about in the wind. A strong gust grabbed my bow and tossed it into the street. Not wanting to lose it, off I went, chasing it as it tumbled away. Frances shrieked, "Patty, let it go, go home, hurry, hurry!" As glanced her way, I saw a monster black cloud surging towards us. It spread out across the horizon like a rolled-up carpet. I stared in awe as it lumbered my way, while billowing higher and higher into the sky. I turned and ran as fast as I could, straight for home.

Mom was standing on the corner, watching and waiting as we ran to meet her. We knew what to do next. While Dad locked the animals in the barn, Chuck threw wet gunny sacks over the cages and Billy brought the dogs in. Ardie and Helen ran through the house shutting doors and closing windows, while grabbing up towels, sheets and blankets to throw over things to protect them from the dust. Jo rolled up wet towels and laid them along the door and window sills to catch seeping dust while Mom and Frances hung damp sheets over the windows. All rugs were rolled up tight to help keep them clean. I took Dad's handkerchiefs from a drawer and wet them down for future use. Then Billy and I covered the canary cages. Eddie wandered from room to room, curious to see everyone scurrying about, unaware of the dreaded storm about to engulf us.

When it hit, it smothered us in a black blanket of dirt and dust that blew and seeped through every crack and into every nook and cranny. We covered our faces with wet kerchiefs so we could breathe and groped our way around the house like the blind. Even with lights on, it was so dark and murky we couldn't see anything. Meanwhile, the dust continued to seep in and pile up, reaching two to three inches high against the walls. The storm came on the weekend and lasted two days. It was called "Black Sunday," and was the longest and worst storm of all. A few people and many animals died. I was really afraid; we all were. But thankfully everyone was safe, including Grandpa.

Cleanup was never-ending; it was a mess. Every time we moved something, the dust flew. It took weeks to sweep the house clean. Walls had to be washed down and bedding and clothes were washed and dried outside in the sun. Curtains were washed and placed on stretchers to dry. We carried the rugs out and flopped them over the clothesline to be beaten. Rug beaters were like tennis rackets only made of wire and were used to get the dust out. Billy and I helped but we weren't strong enough to do a good job so I helped Jo and Frances clean cupboards and wash dishes. I liked working with them. I pretended not to listen but I did. Jo had a new boyfriend and Frances had a crush on one. I couldn't wait to tell Grandpa.

The Depression added to everyone's woes, including ours. There were no jobs or work for people so they didn't have any money to pay their bills or to buy anything, even food. Many friends lost their farms, homes, and businesses and some lost everything. It affected every part of our lives.

Dad's business went kerplunk. Cattle died by the thousands in the storms and most people quit buying things because they were out of money. Without freight to haul, Dad had no choice but to close out Walker's Transfer. He sold it all and it broke his heart but he never complained. With 10 mouths to feed, he decided to run for County Sheriff, a position his father held in earlier years. He ran but lost by a small margin. That hurt, too. There was nothing left for Dad in Franklin County.

First Sighting

I heard a low rumble in the distance. It wasn't like thunder but steady and low to the ground and it was something uncommon. It seemed to be coming our way. The closer it came, the louder it got. Billy stood up and asked, "What's that?" Prince and Lady perked up their ears and started barking while Chuck tried his best to hush them. I hoped it wasn't a new kind of storm. Helen and Ardie dashed downstairs to see what was happening while quiet little Eddie ran to Mom and grabbed her hand as she stood in the dining room doorway, smiling. Frances stepped to the window, pulled aside the curtain and peeked out. "Golly, it's Dad in a big car," she hollered.

We all reached the door at the same time. Chuck shoved his way through and pulled me with him. He always looked out for me. Sometimes I liked it and other times I didn't; this time I did. The rest scrambled off the porch behind us, while Mom and Eddie tagged along. We were dumbstruck. There was Dad, sitting in a big, long car in our driveway. What did that mean? Was it our car? It was all shiny and a pretty deep green. It had four doors, big windows, and a tire on the back. Mom said it was a Buick.

I thought it was beautiful and Dad said, "Yes, it's ours." He hollered, "Climb in, let's go for a ride." We all piled in—three up in front with Dad and the rest of us in the back. It was kind of like sardines in a can but what fun! Before we left the yard, Dad said in his deep voice, "There are certain rules you must obey when riding in a car. Number One is: Sit still. Number Two is: Don't touch the door handles. Number Three is: Don't stick your arm out the window. Another car might pass by and rip it off." I thought about that and I kept my hands in my lap.

We drove through town and I was as proud as punch. I hoped my friends would see us but nobody was around. Dad drove us out west of town, down a dirt road, and stepped on the gas. We were off like a shot. He said we were going 25 miles an hour. It was the fastest I had ever gone and I felt like the wind. Usually we walked everywhere we went. I looked out the window and noticed how flat and dry everything was but I had to look fast because it made me feel a little icky.

When we got home, the boys were busy looking under the hood and checking out tires and wooden spokes while my sisters were deciding where we should sit. I was fascinated by the color. It was such a rich deep green. I asked Dad what it was called. Opening the car door, he leaned inside and popped open a little drawer that he called a "glove box." In his hand was a small booklet that told him all about the car. It was a 1929 Buick Sedan, not new but new to us, and the color was called Boise Green. I loved it.

Chuck asked why Dad got a car. Then Dad and Mom told us that we would be moving to Oregon, where Dad hoped to get a job so they could take better care of us. He explained that because of the Depression and dust storms, there wasn't any work left for him in our area. Dad said he had a cousin who had written about job opportunities in Oregon so it would be best if we moved there. I knew some geography about Oregon, the Pacific Ocean, and Lewis and Clark, too, but I didn't like the idea of traveling the Oregon Trail or Indians either. My friends said Oregon was Indian country.

Dad told us we would be leaving the day after Decoration Day, on Friday, May 31st. Decoration Day was a day when we decorated the graves of those who died in any wars. Mom handed me a flyer to read. It was being posted around town to announce a big auction coming up on May 21st. Looking it over made my stomach churn. It listed our horses, cows, pigs, chickens and Dad's farm equipment, along with our kitchen and dining room tables and chairs, the parlor set and stands, bedroom sets and springs, lamps and fans, two rocking chairs, the icebox, even old "Black Magic," the cast iron kitchen stove. Also our Majestic radio, Mom's electric washing machine, and worst of all, her sewing machine. I wondered what Mom would ever do without it. The list was longer but I didn't want to read anymore. I was heartsick, especially for Mom. She said I would make new friends in Oregon but I knew I was going to miss my friends here.

Friday, May 24th, was my last day at school. The plan would give us a several days to spend with family and to clean up the Walker place before we closed the door of our big house on the prairie. My favorite teacher, Mrs. Royal, helped me learn a lot; I was really going to miss her. I was thinking about all of that as I reached for my pen to practice Palmer Method penmanship. I dipped the pen in the inkwell just as Mrs. Royal called, "Patty, it's task time. Please take this plant to the basement for watering," so I slid from my seat, picked up the plant, and pranced out of the room.

When I returned to the room a few minutes later, everyone was gone except Mrs. Royal. She called me to her desk up front and handed me a book, saying, "This is for you." Thanking her, I turned back to my desk when all of a sudden the line of coat closets at the back of the room flew open and all the kids jumped out, hollering, "Surprise!" I stood there astounded as they rolled a stream of little going-away gifts down the aisle towards me. There were pencils and paper, several oranges and apples, a funny book, candy bars, gum and even an autograph book. They were all gifts that would be useful on my trip to Oregon and appreciated. As tears rolled down my face, I thanked them for being so nice. All my sisters and brothers had farewell parties, too. Walking home that afternoon, my sisters were very quiet and my heart felt heavy. But my brothers were raving about the big adventure coming up in a few days.

On the following Sunday, I was feeling downhearted because I knew all my friends would be going to school the next day but not me. Then we heard more terrible news. Dad said we had to leave Prince behind and had found a home for him in the country. It was bad enough leaving my friends and Grandpa Walker but Prince, too? I cried for hours. Tuesday morning we all hugged Prince goodbye. I think he knew something was wrong because he was whining a lot. When Dad put him in the car and drove off, Prince was looking out the back window at us. It was an awful day plus it was our last few days in our hometown.

When I got home from saying goodbye to Grandpa, Prince was sitting on the front steps waiting for me. He sat in the exact same place just like he did everyday when we got home from school. He'd run all the way home to us. Dad put him in the car and returned him to the family in the country. Wednesday I was in the barn when I felt a cold nose on my leg; Prince was back again. I tried to hide him but Dad found out and took him back to the farm. Thursday, after breakfast, we were running back and forth loading up the trailer when I heard a familiar bark and there was Prince running across the yard towards me. He wanted to be with his family. We begged Dad to let us keep him. We said we would hold him on our laps in the back seat and I promised Prince wouldn't be any trouble but Dad said no again and took him away. I didn't like my Dad very much for a long time.

Oregon or Bust

Early on Friday, we left Bloomington. I felt miserable. Not only were we were leaving our home and friends, but also Prince. If Prince returned again that day, we would never know. I could hardly bear thinking about him running home again and finding we were gone and had left him behind. I was furious at my Dad; we all were. He made room for his dog, Lady, but we couldn't take our little dog, Prince. I didn't understand; I was heartbroken and cried off and on for days.

The Boise Green Buick was a big car and the seats were wide but six kids crammed in the back would be a bit too cozy so Dad placed two five-gallon lard cans on the floor next to the back doors. Chuck and Billy sat there while the girls got the back seat. We traded places when we wanted to. I did because it was neat having a seat all to myself. Mom and Jo sat in front with Dad and took turns holding Eddie.

Dad had it all figured out. It was 1,500 miles to Oregon. If he drove 100 miles a day, it would take about two weeks to get there. After Dad paid everything off and bought a car and materials to build a trailer, he had $300 left in his pocket. I hoped it would last until we reached Silverton.

It was 120 miles to Maywood, where Grandma Lorimer lived. She was Mom's mother. One of the first towns we passed through was Alma, where Mom was born. As we crossed the Republican River, she pointed out where she had lived as a child. I saw land parched and dotted with deserted homesteads. Many had already headed west in search of jobs. We weren't the only ones seeking a better life.

We traveled 35 miles north from Maywood to North Platte, where we crossed the Oregon Trail, then over the Platte River to the Mormon Trail. Buffalo Bill's ranch was nearby and we hoped to stop there but Dad said no. Instead, we had stopped in North Platte to stretch our legs, get supplies, and gas up. Gas was 10 cents a gallon and bread was eight cents a loaf. When we left town, we were on the north side of the river, heading west on old Highway 30. The Platte River and Oregon Trail were on the left. I was excited because there we were, traveling the same route as the pioneers did way back in the 1840's and 50's.

We pulled over along the river to let the dog out and eat a lunch Grandma had packed for us. Lady was a nuisance and the river made me nervous. Then it was on to Ogallala. Towns in Nebraska had interesting names, like Ogallala, Naponee, Omaha, Pawnee and even Oshkosh, by gosh. I figured they were probably Indian warriors. The Oregon Trail country was as flat as a pancake and boring. I tried to add some excitement by imagining a prairie schooner racing across the countryside, dust flying, with Indians swarming all over the place whooping it up and shooting arrows. Dad was hoping to make Big Springs before dark. I sure hoped so; it was lonely out there all by ourselves.

After a good night's sleep and a quick breakfast in Big Springs, we were off to higher ground. Saying goodbye to the Snake River, we piled in the car and aimed west. Still on Highway 30, called the Lincoln Highway, we crossed the rolling plains of western Nebraska, and began a straight but gradual climb through sagebrush to farmland and up to high country. We spotted a sign pointing out Nebraska's highest peak at 5,426 feet. In the distance, we could see valleys of timber and snow-covered mountains. It was the highest I'd ever been.

We stayed all night in roadside cabins at Kimball. Dad and the boys slept in one and Mom and us girls slept in the other one. At 4,700 feet it was cold and rainy. Early the next day, we headed due west to Wyoming. Pulling the 6 x 8-foot trailer slowed us down but by 11 a.m. Mom pointed out a big "Entering Wyoming" sign. We were across the state line and into Pine Bluffs, Wyoming. Mom said it was Indian country and the hunting grounds of numerous tribes. After a break there, we left for Cheyenne, 40 miles west. Helen was happy to be in what she called a "cowboy state." So were the rest of us. The highway was flat and straight and we could see distant mountain ranges in all directions. Driving on the flat plains even at 6,062 feet was a relief.

Dad was keeping a sharp eye on the weather. If caught in a storm, he was told to stay out of the high country to avoid lightning and out of the low country to avoid flash floods. There we were, in high country, with rain and flooding. Already water was running across the road and pooling in low places. I could tell Dad was concerned as he hightailed it to Cheyenne. Arriving there earlier than expected, he decided to continue to Laramie for the night in search of even higher ground.

It was 47 miles to Laramie and the high plains. We were about 10 miles out of Cheyenne when we had our first real mountain experience. It began as we started a steep 33-mile climb to the crest of Sherman Hill and to Laramie beyond. The higher we climbed, the quieter we got. When the chattering stopped in our car, it meant we are either scared to death or speechless; we were both. At the summit, the road topped out at 8,800 feet. We could see the mountains of Colorado to the south, rugged pine-covered ridges to north, and straight ahead were the rolling Great Plains. The view was breathtaking. We were still on the Lincoln Highway and nearby was a large bronze bust of Abraham Lincoln. After leaving the summit, US 30 dropped 1,700 feet in nine miles, through a canyon, past aspen trees, lodgepole pine, and out into a land of sagebrush and prairie, and on to Laramie.

Laramie, over 7,100 feet above sea level, sits in the middle of the Laramie Plain. It is great hunting country, with elk, deer, and antelope nearby. Tribes of hostile Indians once camped there. Mom suggested we camp there, too, but in cabins. The altitude and fresh mountain air were invigorating. After a quick meal and a few chores, everyone was ready for bed. Dad reported things were going good and no car problems.

Our next overnight stop would be Rawlins. It was at a higher elevation and a 100-mile drive. When we left Laramie that morning, it was windy and raining again. I remembered Grandma Walker's Bible stories and thought about Noah's Ark; we might need it. There were no towns between Laramie and Elk Mountain. It was 60 miles to the summit but the roads were good. We saw odd rock masses and the pass topped out at 8,400 feet and was beautiful.

The town of Elk Mountain sat at the base of the tallest mountain we'd ever seen—over 11,000 feet. It was mostly covered with snow and clouds. It was pretty country but all of us felt better after we reached the summit and headed for Rawlins, 45 miles away. Not knowing what was next, we were a bit uneasy. Mom made up a game of counting deer to get our minds on other things. I started humming, "Coming 'Round The Mountain" and everyone joined in singing, even Dad and Mom. From then on, when we got nervous, we sang. It was fun and helped us relax. Eddie never got nervous; everything was fun to him.

After we left Rawlins the next day, we entered desert country. The road was straight and nearly level for over 30 miles but here was nothing but flatland, sagebrush and weeds. At the Great Basin, we crossed over the Continental Divide. Jo explained what that was saying, "The Great Basin is like a huge bowl, surrounded by mountains, where rain waters drain in and flow out the west side towards the Pacific Ocean or to the east side towards the Atlantic Ocean." Mom added, "Where the waters split is called the Great Divide." I liked geography so it was really interesting and exciting, too. I knew Mrs. Royal would like to know that.

As we crossed the Continental Divide, the wind was picking up and clouds hung heavy over the desolate countryside. We passed Wamsutter and the Red Desert Flats where antelope grazed and nobody lived. It was a barren, uninhabited area, plus monotonous. Off in the west, the sky was black. All of us were tired and a bit edgy. It was cloudburst country, where sudden storms and torrential rains could wash away roads and even the sagebrush. Maybe us, too. "Dad," I cried, "When are we gonna get there?" Dad had a doctor friend in Rock Springs. We were looking forward to seeing someone we knew.

We could see no signs of human habitation, only a brewing storm. I was in a dither. After we passed Bitter Creek, it happened; a storm hit fast and furious. Black, rolling clouds hovered low overhead. In minutes, it was hailing and pouring rain. Strong winds pushed at the car and whipped the trailer about. Dad sat as straight as a rod, gripping the wheel with both hands while Mom sucked in her breath. Suddenly there was a loud clap of thunder followed by a brilliant flash of lightning and the screeching of metal. Chuck yelled, "Dad, it's the trailer."

The hitch had broken. Dad pulled off to the side of the road and jumped out, followed by Chuck who pulled Lady from the trailer. She was howling but not hurt. Helen was crying and wringing her hands. Mom told us to stay in the car. Dad found a heavy cable in his tool box and, working with Chuck, they were able to wire the trailer and car together. They were soaking wet. It was a temporary fix but hopefully it would hold until we found shelter. Driving slowly, Dad continued down the road until he spotted an abandoned cabin. He said we would have to stay there until help came. After checking out the place, he pulled the car up close to block the wind and we spent the night there.

The storm raged for hours. We were like sardines in a can but we made it work. It was midmorning the next day before a car came by. Dad stopped it and asked the man to notify our doctor friend in Rock Springs who came out that afternoon with help. They hooked our trailer to theirs and we all drove to town. We stayed there a couple of days while the hitch was being repaired. Rock Springs was a coal mining town.

We said goodbye to Rock Springs and moved on to Little America where we turned north towards Kemmerer and eventually to Idaho, following Highway 30 all the way. I didn't know it but Highway 30 was the first paved route from coast to coast and out west most of it follows the old Oregon Trail, like we were doing right now. Mom suggested we sing a few songs, starting with "Back In The Saddle Again."

After leaving Wyoming and entering Idaho, we traveled through fertile valleys, forests and rugged mountain country. Near Montpelier, we crossed a 6,000-foot pass and started downhill. It was another harrowing experience. I clutched the back of Dad's seat and closed my eyes. I was hoping he would slow down. The highway was steep and narrow, with tight curves. There were valleys, ravines, and gullies full of runoff water. I felt queasy. Mom told me to take a nap but that made it worse. Billy called me a "Nervous Nellie."

We all felt better when we left the mountains and reached Pocatello. Twin Falls was even flatter. Entering town, we crossed the Snake River Canyon and all of a sudden we were at the edge of a sheer drop-off that plunged into a deep gorge. It was like a giant gash in the earth. The Snake River moved swiftly through the canyon and over a magnificent waterfall. We stayed for two days with Dad's cousin Earl and his wife, Noma. Before they married, she was Ardie's teacher back in Bloomington. We visited our great-grandfather, William Daniel, who was a homesteader. He took us to his farm where we played with piglets.

It was a five-hour drive to Boise and mostly uphill. We spent the night there. Oregon was just across the river. Here the Snake was a lot wider and swifter. A sign said, "Entering Oregon." It looked a lot like Nebraska before the Dust Bowl days–a land of open spaces, grassland and blue skies. I could imagine how happy the pioneers were to be here because I sure was. It was exciting to see real cowboys and coyotes, too. I remembered the coyote hunts Dad went on in Nebraska. He even had a coyote skin rug with its mouth open showing long teeth. I used to lie down on it but never at that end.

In eastern Oregon, we were surrounded by country that reminded me of Wyoming and Nebraska but greener. There were no Indians but we did see some cowboys and jack rabbits. Helen liked it and wanted to stay there. Jo and Frances checked out the boys while I searched for wildflowers and fireflies. Eddie tagged along, carrying a fruit jar. While winding our way north we passed some good motels but Dad said they cost too much. I still hoped we wouldn't run out of money.

As I stood marveling at the mighty Columbia River, I remembered what we learned in school about the Lewis and Clark Expedition and their journey down this very same river. They were looking for places to spend the night, just like we were. They wound up at the Pacific Ocean and we wound up in Arlington, in a roadside court tucked away in the hillside of a grassy bluff. A hot wind was blowing through the gorge so it was a welcome break for Lady and the rest of us, too. We took two cabins, as usual. They faced west so we had a good view of the river.

Later that afternoon we heard much commotion and rushed out to see what was going on. Men were running and yelling. We looked up to where Dad was pointing and saw smoke and flames racing over the hilltop and straight for us. It was a prairie fire and there was nothing to stop it except the brave men who were smart enough to make a fire line and the others who grabbed wet gunny sacks and beat out the flying sparks. Dad and Chuck helped, too, while the women soaked gunny sacks and poured buckets of water along the fire line. The fire came close to the cabins where we were staying. It was terrifying and we were glad to move on.

The Columbia River highway was a one-lane road. It rims the canyon walls through rocks and dark forests for miles as it follows the winding river to Portland. There are sharp curves, breathtaking views and beautiful waterfalls. We stopped to change a tire at Crown Point Lookout. The wind was strong and the air smelled like fir trees. Eddie's cap blew off and my hair was flying. Mom grabbed our hands so we wouldn't get too close to the edge. It was a long way down to the river. When we piled back into the car, I asked Dad, "When are we gonna get there?" He replied, "In a few hours." From then on, every time we stopped, someone asked, "How far now?"

At Oregon City, we stopped to stretch our legs and heard a tremendous roaring sound. Curious, we peeked through some bushes and saw the most spectacular waterfall ever. It was huge and horseshoe-shaped. Frances read the sign and pronounced it Will-am-ette Falls. The sign said the falls are natural and the 17th widest in the world. They are 1,500 feet wide and 40 feet high. We were now in the Willamette Valley—a 120-mile-long, 60-mile-wide valley, where everything was lush green. This would be our new home. Before we could say anything, Dad said, "We should be in Silverton in a couple of hours."

The countryside was beautiful, with orchards, green pastures, rolling hills of timber and a clear view of Mt. Hood in the distance. There were flowers I had never seen before and fresh fruit. I thought I was in Heaven. We stayed the first two weeks with the Waltman family on a beautiful farm between Salem and Silverton. Charley Waltman was Grandpa Walker's cousin. He was sweet like Grandpa and they kind of looked alike. It made me feel like Grandpa was there with me. Dad spent most of his time in Silverton looking for a job and a house to rent.

Meanwhile, Dad received word that the terrible rainstorms we went through in Wyoming and also in Colorado had caused horrific flooding along the Republican River in Nebraska and especially in Bloomington. It happened fast, like a flash flood only worse because it was at night, without warning, taking out towns and bridges. Many lost their lives. People heard it coming but they didn't know what it was. By the time it hit Bloomington it was two miles wide and nine feet deep. Dad's best friend was caught in his basement and drowned. We lived at the top of the hill going into the valley so we would have been safe, but the sight itself must have been something. I didn't know what happened to Prince and I didn't want to think about it.

Upon arrival in Silverton, Dad immediately applied for work at the Silver Falls Lumber Company. He went back everyday, sitting all day on the office steps, waiting for a job. They knew him by name and sight. Two weeks later, the owner came out and said, "Walker, we're tired of you sitting on our steps. Go home, get something to eat and be back here at 1 p.m. We have a job for you." Dad was ecstatic, but instead, he went across the street to a little grocery store, bought a can of sardines and some crackers, ate them in the Buick and turned in for work early. Mom always said Dad was a good worker because he was honest, dependable and strong. They gave him the hardest job in the mill—pulling on the green chain. He did that for a couple of years before they made him a lumber grader. He liked that better. He worked at Silver Falls for about 10 years. During World War II, he worked at the shipyards in Portland.

We rented a house on Welch Street and lived there for two years. When I was 10 years old, I started working in the fields, picking strawberries and hops along with my sisters and brothers. We didn't mind because most of our friends did that too. Dad let us keep the money we made but we had to spend it wisely. My youngest brother David was born there. When we ran out of room, we packed up the Buick and trailer, plus nine kids and everything else and moved over east hill to the Casperson home where we lived until the war. Dad got us a dog and we named him Pooch. He was black and white like Prince; it lessened the hurt a bit.

We still had the Buick but mostly we walked everywhere. Dad walked to work and we walked to school, rain or shine. The Buick was used only on special occasions. Sometimes we went sightseeing or on a picnic to Silver Creek Falls. Dad took us to the State Fair and Mom shopping at Montgomery Ward in Salem. When friends came from Nebraska, we took them to the coast or the Falls. Occasionally Dad would drive to town. He came home one night with the car door all banged up. I guess he didn't have enough money to fix it because he parked it under the chestnut tree and never drove it again. I didn't ask any questions.

The Door Closes

One day I came home from school and the car was gone. Mom said we were moving to town so Dad sold it. That old car was a faithful friend for a number of years. It transported me and my family from Nebraska to a new life in Oregon.

The Boise Green Buick was my shelter in the storm as we traveled west, and my haven of rest for several years by providing a special place for me to be alone, to play with my dolls, study, read and write. Once I wrote a mystery story about twin brothers while sitting in the back seat. My brother made fun of it so I never wrote again—until now. So thank you, Boise Green Buick, for opening your door to me, a little girl, and bringing enjoyment, intrigue and adventure into my life. You were not just a car but an old friend whose journey on land ended, but continues in my heart.

About the Author:

Patty Walker Riley was born in Nebraska before the Great Depression and moved with her family to Oregon in 1935. There were nine children in the Walker family. She and her brother David are the only survivors.

After her marriage to Del in 1952, they moved to Albany where she gave top priority to rearing their family. Now the family matriarch, she is the mother of three, grandmother of 10, great-grandmother of

14, "Patty" to her in-laws, and "Aunt Patty" to dozens of nieces and nephews.

Patty turned 90 in March, 2016. Throughout the years, she was involved in church and community work. Her hobbies included reading, wood carving, oil painting, camping, travel and snow-birding. God has greatly blessed her life.

.

14

The Weathered Gray Door
Carol Crespi Green

Una porta del giardino esposto, a weathered
garden door symbolizes the imaginary portal that
opened to my grandparents, Chiara Bolognesi and
Paolo Crespi, upon their arrival from Northern Italy
to America…a door beyond which lay their hopes for
a new life in a new land… a door opening for an
opportunity to live in self-sufficiency, denied them in
Italy but possible in this country. As they ventured
through that door, resolutely taking hold of that
promise, their story and that of their family unfolds…

Heading to Cle Elum

Summer 1950—a day that began warm in our
small farm town. Our family was busy packing up the
1948 Chevy. Soon we would begin our journey across
the state of Washington to visit our grandparents in
Cle Elum. We climbed into the car, one we had been
very lucky to purchase after Dad returned from the
South Pacific. With the metal shortage during the war,
car production had all but stopped. Mom's father was
able to make some kind of special arrangement with
the local dealer for Dad, a navy veteran. The folks
were in front for now but we all knew that sooner or
later we'd need to yell at Dad to pull over so I could
change places with Mom. Car sickness would take

over and I would spend the rest of the trip chewing
Spearmint gum like crazy, with my six-year old nose
sniffing the breeze from the open window in the
front seat. She and my younger sister would share the
back seat for the duration of the five-hour trip. Now,
I'm not saying that the folks were wholly to blame for
my bouts of nausea in the car, but I can partially
attribute them to certain behaviors on their part. First,
Dad was a terrible driver. There was just no getting
around it. He charged up almost to the bumper of any
car in front of us, cursing loudly. There was often
sudden braking which, in the days before seat belts,
would send us pitching forward with regularity. Then
there was the smoking. Both of them smoked. They
smoked a lot. They smoked even more frequently
while held captive in the car. Camels. Two packs a
day. Each. It wasn't quite as bad in the summer with
the windows open but one can only imagine how we
all smelled piling out of that car when we reached our
destination. The grandparents, aunts, and uncles were
kind, but looking back, since most of them had not
bought into the coolness of smoking, it must have
been a bit of a put-off.

The Grandparents

Grandma was short and round. Summer and
winter she wore loose-fitting little floral print dresses
with short sleeves, and belted at the waist. In the
winter or on breezy days, which were frequent in Cle
Elum, she would add a maroon wool cardigan. A
woman of few words, at least in English, she was
rarely idle as there was much to be done on the five-
acre property. She only had three grandchildren—my
sister and I and our cousin Paul who was several years

older. She was always happy to see us, but she spoke broken English so our conversations were never too deep. Grandpa was thin and wiry. We never saw him in anything but denim overalls and a plaid shirt. Most days he donned one of those flat caps with a small brim. He had spent a lot of years in the mines and by the time we knew him he just sat in his chair on the porch with one of those small cheese glasses of wine. He could only speak Italian so there was not much going on with him. My sister and I got a lot of attention in Cle Elum because Grandma would take us around to visit the other ladies with last names like Zaffaroni, Cappelletti, Mattielli and Rosetti. In the summer we were, as Mom used to say, "black as berries," having picked up the northern Italian genes, and they would stroke our tanned arms, and say nice things in Italian. They had smiles and oohs and ahhs and they would offer us torchettis fresh out of the oven— twisted sugar crusted cookies with caramelized bottoms, soft on the inside, crunchy on the outside.

When we were small they still lived in the house they had built on five acres in a section of east Cle Elum called Steiner's Addition. There was a barn, a "batch" house, and hutches and pens for rabbits and chickens. The "batch" house held the laundry and ironing equipment, and a spare bed that they sometimes rented to a single man or bachelor. Perhaps that is how the little building got its name. Next to the barn sat a lean-to that held a large metal vat used for crushing grapes. The men would pull on hip boots and jump in, compressing and reducing the grapes until they considered them ready to be relocated to the underground wine cellar across the yard. At night we would sleep upstairs in a large attic room, resting our heads on pillowcases made of scratchy flour bags. During the day we would play outdoors in the large gravel yard, explore the outbuildings and talk to the rabbits and chickens in their pens. Cle Elum didn't offer a whole lot of entertainment for young girls but we didn't seem to mind. The town itself seemed gray and drab to us, with lots of older wooden homes, one main street that ran through town, and the intermittent shrill sound of train whistles, loud and then fading into the distance, day and night.

Chiara's Cucina

The best memories are of the fabulous food that Grandma would cook on the wood stove in the kitchen. She would be standing over that stove most of the day it seemed. She showed us how to pick dandelion greens from the yard for salad. She would go into the woods and pick porcini mushrooms in the fall; dry them, and put them in risotto and her sauces. We would traipse down to the cellar where the smells were musty but good, with big wheels of white cheese curing on wooden shelves, and jars of canned fruits, vegetables, pickled peppers and antipasto lined up in rows. A case of Orange Crush sat by the door. A large barrel of wine sat in the corner, aged and ready to drink, where small traces of red zinfandel had leaked in a thin stream out onto the dirt floor. Large gallon jugs of pale rosé wine vinegar sat lined up against the wall.

Lunch was a hunk of one of those cheese wheels, a loaf of crusty just-baked, twist bread from the Cle Elum Bakery, a bowl of her antipasto she had canned in the fall when the vegetables were prime, some albacore tuna, and aged Italian salami sliced so thin and transparent you could almost see through it. The antipasto, with its tomatoey vinegary sauce, was filled with mushrooms, carrots, celery, olives, peppers, little pearl onions, green beans, tuna and even a few anchovies—indescribably delicious.

Dinner might be chicken cacciatore with polenta, or a similar dish made with cod. Her spaghetti was primo with a thick Bolognese sauce simmered with cut up pieces of tender steak. There would be no ground beef in her sauces! Raviolis were the crowning culinary achievement and after roasting beef, pork and veal cuts, grinding them along with other ingredients, spices and parmesan cheese, making pasta dough and carefully filling and pinching those tasty pockets of goodness, we were truly in heaven. One morning Grandma headed out of the kitchen and through the screened front porch with a humongous butcher knife in hand. We innocently asked where she was going and she said, "I'm going to get a rabbit for dinner." Oh no! One of those soft, furry rabbits in the pens! My sister and I were not in favor of it at all. Noting our alarm over the situation she quickly said she would make something else and retreated to the kitchen with the knife. That evening, as usual, we had a delicious dinner. Everyone exclaimed over the tenderness of the meat. Somehow we figured it out—even at six and four we had had enough chicken legs to know that something was different about that leg, but it was so good we ate it anyway. That's the way it was in Grandma's kitchen.

The aunts were close but had two very different personalities. Aunt Rose, the older one was as calm and unruffled as they come. Aunt Mary, two years younger, was a bit of a worrier and perfectionist, but both loved us, we loved them and they were fun to be around. William, our Dad, was the baby, born in 1909 in Turbigo, Italy. But before I begin the account of his life and why he happened to be born in Italy, the story of how this Italian family got here in the first place needs to be told.

Coming to America

Paolo Crespi was born in or near Turbigo, Italy in 1871 to Vincenzo Crespi and his mother, whose name we do not know. Paolo had an older sister named Rosa who was born with a very large birthmark covering half her face. When their mother died Vincenzo married a woman named Maria and they had three children, half-siblings to Paolo and Rosa. An uncle, who had settled in Buenos Aires, returned to Italy to visit and offered to take Rosa back with him to Argentina. At that time they believed it would be impossible for her to ever get married. He would take care of her; he had the means to do so as he worked in or owned a Panama hat factory and knew she would have a better life with his family.

Paolo was very unhappy at home when the stepmother arrived and at about 16 struck out on his own. Being somewhat industrious, he discovered that he could make money by diving off a very high bridge for the tourist crowds. A short time later, in the late 1800s, his father Vincenzo left for America to find employment. Fueled by the Industrial Revolution and needing workers, American glass, coal and steel companies recruited all over Europe. Workers from many nations would cross the Atlantic and labor for eight or nine months and then return to their native countries for Christmas, traveling back again in the spring. Vincenzo was a brick maker in the East for a time but eventually ended up in the small town of Helper, Utah, working in the coal mines. Other Italian relatives had preceded him and he lived in a boarding house run by a woman from Turbigo, Italy named Luigia Langé. Vincenzo sent for Paolo when he was about 17 to join him in Helper. There was work in the mines and a place to live with the Langé family.

One evening, when Paolo was about 22, he noticed a photograph of a young woman on Luigia's dresser, and asked about her. Luigia remarked that she was her niece, the daughter of her sister-in-law Teresa Langé Bolognesi. The family and four nieces, including Chiara, 19, had remained in the small town of Turbigo, west of Milan. Although we don't really know if Paolo fell in love with the photograph, we do know that he was interested enough to write to Chiara Genoveffa Bolognesi and offer to pay passage for her to come to America and live with her Aunt Luigia and Uncle Eduardo for six months, giving her time to assess whether or not he was marriage material. At the end of that time, if she wished to marry him she could, otherwise he would pay for her return to Italy or she would be free to marry someone else.

In 1898 Chiara packed her belongings and left her mother, Teresa, her father, also named Vincenzo, older sisters Annunciata and Giuseppa, and younger sister Maria Assunta, and headed northwest to the port of Le Havre, France. It was common practice for all ticket holders to undergo a rigorous medical examination. Some companies, as required by American authorities, went so far as to require a disinfectant bath, fumigation of luggage, vaccinations and quarantine for several days to make sure they were fit to travel.

Here Chiara boarded a steamship, and like many Italian immigrants before her, probably spent up to 12 days crossing the Atlantic in the least expensive quarters—steerage. It would have been crowded and noisy, as there were no cabins. Double bunks with straw-filled mattresses were the norm and let's just say the food was downright awful. Combine this with a lack of showers and toilets and it was no wonder that over the years 1880 to 1920, during the mass immigration of 15 million Italians to the United States, over 250,000 would be held or turned back because of their diseases. As they came into New York Harbor the sight of the Statue of Liberty greeted the passengers and Chiara told me years later how excited she was. Coming to America was a dream for many from Italy. Upon disembarking the ferry that shuttled passengers to Ellis Island, she would have undergone another medical inspection and then spend three to four hours in the Registry Hall answering questions about money, jobs, and where she was going. If all questions were answered to the satisfaction of the immigrant clerk, she would proceed to the currency exchange counter and then the railroad ticket counter, exiting down the "Stairs of Separation" to the rail stations for immediate passage to various cities. After a long and tedious train ride across the United States she would eventually be reunited with the Langé family and maybe, just maybe, the man she would choose to marry.

Chiara and Paolo

It appears that it didn't take long for both of them to decide that they liked what they saw as Chiara Bolognesi and Paolo Crespi were united in marriage in the adjacent small town of Castle Gate, Utah, on May 13, 1899. From then on, Chiara always referred to Paolo as "my man."

This was coal country with some of the best quality ever to be mined in the United States. They most likely would have set up housekeeping in one of the frame homes built by the Denver and Rio Grande Western Railway when Helper became a freight terminal for coal hauling. In 1901 they welcomed their first child, Rose and later a son, who died at birth. Rose only made it to the age of three. Grandpa always felt that she had died of fright—he had left her alone in the wagon while he tended to some business and the horses ran away with her. He believed she was never the same after the unfortunate incident but Grandma was fairly sure that she had been ill and actually died of pneumonia. Fortunately for them, another girl was born just after Christmas, on December 31, 1904, and as was sometimes the custom with one recently deceased, they also named this child Rose.

When Rose was still a baby the family moved to Kansas, following work in the mines. One might wonder why they would leave Helper with a small baby but the mines were booming near Fort Smith in 1900 due to the expansion of railroad lines into

Choctaw Indian country. Between 1901 and 1903 coal production increased from two million to three million tons. These companies needed workers and one must imagine that, given supply and demand, higher wages most likely played a part in the decision to make the journey east. However, after a time all was not well in Kansas. For the first time they were by themselves with no family. Paolo, whose name was now Americanized to Paul, worked long hours. Chiara (now called Clara) home by herself with a small baby, had the misfortune to come down with malaria. Although the initial symptoms of fever, chills, and nausea may not have lasted too long it appears that she may have had the bad luck to suffer from "relapsing" malaria which could bring symptoms back every few days. On doctor's orders that they should move west, at some point in the next year they made the decision to leave Fort Smith and move to Cle Elum, Washington. A man named Charlie Cappelletti was known to be there, and may have been a great uncle to Chiara, originally from Turbigo.

Arriving in Cle Elum

Cle Elum was also a coal mining town located in central Washington at the base of the Cascade mountains. The prospect for a job was good. Coal had been discovered in the 1880s in Roslyn and in 1894 in Cle Elum. Coincidentally, the Northern Pacific Railroad was pushing forward on its way through the Stampede Pass to Puget Sound, the end of the line. They needed coal and timber to build the tracks and Cle Elum had both. The news of mining jobs spread quickly. The population went from four hundred to over three thousand in the first decade of the century and brought hundreds of Italians, Poles, Croatians and Slovaks to work in the mines and lumber industries.

One business that developed shortly after the family moved to Cle Elum was the Cle Elum Bakery. Clara visited it most every day and would bring the famous, still warm "twist" bread back home for the family to enjoy. The owners, John and Letizia Pricco, both from the Piemonte area of Italy, found each other on the same ship coming to America in 1902. They married in 1903 and were drawn to Cle Elum because of the number of Italians already settled there. Building a wood-fired brick oven, their old-world style bread became famous, and when the Snoqualmie Pass road opened in 1915 many travelers now driving through Cle Elum had to stop, not only for bread, but also for torchettis, cannoli, biscotti, sweet rolls and the like.

So it was in Cle Elum, arriving during an exciting "boom" era, that the Crespi family set down roots. They purchased a home on 2nd Street and Paul walked several miles a day to Roslyn Mine #5, putting in grueling days, summer and winter. Sometimes in the winter he would arrive home and his clothes would be frozen stiff. Mining was extremely dangerous during these early years. Methane gas was always a problem and so was the coal dust. Miners worked with the help of light from open flames attached to their hats. Thirteen years earlier, in 1892, a terrible explosion had occurred in Roslyn mine #1, killing 45 miners. The mine reached down seven levels. There was a main airway down to the fourth level, which provided some ventilation. Furnaces burned night and day to disperse the methane gas. The workers were in the process of building another ventilation shaft to reach the lower levels when a dynamite blast was set off to break rock for the tunnel. It is believed to have released a pocket of methane, which was set on fire by one of the miner's lamps and coal dust fueled the flames. Those who were not killed outright by the explosion were quickly asphyxiated. The disaster left 29 widows, and 91 fatherless children. In later years precautions were taken to dilute the coal dust, but even today it continues to be a dangerous occupation.

A Return to Italy

The small family settled into their new life in Cle Elum, with its warm summers and snowbound winters. Two years after the birth of Rose, daughter Mary Julia was born on November 13, 1906. By fall 1908, Chiara was pregnant with her fifth child and at some point the decision was made that she would return to Italy for a visit. Perhaps the harshness of her new life in the States, the loss of two children, malaria, and two long moves weighed in the decision to make what seems to be a very unlikely journey at this point in her life. Perhaps she was homesick for her family. She traveled across the United States by train with girls ages three and five, and was several months pregnant with a third child. Although no records exist of their journey back to Italy, they arrived before April 4, 1909 when son Guido was born in Turbigo. They lived in a horseshoe-shaped court with a tall iron gate on or near Main Street. Rose was school age and would walk down that street to the building that housed her classroom. No one is sure how long they planned to stay in Turbigo but baby Guido became ill with scarlet fever and they were quarantined for two years and not allowed to board a ship for home. Scarlet fever was one of the most common childhood infectious diseases causing death in both Europe and the United States, with fatality rates that reached 30% in larger metropolitan areas. Rose came of age and began school in Turbigo, walking down Main Street to her classroom. They enjoyed the company of Clara's family. Her sisters had married and family occupations included a tailor and a baker. Fortunately, young Guido made it through the illness and they were finally able to secure passage back to America on the ship "La Savoie" out of Le Havre, France. Upon arrival back in the United States, documents show that Chiara, 31; Rosa, 7; Maria, 5; and Guido, 22 months, proceeded through Ellis Island on April 22, 1911.

During this time Paul rented out the house on 2nd Street and is believed to have boarded with the Cappellettis while his family was in Italy. The Cappellettis lived in that section of east Cle Elum called Steiner's Addition, and Charlie and Paul owned cows and sold and delivered milk around town. Shortly after the return of the family in 2011, Paul and Clara rented the house on 2nd Street and purchased a five-acre parcel near the Cappellettis. By 1912 they had begun building the home where they were to spend the next 40 years, working and raising their family. It was clear that they had little money but they were amazingly creative and productive. The barn housed a horse and some cows and heifers, the cows for milking and the heifers for meat. Paul would rise at four in the morning, do the chores and milk the cows for delivery around town before walking the three miles to work. Alfalfa and other kinds of feed crops were grown on the acreage. Across the gravel yard sat chicken pens and raised enclosures with wire screens for rabbits. To the side of the home, away from the road, lay a large garden, tended for hours in season by Clara. There were fruit trees and even a hazelnut tree.

Paul had his own cellar, dug deep into the earth and somewhat hidden behind the rabbit pens. It was rumored to have several large 50-gallon wooden barrels of deep red zinfandel wine and one of white wine, aging in the coolness and fairly constant temperature underground. In later years the men in the family—Dad (Bill), Uncle George (Mary's husband), and Grandpa Paul would disappear down there for an hour or two, just to make sure things were going okay. One time, after they had been absent for some time, the three returned to the house in a very jovial mood, covered with large deep red splatters of wine. When uncorking a barrel, it seems that some kind of pressure had built up, resulting in a crimson explosion. The sight of the somewhat raucous men was not met with the same enthusiasm by the women, who had to deal with the stains.

Clara had to learn enough English to do the daily shopping, pay bills, and interact with the children as they grew up in the public school. Rose and Mary had learned Italian during the time spent in Italy and were able to communicate in the language with their parents. Bill was either too young or, if he did have memory of the language, simply rejected having much to do with it. He desperately just wanted to be an American kid. Each night he would wet down his wavy black hair and pull a tight-fitting stocking cap over his head so his hair would be straight the next morning. When asked what his favorite meal was, one would be almost sure that he would mention one of the wonderful meals that his mother prepared, but instead he would answer "steak and apple pie." His given name, Guido, was never mentioned. Somehow the name, which translates to Guy in English, became the translation for Guillermo, or William.

Sometime in the years between 1916 and 1918 a very serious diphtheria and flu epidemic occurred in Cle Elum and both Rose and Mary became ill. Mary's case was not as serious but poor Rose was in such bad shape she became delirious. The doctor felt that she wouldn't make it without trying a new antidote that was still in the experimental stage, but had been tested in Europe and New York State with success. An antitoxin made from horse's blood had been developed and in 1914 a newspaper in France had declared it one of the "seven wonders of the modern world."

Somehow Dr. Kheel was able to get hold of this diphtheria medication, which required mixing a combination of a toxin and antitoxin in just the right amounts. Clara made the difficult decision to give it to Rose. I am sure everyone was thrilled and thankful when she recovered. Interestingly enough, that antidote was not widely distributed until 1921, so it was truly a risk prior to that time. Many people died in Cle Elum. So many died that they buried them without a funeral for a time so all efforts could be turned to caring for the ill. Their home was placed in quarantine and Paul was prohibited from entering; an edict he promptly ignored, sneaking in the back window each night after work. Aside from that experience, the children led normal and happy lives during their youth. In the hot Cle Elum summers the family would load up the wagon with food and bedding and make their way down to the Yakima River with other families to swim and camp. In the winter Paul would take them on sleigh rides in the deep snow around town. They all took part in activities in school, and Mary and Bill would leave home upon graduation from Cle Elum High to pursue college degrees.

Rose, Mary and Bill

Each one of Paul and Clara's children lived lives with purpose. Each in their own way felt the need to "make something of themselves." This desire partially came from the excitement of changing times—they all graduated from Cle Elum High in the 1920s after the end of World War I. It also came from the example of parents who took advantage of every opportunity in their new country to become self-sustaining and to make better lives for their children.

Rose, the oldest, stayed in Cle Elum, worked in the office at the laundry for 15 years and married Uncle Butch Micus when she was 37 years old. He was a bit rough around the edges and also worked in the mines. Butch drank a lot but was good to us when he was around. He died fairly young of a cerebral hemorrhage and secondary complications of the dreaded miner's disease—black lung. They had a wide circle of friends and when he died there was standing room only at his funeral.

Rose was calm and collected, not much bothered her, and she was a lot of fun. After Butch's death she carried on over the years with an active social life, never remarrying. She advanced through the chairs and became the Worthy Matron of the Eastern Star, spent weekends at the Fraternal Order of Eagles and was famous for the raviolis she would make for the Eagle's Italian dinners—500 at a time. She was a one-woman ravioli machine! It was rumored that she was a loser at a couple of strip poker games, although none of us was there to witness it. When she was in her late eighties she decided to sell the home she had lived in for 50 years and was eager to move into one of the new senior apartments on Pennsylvania Avenue. She was amazingly healthy, and with the exception of two hip replacements, needed little medical attention. Her door was always open, the coffee pot always on, and apartment dwellers and visitors would drop in all day long. She died in her sleep, but not until she had reached the venerable age of 98.

Mary worked as a waitress during high school at the Auto Rest Café and was the first to leave home. Upon graduation from Cle Elum High, she enrolled at what was then called Washington Normal School in Bellingham. In two years she received her teaching degree and moved to Seattle where she met Uncle George, an accountant with Boeing. They were married in July 1934 and settled in the South Seattle area. Several years later cousin Paul was born on the Fourth of July, and attended school at Highland Park until they moved to a lovely spot in Woodinville, part of 160 acres of land that had been homesteaded by Uncle George's father. Each child received 40 acres and built homes nearby on their land, so family was never far. As kids we loved the property with a meandering creek running through it, just below the house. Aunt Mary continued taking classes at the University of Washington, teaching elementary school, and reading until she retired. She was much more cautious than her sister Rose and sometimes decisions were elusive. She would make a trip to a department store, Frederick and Nelson, bring home two dresses, and try to decide which one to keep. She often returned both of them, months later. Mom, who was very decisive, would say, in jest, "Mary, I am sure you are one of Frederick and Nelson's favorite customers!" Uncle George was jovial and great company.

When they visited us, Aunt Mary loved to fool with our hair, and even though it didn't "turn out" like we hoped, we always let her do it. She didn't have little girls on which to practice her hairdressing expertise! One time she insisted on helping me with my Camp Fire Girls headband. Tiny beads had to be threaded and woven on a loom in a design that represented our chosen name. Her eyesight left something to be desired, as I discovered when I was almost done with the rather complicated thing. She had mistaken navy blue beads for black way back in the middle of the headband. I wasn't very happy. Today, it rests in a memory box on the wall and with the passing of time, every time I look at those blue beads it brings a smile and warm memories of those days.

One summer, when we were ten and eight, our families took a trip together to Banff and Lake Louise, renting a log cabin and warming ourselves in the Radium Hot Springs mineral waters. We had many happy days with Aunt Mary, Uncle George and Paul. After Uncle George passed away, Mary sold the lovely ranch-style home on the creek and moved into an equally lovely but smaller patio home in Issaquah, living into her nineties.

Dad had a very normal life in Cle Elum, and took part in many activities while in school. He was a halfback and captain of the football team; he played baseball for three years, was vice-president of the "C" club and (who knew?) even took part in Glee and an operetta. After graduation he too left Cle Elum for college, but instead of following Mary north, went southeast to Washington State University in Pullman. He lasted all of one week when he got so homesick he hitchhiked home, arriving at three in the morning, much to his family's surprise. He said, "This is not for me; they don't cook like mother does!" His father told him that if he was going to be home, he darn well had to go to the mines and work. What could Bill say except, "I would be glad to." However, after one year in what turned out to be extremely onerous and laborious work, he had a change of mind! The next fall he made his way back to Pullman, took up residence in Ferry Hall and later joined the Sigma Phi Sigma fraternity. There was no more hitchhiking home and either he got used to dormitory meals or quit complaining about them. While he was studying for his teaching career he caught the attention of Ike Deeter, a nationally known boxing coach at WSC. He began training with the boxing team and earned several Golden Gloves awards during his time at college. One summer while home from school, he, Rose and Mary decided to drive to a dance at Liberty Hall, located on the way to Wenatchee over Blewett Pass. At some point during the evening a fight broke out and someone said, "You'd better not get Bill Crespi in there; he's a Golden Gloves boxer!"

When Dad graduated in 1934 he completed the lengthy process of becoming a naturalized citizen, and took a position as a history and industrial arts teacher in the small town of Kapowsin. Perhaps he did some coaching too. Teaching in small schools usually involved being coerced into overseeing a few classes that you hadn't necessarily been trained for in college.

After a stint in another small town in 1937, he found a job in Edwall, Washington, the same year a pretty English teacher was hired, who had just graduated from WSC. Over the course of that year he fell in love with Faith Warwick and in June 1941 they were married at Springbrook Farm, her family home near Oakesdale, Washington.

After the bombing of Pearl Harbor in December of 1941, Dad completed the year at Edwall High School and enlisted in the Navy. He applied to Officer Candidate School in Annapolis and was well qualified with his degree for admittance. To his disappointment he was denied because he had only been a naturalized citizen for eight years. One had to be a citizen for 10 years before consideration. Instead, he was sent to San Diego for Navy duty and Faith went with him. They found an apartment and made friends with many other Navy families. Faith worked for Lockheed Air, which was disguised as a chicken farm on the roof. This was to make sure that if the Japanese bombers managed to get that far over the Pacific, they wouldn't recognize it.

All along the West coast everyone was ordered to adhere to total blackout in the evening. By the fall of 1943 Mom was pregnant with me and continued working. One day in the ladies' restroom at Lockheed, a woman noticed Mom was pregnant and asked what she and Dad were going to name me. Mom said, "If it's a girl we are thinking of naming her RoseMary." The women replied, "Oh that's such a wop name!" There had been plenty of discrimination against Italians when my grandparents arrived in the early 1900s but Mom had never experienced it. She replied, "My husband is 100% Italian and so are his sisters, Rose and Mary." That pretty much ended the conversation.

I was born in May 1944 in the Balboa Park Naval Hospital along with 84 other wartime babies. The pictures sent home to family in Washington show a suntanned, blue-eyed baby…the blue eyes being a bit of an anomaly among all the brown-eyed members on that side of the family.

Dad was assigned duty in the South Pacific in the fall of 1944 and sent off to Ulithi Atoll, a naval resupply station. Mom packed up and she and I drove back to live with her family on the farm near Oakesdale while Dad was away. Mom was asked to take a substitute teaching position in Tekoa for a while which she could do, as Grandma and Grandpa Warwick were on hand to care for me during the day.

When Dad was deployed back to the States in 1945, we joined him in Bremerton, Washington until he completed his time in the service. By the summer of 1946, Dad had been offered a teaching job in Quincy, Washington. Mom was six months pregnant and we moved in time for school to begin. In early November, sister Marjorie entered the world in a hurry. Mom barely made it the 30 miles to the Ephrata Hospital when Marjorie was born. Her water broke in the parking lot and 20 minutes later the brown-eyed baby arrived with Mom on the gurney with her garter belt and nylons still on and no doctor in sight! She was always miffed that the doctor charged them for his services when he hadn't shown up until 20 minutes after the blessed event.

After two years in Quincy Dad applied for the high school principal's position in Tekoa, Washington. In June of 1948 we arrived back in Palouse country in that Chevy that Grandpa Warwick had miraculously wrangled out of the Redfern Chevrolet dealership. We bought a small home and spent five nice years there. An aunt lived just down the street, and grandparents, other aunts, uncles and cousins on farms nearby. We swam all summer long in the city pool, roller skated, rode our bikes and played 10 kinds of tag with neighborhood kids on the high school lawn. We ran through sprinklers even though mothers worried we might get polio.

The winters in the early 1950s were harsh with snow so deep that sidewalks became tunnels and icicles hung down so far that they reached the ground. At the end of the street stood a fence with vacant land beyond. The snowplows would push all the snow down there and make a giant snow hill that was great fun. We would wet a path down one side and, once it turned to ice, made a terrific slide. One of those winters I begged for white boots. Those old-fashioned black galoshes just wouldn't do. I think they were kind of expensive but Mom and Dad finally broke down and the day they brought them home I was so excited I tried them on without shoes, just my stocking feet. I decided I had to go down to the snow hill and show them off to the other kids. Out the door I went and no sooner did I ascend the hill than one of the boots sunk deep, deep into the snow. Of course, since I did not have shoes on, my foot came up without the boot. Everyone tried to find it. I ran home crying and Dad went out with the snow shovel. We could still see him out there after dark, shoveling away. The boot never did surface, even after things thawed and the snow hill melted away. I was destined for black galoshes.

Orofino, Idaho

In the summer of 1953, just after we had purchased a new turquoise and cream Chevy Bel Air, the school board decided to fire everyone except for two teachers at the high school. My aunt, who was one of five members of the board, was the lone dissenting vote. It came as a surprise to everyone, coming so late in the school year, and Dad looked all over for a job. It was getting very late in the summer and it was one of the only times I ever saw Mom cry. Finally, two weeks before school started Dad was offered the high school business manager's position in Orofino, Idaho. There wasn't a lot of choice in housing, and we had to get settled so we rented the main floor of what had been the downtown mortuary. The lawn in front was very long and terraced, with identical plantings on each side. Mrs. Blake, the widow of the funeral parlor director, lived upstairs. My sister's room was where the bodies would lie in their coffins for viewing. The living room was so large that you could roller skate around it. Of course one can imagine what happened in the kitchen. What a year that was! My classroom was a World War II quonset hut because the town had outgrown the brick elementary school building. Nine classes were out on the property, quite a distance from the main building and the bathrooms. The town itself was bustling, full of loggers and huge logging trucks passing through. There was an air of excitement never present in the sleepy farm towns we had been used to. The mortuary-turned-residence also sat across from the hospital emergency room and there were lots of ambulances, being timber country with numerous logging accidents. Marjorie, (now shortened to Midge) and I would turn off the lights at night and stare out at the ambulances unloading the accident of the day and wonder what befell the poor soul. It was the kind of place where your folks told you not to go into the part of town past the bridge. It always did look tempting, as it seemed like there was a lot of activity down there.

We took Sunday drives. Mostly Dad would want to venture up one of the many logging roads in the hills. Did I mention he was a bad driver? We would keep going up and up until the road got so narrow and the drop-off so far down that Mom would finally say, "Bill, I think we should probably turn around, don't you?" She would then order us out of the car while he attempted the time-consuming maneuver to get the car turned around, coming perilously close to the waiting precipice. When we were older we simply refused to go on any more Sunday drives. The other driving experience was his insistence on taking what he called a shortcut on the way back to Orofino from visiting the family. Instead of driving down the Lewiston Grade, he opted to take the much lesser traveled Coyote Grade. Though it might have saved a few miles, it was less traveled for a good reason, being all gravel with no guard rails, and so narrow that two cars could not pass each other without pulling over. Usually we drove it during the daytime but somehow, this particular time, we had gotten a late start so started down the Coyote on a particularly dark night. It had the worst drop-offs of any road we had ever traveled and switchbacks one on top of another. As we were still near the top we started around a corner when Dad let out an expletive yelling, "Faith, we've lost our lights!" Well, thank goodness he kept turning the steering wheel in the direction he thought we should be going, avoiding a sure fall hundreds of feet below. As we headed down, lo and behold, back came our lights. It was so dark and we were up so high, there was nothing but space. We hadn't lost our lights; there was just nothing out there to reflect them. That was the end of the Coyote Grade adventures, in daylight or otherwise.

The one rule I did break in Orofino had to do with Coca Cola. We could have soda pop, like Orange Nehi and grape, even Seven Up, but never Coca Cola. Dad said it would rot our teeth and insides. We were always allowed a wide berth for exploring the places we lived and Orofino was no exception. I had gone to a movie and decided to walk a block farther when I passed the pharmacy. Inside it had an old-fashioned soda fountain, but there was also a window to the street where you could order things to go. I saw the big Coca Cola sign and just had to try it. I looked both ways, just to make sure Dad wasn't around, and ordered a five-cent Coke. Oh my goodness! I have never forgotten the taste of that drink. It was like nothing I had ever experienced...a sweet and fizzy brain explosion! So ended the prohibition of Coca Cola. I snuck around drinking Cokes on the sly that year but after that I had to come clean and by the time I was in fifth grade, Dad gave up.

We only lived in Orofino one year. The folks said we had to get back to Washington because the salaries were so pathetic in Idaho. Even with Mom being offered the school secretary job and going back to work, it wasn't going to work out financially. I said goodbye to my Pepto Bismol-pink room with the French windows that looked out over the terraced yard, to the caretaker's wife in the little cottage at the bottom of the property who had been so kind letting me hold her darling baby Johnny, and cutting oranges up in quarters to share, to the movie theater and the pharmacy with the soda fountain, to the library where I stopped every day to get a new book.

We moved back to Washington; we took vacations to Disneyland and San Diego to visit Navy friends; we had cousins on Mom's side close at hand; Mom started the Camp Fire Girls; and every summer I went to Camp Sweyolaken on Lake Coeur d'Alene, and we had a lot of wonderful times. We were certainly not rich but, given Dad's position, we had some status in the towns where we lived and we found we could be happy almost anywhere. It was here in Rockford in 1954 when we bought our first television. In earlier years, we would sit around the radio and Dad and I would listen to boxing bouts on the Gillette Cavalcade of Sports. Names like Rocky Marciano, Sonny Liston and Carmen Basilio were big in the 1950s. After we got television, his favorite shows were Groucho Marx's "You Bet Your Life" and "The George Gobel Show." You could hear him laughing all the way upstairs.

From the time I was born we made seven moves, and because Dad didn't want to get stuck with a house in case he was offered a new position, by the time I was a senior at Grand Coulee High School I had lived in 14 homes! Truthfully, it was quite an adventure, and we have to hand it to Mom who made those chiffon-like Priscilla curtains work in almost every one of those houses.

Dad went back to WSC to summer school several times, wrote his thesis, got his master's degree and superintendent credentials. Mom commuted at night to Cheney and Eastern Washington College to get her master's degree, teaching junior high and high school language arts and English during the day.

After four years as Superintendent of Schools in the very small town of Rockford, Washington, the school boards of both Rockford and Valleyford decided to consolidate and build a new school in between the towns. Since the Valleyford educator had been there longer, they made him superintendent and Dad was offered the same salary but his title was to be Business Manager. This didn't sit well, so once again he went out looking for a new job and was offered the position of Superintendent of Schools in Grand Coulee, Washington. We were glad to move. Rockford only had one restaurant and it closed at 5 p.m. The town didn't even have a movie theater. The grade school and high school were in the same building. They combined the fifth and sixth grades, and the seventh and eighth grades. Most of the kids lived on farms so the town's population was reduced to 400 people after school as the buses pulled away.

Grand Coulee was a big step up! The town had restaurants that stayed open long enough for dinner, a movie theater in the area, and a high school completely separate from the elementary school. To a teenager it was life in the big city!

It was also here that Dad acquired a middle name. He was born simply Guido Crespi. We didn't know about this name until many years later while going through some old papers. When we mentioned it to him he was not happy, in fact he was downright mad! We didn't bring it up again. When the folks took out a Sears and Roebuck credit account in Grand Coulee, the clerk asked Dad his middle initial. He said he didn't have one so the clerk placed a zero in the space and after that all of our packages arrived addressed to William O. Crespi. People sometimes tried to guess what his middle name was. Oscar? Oswald?

As it turned out, this would be Dad's last job. He and Mom were very happy there and he oversaw the district for 11 years. Grand Coulee gave him the opportunity to fish close to home. The biggest lake trout he ever caught was at the Banks Lake reservoir when we first moved there. The excitement of that fish kept him going back for years. He caught a lot of fish, but never again landed an eight pounder. Dad was also a golfer, but not until later in life. He got clubs for a retirement gift, about the same time Wilbur, a community 20 miles away, opened a golf course. He and his friend Cliff left in the morning and many days they would play 54 holes. I guess with all that golf, one's chances of a hole-in-one were better than average. Dad, as a left-handed golfer, got two in his lifetime.

As teachers' unions were forming across the country and faculty and staff were talking of striking for higher wages, the climate had changed so much that he couldn't do it anymore. He didn't understand it—to him it was a privilege to be in the teaching profession and unions and strikes were simply beyond him. He retired a little early at 61, making it through a difficult year with Mom, who had been diagnosed with breast cancer and gone through a difficult surgery. After she got a bit better, they tried to take the long-awaited "retirement" trip, but in the middle of it, somewhere near the Philippines, she had a relapse and they had to return home. After a four-year struggle, some ups and quite a few downs, she passed away in 1974 at 59 years, after 33 years of marriage. I had just turned 30; Midge was 27.

Dad had a tough time living alone without Mom. He just didn't do well by himself. When Aunt Mary introduced him to a lovely retired teacher friend named Hazel Matson, they were married the next year. She was delightful and we were happy for him. They had a beautiful, but short marriage as Hazel succumbed to bone cancer six years later. Dad kept going to the Bothell Methodist Church…seems there were many more widows than widowers there and lots of Sunday dinner invitations. By golly, he met Blanche a couple of years later and soon they were married! Around 1990 he began to show signs of dementia, getting up in the middle of the night and forgetting names and faces. One day he took his brand new very expensive hearing aid out of his ear and cut it up into pieces. He struggled with short-term memory and had difficulty recognizing even Blanche, although he always seemed to know my sister and me. In March of 1992, just before his 83rd birthday, he caught a cold and very suddenly passed away of what was diagnosed as kidney failure. Both he and Mary had become ill with nephritis in the 1950s and we have always wondered if there may have been a connection.

A Return to Italy

In 1988, my husband Jim and I took advantage of the opportunity to join Willamette University's Renaissance Art and Literature program in Florence. We flew ahead a day as we had discovered that the town of Turbigo was only 40 miles south of the Malpensa airport where we would arrive. We had decided to take a cab there to explore the area, staying overnight. Storms had preceded us on the trip and we were delayed taking off in Chicago as thunder and lightning descended on us sitting in a grounded jet on the tarmac. Delayed two hours, we made it with only minutes to spare at JFK in New York, where our Alitalia plane was ready to take off. As expected, our suitcases didn't make it, but in a way it was a blessing, as following our "Europe Through the Back Door" advice, we had packed extra socks, underwear, and toothbrushes in our carry-ons. We arrived in Turbigo in time to walk around town, attempted to converse with a couple of wonderful ladies in a book shop about what we were doing there, and followed their advice to go to the "cimitero" and look at the headstones. We did find a few familiar names but not the exact ones we were looking for, and vowed to return next time with more information. Later we enjoyed a wonderful meal in the only hotel in town and were grateful for a comfortable bed and the deep sleep that one hopes to have after spending almost 24 hours in transit. Upon returning home I decided to write to the Catholic Church in Turbigo and ask for some information from the records held there. In due time I received not only my father's birth certificate, but the priest had researched all of the children of Vincenzo Bolognesi and Teresa Langé who, somewhat to our surprise, not only had four girls but also three boys! He had been kind enough to trace the families down to the present day, including those who still remain in Turbigo, underlining the names in green. When I mentioned this to Aunt Mary she was a bit puzzled and remarked, "That's funny. I don't remember mother mentioning any brothers."

Two years later, in 1990, I was fortunate to return to Italy, this time with sister Midge, and armed with our newfound genealogy, we made plans to travel to Turbigo to meet up with relatives. Since we do not speak Italian well enough to converse, we requested that Andrea, the proprietor of our hotel in Cinque Terra, make the phone call to one of the chosen relations and ask if we could visit on our return to Milan. Taking out the papers, and finding lots of green underlining under Francesco Bolognesi, he obtained the phone number, made the call and relayed to us that indeed, the family would expect us on a Thursday afternoon. Midge and I made the rather complicated trip from Milan to Turbigo, taking a train and two buses to get there. We refreshed ourselves at a local bar and walked down the street to the apartment building where we were eager to find our Italian roots. The door was opened by a younger man named Renato Cardani, the husband of Luisa Bolognesi, granddaughter of Francesco. Luck was certainly with us as Renato just happened to work for United Airlines at Malpensa Airport and spoke fluent English. He took us upstairs to meet not only Luisa, but their three small boys AND her father Ugo, son of the now deceased Francesco. We sat and talked for a while and they were trying to figure out exactly how we were related. They had had some other family visit from the States a couple of years earlier. I thought I should get out the papers that the priest had sent and Ugo, after looking at them for a few moments, began to shake his head back and forth saying, "No sorella! No sorella!" Uh oh…even in my pathetic Italian I knew that meant, "No sisters! No sisters!"

Could it be? We were at the home of non-relatives! And they had prepared dinner for us! Remembering Aunt Mary's puzzlement over not remembering any brothers, I realized that somehow the priest had made a BIG mistake in our family tree! Same last name…no relation! Luisa and Renata started laughing and so did we. But wait! You haven't read the END OF THE STORY! Renato took a look at the family tree and found that they knew some of THE REAL RELATIVES! They lived just down the next street. He called them up and we went over to meet Teresa and Decimo Zoia and their children, Manuela and Luigi. We knocked on the door and walked into a small living room. Everyone was standing. Our eyes went to Teresa, then in her eighties. Midge and I looked at each other in amazement. She was the picture of our grandmother Clara, just as we remembered her. The likeness was astonishing. Teresa fondly remembered her mother, Maria Assunta, telling her about her sister Chiara, far away on the west coast of America. We did our best to have a conversation, difficult with my very limited Italian, but thanks to Renato's translation skills, we spent an hour and a half doing our best to make up for the 90 years that had passed since Chiara left home. It was almost dinnertime and Luisa had a special meal waiting for us back at the Cardani's. Over dinner we laughed and Renato couldn't wait until Sunday when he'd get to tell the priest about his mistake. The little boys begged us to stay but we could not. We had planes to catch in the morning and other places to go.

As generations move on, doors close and new ones open. The home in Steiner's Addition was sold in the 1950s and Grandma Clara and Grandpa Paul built a small home on property behind Aunt Rose's. Grandma moved her wood stove with her and continued cooking great meals on it until, after Grandpa Paul's death in 1958 at 88 years of age, she moved into Rose's home. The wood stove was moved again, this time to the basement and was fired up only during canning season. Here they lived quietly until she passed away in 1968 at age 89.

The three of us grandchildren grew up, went to college, married and now retired, have settled in Seattle, Washington; Salem, Oregon; and Phoenix, Arizona. Cousin Paul had been a human resources manager at Boeing; sister Midge and I became teachers; and later I was a nonprofit executive, and Midge the owner of a successful insurance brokerage. Six great-grandchildren came along, all college graduates, moving into professions in sales, marketing, medicine, and the law. The fifth generation now numbers 12. The oldest will graduate from college in June 2016 and move to Chicago, taking a position as a project manager in an internet company, a job not even on the horizon when the fourth generation ventured out into the world of work. Time passes. The weathered gray garden door, which Chiara and Paolo bravely stepped through so many years ago, has swung wide open, allowing each of us on the other side a life filled with more love, adventures and blessings than could possibly be imagined in 1900. Con la nostra profondo gratitudine e amore e Chiara and Paolo. With our deepest gratitude and love, Clara and Paul.

POSTSCRIPT:

We never heard back from the relatives in Italy. I tried writing to them with assistance from my Italian teacher and sent Christmas cards and letters for several years, with no response. The language barrier may have been too difficult and Teresa Zoia, being in her late 80s, may have passed away within a few months or years after our visit.

The small town of Helper, Utah lives on today but Castle Gate was abandoned in the 1970s and the residents relocated to an area west of Helper. All that remains after the town was cleared is a coal loading facility near the railroad line. A piece of news that put the small town of Castle Gate on the map was a robbery in April of 1897. A young "Butch Cassidy" along with a partner (not the "Sundance Kid!") held up an employee of the Pleasant Valley Coal Company midday at the busy railway station, making off with $7,000 in gold, worth $1.8 million today.

Mom had four brothers and sisters. We had 20 cousins on that side of the family. Our grandparents were Irish and Swedish. I've been to Ireland to find those relatives too, but that's a story for another day.

After Mom died, and the folks never got to realize their retirement plans for travel, my husband Jim and I decided not to wait. This was back in the days when you only borrowed money for appliances, a house or a car. Our new friends in Anacortes, Washington, where we moved after graduating from WSU, had borrowed money from the credit union to go to Hawaii. They wanted to start a family after they returned and figured they wouldn't get there for years if they didn't do it then. She said that every time she sat down to pay the bills, the only one that made her smile was the $30 to the credit union. What a new perspective! We've been traveling ever since.

The Cle Elum Bakery is even more famous today. With only three owners in the 110 years it has been in operation, the "twist" bread coming out of that same wood-fired oven sells out by mid-morning. If you make it to the bakery you also need to cross the street to Owen's Meat Market. In business since 1887, this store began even before the bakery. Their large assortment of meats and freshly smoked items make it a must stop. Bring a cooler. After that, move on down 1st Street to Glondo's Sausage Company for sausages, pepperoni, imported Italian cold cuts and cheeses. If you're still hungry and want a sit-down meal try Mama Vallone's, two or three blocks northwest on 1st Street. Visit Cle Elum. You'll be glad you did!

About the Author:

Carol Crespi Green is a retired elementary schoolteacher, real estate sales associate, fundraiser and nonprofit executive. She is married to Jim, her high school sweetheart, and they live in an old 1877 foursquare home on Mill Creek in the heart of Salem, Oregon. Their two children and families reside in Seattle. Four of five grandchildren are scattered around the country in college; one is in high school. Carol has traveled to Italy five more times since the first trip in 1988 even though she is terrified of flying and it takes Xanax and vodka to get there. The family often cooks Italian using Chiara's recipes, canning antipasto and peppers in the fall and enjoying her raviolis on Christmas Eve. Buon Appetito!

33753009R00214

Made in the USA
San Bernardino, CA
09 May 2016